A
Wonderful
World

A
Wonderful
World

A Gentleman's true story; Yorkshire in 1937;
serving in the British Army; to fighting with Dementia

PETER HORN

THE CLOISTER HOUSE PRESS

First published in the United Kingdom in 2018 by
The Cloister House Press

ISBN 978-1-909465-77-0

Contents

Foreword   ix

Chapter One   Bradford 1937   1
Chapter Two   Green Mount Road 1944   21
Chapter Three   1948   45
Chapter Four   Leaving School 1952   57
Chapter Five   National Service 1955   72
Chapter Six   Leaving Home   78
Chapter Seven   Off to Germany 1956   90
Chapter Eight   Back to Civilian Life 1958   111
Chapter Nine   Back in The Forces 1963   118
Chapter Ten   Bordon, Hampshire 1966   145
Chapter Eleven   Celle, West Germany 1968   152
Chapter Twelve   Back to The UK – Seme 1972   162
Chapter Thirteen   Off to Cyprus 1974   175
Chapter Fourteen   Back to Bulford 1976   180
Chapter Fifteen   Borneo 1977   184
Chapter Sixteen   Northern Ireland 1979   204
Chapter Seventeen   A Different Life   212
Chapter Eighteen   Retirement 1996   222
Chapter Nineteen   Moira   227

Life's Log Book   281

In memory of our daughter Linda, who taught me so much
and to whom I dedicate the title of this book.

Acknowledgements

My thanks to the late **Ray Scovell** who was such a guidance during my early years of training. **Francis Wilson** who tried her best to keep the words in the right place for me and **Lorraine Fenwick** who has brought this book into form at its final stages and of course, my 'Rock', **Moira** who has been always at my side.

Foreword

Writing a book is a difficult and demanding activity. Thoughts and ideas need to be ordered and honed to make them fit for their purpose – to be engaging to the reader. Autobiography, perhaps, is even more gruelling than other forms of writing. The author requires an encyclopaedic memory of events in their lives. In addition, autobiography leads to the recollection of both good and ill in a life and forces the author to reflect in hindsight on the meaning of key events both at the time, and from the position of writing in later life, with the benefit of hindsight and maturity. These are inevitably, at times, painful activities. So why would any sensible person put themselves through such tests? More specifically, why has Peter produced this account of his life?

Perhaps the interesting life meriting recording, requires events and incidents of variety, episodes of extraordinariness, challenges met and not met but equally studied, and a tale woven into a backdrop of major world events. There is no doubt that Peter's account fulfils these elements of an imaginary checklist for a successful autobiography.

Peter describes being raised in an England unrecognisable today, where horses and carts, coal ovens and pigs in the public bar were normal and every day. The stark hardship of life is downplayed in favour of clear memories of growing up in a society that it's citizens understood, where hierarchies and age were respected, and strong ties of community led to commonplace acts of kindness and decency to friends and neighbours alike. However, Peter was growing up in a country at the tail end of its Empire, and in a part of the country where opportunity for 'getting on', was limited to the soon to be declining industries of the woollen mills and farming.

With conscious or unconscious insight into this, Peter siezed the opportunity of casting his net wider, to see and experience other cultures. He describes his experiences travelling the world with the British Army, at a time when the reach of his country's influence still offered opportunities for travel to places as far flung and varied as Brunei, Libya and Northern Ireland.

Perhaps simply living through events and travel is not enough alone to make a life of interest to others. Indeed, what grabs the reader's attention is the peppering of his account with anecdotes of the many odd, challenging and just plainly ridiculous life events he experienced with wit and insight, often arising from cultural differences and misunderstandings in the exotic places in which he lived and worked. Peter's meritocratic nature shines through, never judging on the grounds of narrow racial or cultural stereotypes but evaluating those with whom his path crossed by the extent of common decency and morality, and the extent these were manifest in their behaviours.

Later years are sadly characterised by the toll of age, both in the author and loved ones. It is sad, but necessary, that Peter found himself in a position where his story needed to end with a first-person polemic on the treatment of older adults in the UK, and more specifically his beloved Moira. When the support to the state was needed for her enduring and progressive health problem, this was found wanting. This powerfully counterpoints with the strong social structure described, growing up in a small Yorkshire village in his youth. Nevertheless, even with the challenges of dealing with social care systems that were poorly administered and seems barely fit for purpose, Peter's ability to recognise human decency remained. Peter carefully identified the characteristics of empathy, dedication and thoughtfulness in Moira's carers, with his judgement validated by the support and friendship they continue to offer him.

I hope this foreword has given the reader every reason to continue on to Peter's life story. Nevertheless, the answer to the question set at the outset, being why he has written an autobiography remain, I think, unaddressed. The imagined checklist I describe, to decide what merits a life worthy of recording, is well met. However, this list does not explain what drove Peter with the need to write this book. Only Peter, of course, can really know the answer to this question, but I do have a theory.

The Peter I have come to know over almost three decades is driven by, and his behaviours, have always reflected, strong moral standards and duty. His judgement of others has always been meritocratic – with his friendship and trust won on evidence of decency as evidenced by behaviour. These underpinning character traits do not overwhelm a lightness of touch, humour, and a response to adversity that sees only a potential for new beginnings and a new path, not previously countenanced. I believe Peter wrote this book for his grandchildren and great grandchildren to reflect upon, when looking at their own futures. It is, after all, an example of a life where the lack of early opportunities and advantages are overcome by determination, strength of character and the purposeful management of life's challenges and disappointments with wit and optimism – all successfully leading to a life worth living.

❛ An unexamined life is not worth living ❜

PLATO

❛ No spring, nor summer beauty hath such grace ❜
As I have seen in one Autumnal face

JOHN DONNE

Doctor Philip Wynn – Son-in-Law.

CHAPTER ONE

Bradford 1937

**❛ It was the best of times
It was the worst of times ❜**

CHARLES DICKENS

On 5th April 1937 at Hustler Street in Bradford, West Yorkshire, great celebrations should have taken place. Why? On that day I was born, eventually to be the middle child of seven.

In August 1939, we moved to 1 Moss Street, Hill Top, Thornton, a small village to the west of Bradford. Strange as it may seem, I remember with reasonable clarity being on that journey although I was only seventeen-months-old at the time. I was lifted into some kind of vehicle, where all the family sat on furniture or bedding. Once the transport was on the move, out of the rear opening I could clearly see the road passing away behind us on what seemed a very long journey, albeit only four miles up to the village of Thornton.

On arrival, our transport had to climb the very steep, cobbled West Lane, bordered by flagstone pavements and five-foot high, dry stonewalls, which encased undulating fields in various shades of green. On approaching our new home our eyes were drawn to row after row of houses, which would have originally been a beautiful sand colour but had been changed by many years of harsh Yorkshire weather, smoke and moss, to a mixture of sombre colours. Finally, we arrived at the appropriately named "Hill Top" where we as a family were to become part of the wonderful community, which was to play a major part in the development of my young life.

Our new home number one Moss Street had been built many years before, from good old Yorkshire stone dug out of the redundant quarries less than a mile away. It contained two bedrooms, a living room, a kitchen and a front room known as a parlour. Outside was a spacious flag -stoned yard surrounded by a beautiful high stonewall, broken only by the solid wooden gate of equal height. Within the yard was a stone toilet building and the coal store, far too big, for the amount of fuel our family would ever need or be able to afford.

The kitchen, could only be described as very basic. In one corner, it had a stone trough-like sink with a cold-water tap and on the opposite outside wall there was a pantry in which, from that day on, we would keep all our food and drink fresh. The floor was flagged as if an extension of the outside yard. And in the very centre Mum had positioned our large wooden table, which was to be a very useful item in the years to come, especially during the night. Upon that, she had proudly placed our oversized enamelled bread bin. To complete the picture there was a floor-to-ceiling cupboard, a couple of buffets and a bench seat, all brought with us on the vehicle.

Every Monday Mum would fill a 'Peggy' tub with boiling water in which she threw a couple of soap blocks followed by the clothes in need of washing. Then I would do the 'possing'. Our Kath would always try to help but she was too small to be of much use. However, when Tony or Barbara were at home from school they would share in the duty with me. The secret was to give all the clothes a good dunking and twirling with the plunger-like tool. That would be my job until Mum called a halt, and placing a washboard in the tub, scrubbed each piece of clothing with great energy for what seemed like hours.

When they were to her satisfaction, all the items would be rinsed under the cold tap in the trough, before being carried into the yard and squeezed between the rollers of a giant mangle. Quite often, there would be three of us swinging on the handle to keep it moving. Finally, when the clothes had been squashed until the last drop of water had surrendered from every garment, they were hung on the line to dry and washday had sadly come to an end for us kids.

Sometimes, when the weather was really cold, Mum would bring the clothes back inside frozen solid and would stand them up in the sink, there to remain looking like ghostly human parts, which to us children was quite scary. After a short time, they would lose their power as they thawed out and slowly collapsed to the bottom of the trough. The final stage of drying, especially in bad weather, was over a number of clothes-horses made by Dad from his precious never-ending supply of thrown away timber. Those were positioned in various places about the house, and for that day and many afterwards, the whole house was very humid with a washy smell.

In the living room stood a magnificent fireplace with what seemed to me, all the time we lived there, a very high mantelpiece (at that time most things seemed high to me). The whole unit was called a range and was the most beautiful piece of metalwork I have ever seen.

A fire grate was raised above floor level, and below was a shallow pit to house a metal tray into which ash fell from the fire above. The grate retained the larger pieces until they too were burned enough to follow. In the front, was a fold-down shelf to accommodate a kettle or a pan. One side of the fire was an oven and the opposite side a boiler, complete with a lid to allow the filling and emptying of water. Beneath each of those two units was a space with a heavy metal plate which could be pulled outwards from the front to allow hot coals to be raked underneath whichever unit was needed, and when not required the plate was pushed back in to isolate that area from the heat.

The relighting of the fire each morning was a job we, kids had to do from a very early age. Our first task was to rake out all the dead coals making the ash fall through the grate into the pan, before raking the dead coals from under the two side units. If, however, there were any bits of coal or coke, which could be reused, they had to be picked out and put carefully to one side in order to be used again.

The next job was to re-lay the grate with rolled up newspapers or chopped wood. That was topped with the partly burnt coal, plus fresh fuel and then lit. Many families had a metal draught plate to draw the fire into life and speed up the lighting process. Unfortunately, we had no such luxury, so we had to improvise. Barbara, our eldest sister, would hold a sheet of newspaper across the fireplace front; it did the same job but was far more exciting. More times than not, the fire would unexpectedly come to life and the paper would catch fire before shooting up the chimney. A very hazardous start to a day but we kids loved every minute of it. When that happened Dad had constantly told us, we must run outside and look to see if the chimney had caught fire internally. I never did find out what to do if that happened.

Once the fire was alight one of us would empty the ash tin into the metal dustbin out in the yard. Finally, the whole fireplace was brushed and dusted. During the winter when the ice or snow lay on the ground, we kids would spread the ashes around the yard and footpaths to stop people slipping. That always pleased the dustman, because he did not have to lift the heavy bin into his cart on the weekly collection of rubbish. The range was cleaned once a week by Mum, helped by me or anyone else who was at home. She would cover all the black parts with black lead and together we would polish like mad until it shone, as she would say, like "a tanner on a sweep's arse". Then all the silver bits were burnished with wire wool. I have often thought what a grotty little sod I must have been in those days; what with the lighting of fires and mixing with black lead, and such a lack of hot water. The only bath we had was a galvanised one, which, when not in use, hung on the yard wall where it would swing in the wind making a combination of squeaking and scraping noises, which we could hear in the bedroom at night, as it gradually wore a nice smooth patch on the stone face.

Every Friday, the bath was brought inside and placed on the rug in front of the fire, then filled with hot water from the fireside boiler and cold from the tap in the kitchen. First in for bath night were Tony and me, followed by Kath and Barbara – no change of water.

One everlasting memory of that range, apart from its sheer beauty, was very sad. It was in fact the first time that death became known to us children. We had at the time two family pets: a fox terrier dog named Rip, who was born the same year as me, and a black cat named Peggy, which loved to sleep in the fireside oven when the door was left open to allow it to cool. That black cat was not very lucky. One night she slipped inside and unfortunately, for Peggy, someone inadvertently closed the door. Come the morning she was found suffocated.

Our living room was furnished with two very old armchairs, a couple of wooden school chairs and a large object, which today would probably be described as a bean bag, but without any beans. It was made from sacks washed and sewn together before being filled with rags, which was great for us youngsters to roll about on. Ornaments were very few, but we did have wall plaques, paintings and embroideries all done by our dad.

A large picture of the Sacred Heart hung on the wall above the fireplace (no good Catholic house would be without). In the bedroom, we had pillows without covers, a mattress but no sheets and a couple of very hairy blankets. The bedroom floors were bare boards that creaked at the slightest of movements (we had no need for burglar alarms). Sleeping arrangements were four in our bed; Tony and me at the top, Kath and Barbara at the bottom.

The few so-called carpets we had in the house, were all home made. The base was once again made up from old sacks which had been washed and cut open, then sewn together to create the required size. Old clothes were cut into nine-inch, by two-inch strips and then using a sharpened stick, we punched through the flat sack base, one-inch apart, over the whole area. Through one hole was pushed a folded strip until the loop appeared then the two loose ends were threaded through the next hole and the loop and pulled tight. That was repeated all over the base until it was finally covered. We kids learned how to do that from being able to walk. The end result was a very hard-wearing tab rug in an array of colours which cost nothing, and we loved making them.

Our only form of electrical entertainment was from a very old radio that we would all gather round every night at 6.45pm to listen to 'Dick Barton Special Agent', a never-ending series about a detective and his sidekicks; Jock and Snowy. Sometimes we were allowed to stay up a bit later at night to listen to a comedy show which Mum and Dad liked and on rare occasions, we heard the news. For more than a year we had been involved in a war with Germany, which didn't mean a lot to us kids but would eventually. At every opportunity, dad would teach us how to write and draw, paint and make games from bits of old card. He constantly encouraged us to be creative in every way possible. Many happy hours were spent drawing farm animals and cutting them out before they were painted and stuck to small wooden blocks in order to make them stand up. The girls made girlie things such as cardboard figures of ladies or children which they could dress up. Probably the first Barbie dolls and

Action Men were designed and made inside 1 Moss Street. We made horseracing, football and cricket games, which with a couple of dice and a little imagination would ensure we were happily occupied for hours.

During those early days, our parents were looking after four of us on a clerk's pittance of a wage because there was a limited amount our dad could do. He had been severely wounded in his left calf during 1917 in the Great War; the result of which was amputation in 1918. Prior to that, he had been bayoneted, from which he carried a grotesque scar across his stomach. If that wasn't enough, he had a hernia and had to wear the most horrible looking truss. We youngsters were used to seeing that monstrosity and the artificial leg many times, before we understood fully what they really were. Later our own children, mine and Moira's, were to see artificial legs a lot because her dad unfortunately had one due to a mining accident. So, when they were little our girls thought all granddads were supposed to have one leg.

Our dad was a quiet, laid-back person. I can never remember him raising his voice except to call us kids in at night for bed, a common practice for all parents at that time. He had a terrific sense of humour and mum told us many times over the years that he had been the runner-up in a Carrol Levis radio show, as a comedian. It must have been the talent show of its day. She said he won a few pounds and a bit of publicity, which helped him get a number of bookings in clubs local to the area where he was living at the time. He still entertained a bit at some of the local pubs when we were small and many times, he brought out the small case in which he kept his make-up. Then, we had great fun when he painted our faces or stuck a moustache on us, especially the girls.

Outside working hours Dad's list of pastimes was unbelievable, all of them were little earners to help provide for the family. He had an allotment about half a mile across a field behind the house, to which he walked most evenings and weekends if the weather was favourable. If not, and during the winter months, he spent hours painting in watercolours or embroidering. The latter I can only think was the result of long periods spent in military hospitals, recovering from his wounds. It certainly was not a usual hobby for a man and he was exceptional at both; as a result, they made him quite a nice little income. There always seemed to be orders for him to paint or embroider regimental badges or floral pictures. He also made a great number of wall plaques from Plaster of Paris, on which he would paint whatever scene the customer requested, before finishing them with a nice coat of varnish. Almost every house in the village seemed to have something made by our dad hanging on the walls.

Each year, prior to Christmas he would spend a lot of his time making toys, from the never-ending supply of scrap timber he constantly brought home. And for weeks right up to the big day, every corner of our house would be littered with toy farms, dolls' houses, carts, boxes of toy bricks and wooden trucks. It was like living in Santa's Grotto. Now, when I think back, what puzzles me most is from where did he get all the energy and enthusiasm? He was five foot nine tall, weighed more than seventeen stone and was severely handicapped. From Monday to Friday, he walked down the very steep cobbled West Lane into the village to his place of work, a distance of about one and a half miles. Then back up at night; all the time having to manoeuvre a very heavy primitive artificial limb with an unbelievable number of straps, which were needed to secure it in place. It squeaked at the most inopportune times much to Dad's embarrassment. I know how much it weighed, having delivered or collected a great number, to or from Thornton Railway Station over the years, when he had sent them away for repair or replacement. That daily journey he did, whatever the weather and I can never remember him being late or having a day off. Many times since then, I walked that journey and it was a real test of stamina even for a young, fit and able person.

Like so many of his generation, he never wanted to talk about the Great War. In fact, when we kids tried to question him about what he had done, which we often did due to our natural childish curiosity. He made it into a joke, and would throw us off track by singing us rather rude songs about the Germans until mum stopped him (I was turned seventy before I knew he had a brother called George, a year younger than him, who was killed and buried in France). We, kids knew more Music Hall songs and jokes about that time, including all about Hitler and Goering's sexual anatomy, than any other subjects before we ever went to school.

Many years later, when mum and dad had long gone, I was thinking about him and became aware that the man I looked up to so much had a weakness which I had never before recognised. It concerned Barbara, my eldest sister, or so I always believed, only to find out when I was nearly fifty that she was only my half-sister. Mum had given birth to her before she met Dad. In those days, secrets of such a nature were not unusual. It was years later when we really found out a lot of eye-opening facts about the villagers, at the time, it was a kind of family censorship. Anyway, I began to understand that he must have thought differently about Sis to the rest of us. He always called her Fanny and made comments about her clumsiness and her long uncontrollable legs. As a young girl at school, she was very thin and gawky and her legs seemed to go on forever, and have a mind of their own. As a result, she often had damaged ankle bones caused by her clog irons and almost every day she would come home with blood on her legs and Dad would ridicule her and say quite nasty things. At that time, we were very young and never thought much about it. Only later, when I saw the same thing happen twice in the family, when fathers took on children from previous relationships, did I understand what Dad had done to 'Babs'. He had provided for her, but he had failed to give her the most important thing a child needs – love.

Mother was quite the opposite of the old man. She was a very feisty Irish Catholic who had been born in Macroom County Cork to a family of Irish Tinkers by the name of O'Driscoll. Like so many Irish children at the turn of the century, she and two sisters, Molly and Mary, were taken into care by the Clonakiltie Convent in Dublin where Mary died. Molly and mum were used as slave labour, as mum would often tell us. Later Molly reached a certain age and was sent to England to a convent in Yorkshire. Shortly after arriving, she managed somehow to get mum to join her. The two sisters never saw home or any of their family again.

Mum was a very short dumpy person with red hair and a constant, cheerful smile – when not upset by anyone. She had an obsession about eyebrows, her theory was, if they met in the middle of the forehead it was the sign of a murderer. As we got older, poor Barbara had to take that into consideration prior to bringing any of her boyfriends home. Kath and Maureen didn't have that problem, as by the time they reached that age they were off to work in America. As time went by, I realised Mum didn't take kindly to any boy or girl we brought home. None of them was ever good enough for us, as I really found out later in life.

The elder of the two remaining sisters, by about three years, was Molly and they were as different as chalk and cheese. She was very tall and ever so thin with the whitest of skins and a head of jet black hair and a huge nose, all the features one would normally expect to see on a witch in story books. When she visited Mum, which was often, she always had a bag of sweets to share between us kids. However, that didn't really endear her to us and we were always quite scared even to approach her. She was married to Bill Hill who had a plumbing business and had transport, albeit an old motorcycle with a sidecar. That was enough for Aunt Molly to treat Mum like lower class. They had two children who were much older than us, Mary (my godmother) and Jack – both were in the RAF at the time.

As a little lad I would play out on Moss Street and the adjoining Reservoir View, which led out onto West Lane. It was a great play area for all us kids because most of the streets were cul-de-sacs, and the only transport which ever came along was the milkman and coal deliveries by the Co-operative horses and carts. A real delight to see weekly was the magnificent two-wheel cart drawn by the most beautiful dapple-grey horse of the Ringtons Tea Company.

One day, Mum returned from one of her many working visits to a wealthier neighbour with a tricycle for me. The lady had brought it back from a visit to her sister in Lancashire, where it must have seen plenty of action, mostly on a mountainside, because the solid rubber tyres were worn to a 45-degree angle. Consequently, the 'trike' and I, leaned precariously to one side and it was a constant battle trying to stop it going around in circles, but despite everything, it was my pride and joy.

The milkman who delivered fresh milk for the whole area daily was one Willie Birch, the local farmer. The milk he brought in big churns on a cart drawn by the most magnificent grey shire horse which he would leave standing unattended and unfastened in the road, while he delivered to each house from a small can and returned each time it was empty, to refill from the churn. I was simply fascinated, by the huge docile animal, which had the most impressive beard and moustache, and feet the size of dustbin lids.

The Co-op horse was even bigger, with muscles rippling over every inch of its magnificent body, due to the very heavy work he and his companions had to carry out. All the time I lived up Hill Top it was handled by Mr Gill (Dad called him Billy and always had a chat with him on lots of different subjects). He seemed to have quite a wide range of knowledge did Mr Gill. His horse, like every single one in the Co-operative's stables, was always beautifully turned out, and he always encouraged me to make a fuss of it. I would follow along when he took it to the horse trough at the top of James Street and West Lane for its much-needed drink after the climb from the village coal depot. Mum would never allow me to ride on the cart as she said it was far too dirty. I myself wasn't too clean after being outside for more than ten minutes and, as for Mr Gill, he was even dirtier. Like all the horse handlers, he loved his horse and was continually talking to it.

One particular sunny morning when the older children had gone to school and I was on my morning wander around my patch, I approached the milk horse as I had done on numerous occasions before, simply to stare into its eyes. They say the eyes are the windows to the soul; in his case it was so true for he always looked gentle and content.

As I got near to him, due to my carelessness and a bit of over enthusiasm plus the deformity of my transport, I was too near the edge of the pavement. I over-balanced and, before I knew it, I was underneath the animal between its four legs. There I was wriggling about looking directly up at the underside of a milk horse, trying hard to extricate myself, and one trike. Thank goodness, what I saw in his eyes that morning was true. He never reacted in anyway whatsoever to an idiot four-year-old trying to view him from a completely different angle. An elderly lady neighbour, by the name of Mrs Cockroft saw my predicament and dragged me and my transport out.

She took me to her house and bathed a cut I had received to my right thumb, a scar I have to this day. The horse was still there when my rescuer later walked me and my bandaged thumb back home to Mum – something Mum got quite used to in the years to come. The horse slowly turned its head and looked at me. If only I could have read its thoughts.

Milkman Willie was a great character with a heart of gold. When he delivered to families that were not very well off he would always pour more milk into the jug than what was asked for. Quite often, he would neglect to take the full payment at the end of the week. He was like many tradesmen of the time, money was not the number one priority; the welfare of the community and the pure enjoyment of his job were. Willie often got drunk during his deliveries, because so many of his customers would ply him with home brews, especially at weekends or Christmas. When he was too far-gone, someone would lay him down in the cart and people would remove his delivery book from his pocket and complete the round for him. Then they would give my friend the horse a slap and it would walk back home to the farm with its inebriated owner. That ritual I saw many times up to being fifteen, when Willie went to the 'big dairy in the sky' as Mum had always prophesied.

The war was in its third year and we children, although quite aware of what was happening, did not know just how serious it was. We did have many sleepless nights due to the wailing of the air raid sirens and the distant explosions of the bombs dropped by the German planes on Leeds or Liverpool, and the occasional one or two on Bradford, as Dad would tell us. We would be ushered down stairs and shoved under our huge kitchen table.

Later when the all clear was sounded, we returned once more to our bed. It was all so exciting, especially during the daytime, when we would constantly search the skies for aeroplanes. More often than not, we would see fighters circling high above, leaving behind their giveaway vapour trails, weaving all kinds of patterns in the great blue space.

On one occasion, when Dad and I were standing in the yard, three German bombers passed over us followed by a Spitfire in hot pursuit. The noise was horrendous and because they were so low, we could clearly see the pilots. That night it was announced over the radio, that three German bombers had been chased out to the coast by one of our fighters, where he had shot one down, damaged another and the third had escaped out to sea. From that day on, I wanted to be a pilot, they were our heroes, protecting us – alas, I never had the education or the opportunity.

At the top of Moss Street lived a couple of playmates of mine, John and Jean Battersby, with their Mum. I never knew anything about their Dad until one morning when I opened our back gate to face the world. Standing on their doorstep in full view, was a very tall slim man with ginger hair, dressed in an RAF uniform. I liked him right away because I had red hair; so did John and his sis, it was like being in a very special gang. Secondly and more important, I learned John's dad was a bomber pilot. Very soon, the neighbours, who had obviously known Mr Battersby before the war, were chatting and laughing with him. He stayed only a couple of days, during which time he had a constant trail of children hanging on his coat tails, like the Pied Piper of Hamelin. Then he was gone, and sadly never seen again. A couple of weeks later we were told that his bomber had crashed into the sea and he had died with all of his crew. The day Mrs. Battersby received that horrific news she seemed to lose interest in everything except her kids, even though all the community pulled together to help her in every way possible. Mum said she had a broken heart, that lady brought those little ones up by herself. I completed my whole school life with them and can say, their Dad would have been very proud of all his family.

Late one summer evening, a group of us kids were involved in a game of King of the Castle. The idea of the game is one of the players is made King. He or she has to find a high point and defend it against all attackers. The point selected by the chosen one was a double thickness stalls in a half-demolished building. The King selected was, nine-year-old Jack Burgess. He stood on top of the wall about ten feet above us (Health and Safety of today would turn to jelly if they knew what we children did in the course of our play). Jack was doing quite well repelling the bigger boys and we little ones were down below shouting, and the girls were doing what girls do best, screaming. Suddenly the lights went out. When they came back on, a crowd was gathered around. My hands and clothes were bright red, many of our neighbours were fussing and showing great concern.

I was lifted up and carried home where Mum and a couple of her friends bathed me, then wrapped my head in a huge towel, before a couple of the men took it in turns to carry me the mile or so down West Lane to the village doctor's surgery, followed closely by a few of the mums. Among them was dear old Mrs Cockroft, who had saved me from certain death or a darn good soaking by the milk horse. She kept saying to me how brave I was, but it was meaningless to me at the time. Many years later, when I was clever enough to understand her words, I thought 'Prat' would have been a better word.

That night the Doctor inserted six stitches into my scalp and for years after Mum would often look at me in a strange way and say; "your head is flatter than it used to be".

I was to learn later that night how Jack had found himself in danger of being overcome on top of the wall, so decided to roll a few of the loose stones down on his challengers. I was the idiot who did not move out of the way fast enough.

The following day, Mum took me to the Burgess house to see Jack's parents. Everyone who was at home, plus a few of the neighbours, were there and took it in turns to inspect my wound very carefully all sighing and making strange grunting noises – none of which helped in any way. When they had seen enough, Mum told Jack's parents that the lad must not be punished in any way because it was a play accident. In those days, we all looked after each other and common sense prevailed. It wasn't that Mum was soft in any way; she would have fought a lion for us kids.

Mrs Cockroft was the very first person to visit me the day following to enquire about my health. She was a lovely lady, never to be forgotten. She and Mr Cockroft lived in the largest house in the area. Unfortunately, I never did see her husband because it was said he was always away on some kind of business. Our parents said he was a very important man in the war effort and it was all very secretive. However, she was always available to everyone if they needed help in any way; to us youngsters she was a constant source of cakes and sweets.

On another evening our usual band of brothers were playing in the fields overlooking West Lane when, to our joy, one of the lads found a truck tyre, a very rare item indeed. (Today they litter the roadsides and ditches of almost every county in England.) We were having great fun rolling our new toy down the field where it came to a stop against a high stonewall. Then we would drag it back up to the top again.

Suddenly, one bright spark a bit older than most of us decided he would take the tyre to the steepest part of West Lane and roll the monster down toward the unsuspecting village. Off he went with us youngsters tagging along behind. At the very top, he started our prize on its downward journey to Thornton Village with no idea at all of what might happen. For the first few yards, everything was going well; then a combination of speed and the bumpy surface caused the tyre to start bouncing, higher and higher with each rotation. Then it was flying more than rolling. By that time, we were off, running as fast as our legs could carry us away from the scene. However, none of us managed to pass the lad who had come up with the bright idea.

A short time later a large black car with a battered front and bonnet pulled up alongside us. That in itself was most unusual because we saw very few cars on the roads of our village and even less with battered fronts like the one parked beside us. The window was immediately lowered, and a very white-faced man stammered, "Have you lot seen a bloody idiot roll a tyre down this hill?"

At certain times, no matter how young you are, the law of self-preservation comes to mind. "no," was the chorus; "but, we will tell him you are looking for him, if we see him". Many weeks passed after that incident before we played in those fields again, for fear of repercussions.

I awoke very early one morning, my head was thumping, and I was shivering although I was wet with sweat. I saw Mum crying and I heard certain words like "rash" and "doctor" and "temperature." Then I saw our village doctor just before everything went black. The next thing I remember was being carried outside wrapped in a thick red blanket and placed in an ambulance. It seemed like all the neighbours were gathered around, talking and all looking very serious. The doors of the vehicle were very quickly shut and off we went leaving everybody behind including my Mum. The next time I awoke, I was in a sparkling white room, which had a very strong smell, which I found out later, was disinfectant and nurses everywhere. At that stage, I was very upset at being with many complete strangers as I had never been away from Mum and the family before.

During the next week or so, I was in and out of sleep and everything was very patchy. I do remember being checked by the nurses quite often and having my temperature taken from various areas of my body. In addition, I certainly remember being injected many times in my bottom or my thigh. After a very short time, those two areas were extremely sore and very tender to touch. I also remember being washed a lot which was most unusual for me. Time passed, and I began to think I would never see Mum or the family again. I really missed Mum's dinners.

We did not have much to live on, but our Mum could make very tasty but, most of all, filling meals from next to nothing. Every so often, we managed to acquire a small amount of bacon on the ration book. The majority of it went to Dad, then Mum; after all, they were the workers. She would cut all the rind and fat off the rashers and fry them until all the fat ran out (that was quite a considerable amount in those days). Then she prepared mashed potatoes with plenty of salt and pepper, added the fat, all topped off with bits of crispy rind and accompanied with a bit of turnip or cabbage from Dad's allotment – magnificent. She also made some very mouth-watering stews – not a lot of meat, but Mum knew which bones to get and boil down before adding vegetables and, finally, her earth shattering Irish dumplings made from suet from the butchers. By the time the stew was cooked, the pan was completely full, with dumplings the size of tennis balls and gravy fit for a king – followed quite often by roly-poly covered in custard.

Then one morning a nurse wrapped me in a blanket and put me in a wheelchair and, to my surprise, she said; "off we go to see your ma." I was pushed out into a corridor and positioned, so that I could see out of a window. There, across a large stretch of lawn, behind some cast iron railings, stood Mum, Barbara and Kath who must have been shattered having walked from home. The very fact iron railings were still in place was in itself most unusual because all other railings, even from churches, had been cut down to melt for the war effort. We faced each other waving continually until my weakened little arms ached. Then, I was wheeled back inside and put back into bed.

From that day, visits of the kind took place once a week for six more weeks. Finally, the day arrived when before taking me out to see Mum, the nurses bathed me in a bath full of white liquid (disinfectant) which smelt and tasted awful. Once bathed, I was dressed in clean second-hand clothes, which I just knew had been delivered by Mum for me, but by the smell of them they had been re-laundered by the hospital staff before being allowed on the ward. Then I was taken out in a wheelchair to breathe my beloved fresh country air, for the first time since my arrival.

It was the most beautiful sensation as the nurse pushed the chair along the path to the gate where Mum and big sis Barbara were waiting to take me home. Our journey that day was about half a mile but to me it seemed like fifty, owing to me being so weak after so many weeks in bed. Not long after being back home Dad told me my illness had been Scarlet Fever, and that was the reason for the eight weeks isolation. At that time, it was still a killer disease.

April 5th 1942, my fifth birthday, Mum called out to me to come and look out of the kitchen window. Looking through from the other side was our Dad; he smiled and held up a small brown object, which meant nothing at all to me. Then he entered the house and said to Mum; "boil that for his tea". I was seeing for the very first time a fresh egg laid by a real live chicken, something none of us kids had seen. Dad said; "That, is your birthday present". It was a bit like the last supper because the following morning I was due to start school.

Perhaps I remember it so well for the following reasons; first, it seems so hard to believe someone not knowing what an egg was, but we kids had only ever seen the powdered version. Furthermore, I remember Dad's face and the smile beneath his flat cap. In later years, whenever I caught a glimpse of myself in a mirror dressed in a similar way when working in the garden, I was aware just how much I looked like him. Then for a short period, both Mum and Dad would be with me once again. Many times since that night Mum would say to me in a jokey way; "The first time your Dad saw you as a naked little lad he said, "He looks just like me" and she had said, "Silly sod, you're holding him upside down."

The following day Mum and I arrived at the junior school entrance in James Street. There myself and all the others whose freedom had come to an end (because we had reached the ripe old age of five years), were nervously gathered and met for the first time, a lady named Miss Wilkinson, the junior school headmistress. That was the start of my education. I still believe today, it was wonderful the way that lady introduced herself to every child – not the mums. She knelt before each and every one and in a grown-up voice asked our names and one or two questions. From that very first meeting she never forgot one of us – quite remarkable really because of the number of children she had under her care. Then it was time for Mum to say her goodbyes but not before she produced a piece of rag serving as a handkerchief from somewhere as if by magic, a couple of quick spits on it and my face was washed in a good old Irish way.

The next day and from then on, I went to school with my sister and brother. I really did feel grown up. Not only was I going out of the street without Mum but, because of the war I had to carry with me a gas mask in a cardboard box fastened around my neck. The nearest we ever got to using them, thank goodness, was when Dad put them on us before stuffing us under the table every time the air raid siren sounded.

The first few months of my school life, I felt trapped. I missed being a free spirit who for two years had wandered my patch of Moss Street and Reservoir View when not helping Ma. I had just got used to knowing the daily deliveries of milk and coal and making my daily visits to Mrs C for biscuits and sweets.

No more would I make my daily visit to old Mr Burdin who kept a few chickens on his allotment patch (funny thing was, I never saw any of the eggs they produced; perhaps he only had enough for his own needs). He would always be sat at his kitchen table as if awaiting my arrival. Our conversation (very limited on my part) was always about animals, especially his poultry. He showed me how to make feed for his birds from scraps of food, which was very useful information for me later in life. Many hours I spent helping him cut old dry bread into small cubes before putting them on a tray in the oven to turn brown. Those he scattered like corn, which was unavailable to everyone except the farmers. The next job was to boil up old vegetable peelings; when they were soft, he would mash them to a pulp with his rolling pin before mixing them with some of his dried bread, which we had already crushed to a powder, and that became a good substantial mash for all his birds. He also taught me how to make Yorkshire puddings, which contained currants and quite often, we had one as our morning snack. I always remember his kitchen had the most wonderful smell all the time.

He was a proper gentleman was Mr Burdin. His persona was very obvious from his dress. He always wore a nice suit, collar and tie, polished brown boots and a beautiful coloured waistcoat complete with watch and chain. There was no Mrs Burdin as unfortunately she had had died many years before we moved into the area.

> **Let everyone sweep in front of his own house
> And the whole world will be clean**
>
> JOHANN WOLFGANG VON GOETHE

I was also missing watching the ladies carry out their weekly task of washing their front steps, and all the times they would let me help with the finishing touch, which was to cover various parts of the step with scouring stone of various colours. It was great fun and the outcome was always a beautiful entrance to a house.

Then there was dear old Mrs Booth, a very dumpy little old lady who lived at the bottom house in the street. It had a small garden in which she spent most of her time. She taught me the difference between weeds and plants on the mornings I turned up to help her. It was another source of cakes and sweets. I have always told our children and grandchildren that I was not only brought up by my parents, but by the community. There were other boys and girls of my age, but none seemed to have the wanderlust like me (I think I must have inherited that from Mum's side of the family). I was a loner but never lonely. After school had finished at night, it was very different; many children would be out playing. So, for the first few weeks of school I felt like a bird in a cage.

Once again, we kids were made aware of death. Cousin Mary, Aunt Mollie's daughter who was in the WRAF, had died from a burst appendix, so Mum told us. I had only met Mary once but to this day, I have a photograph of her. After all, she was my Godmother.

Moss Street, where I spent the first 5 years of my life.

The house was not light-coloured when we lived there.

Dad on his way to the front – seated by the rifles

Close up of Dad

*Godmother Mary,
who died during
World War II*

20

CHAPTER TWO

Green Mount Road 1944

Late 1943 we were on the move again, this time a short journey down the hill to live in the village. Our parents had by then qualified to rent a council house. Nobody asked me if I wanted to leave and I was very sorry to be taken away from my patch and all my grown-up friends. Mrs Cockroft was very upset at losing her regular breakfast visitor, but to Mum and Dad it must have been like winning the football pools especially as we also had an addition to our family, Danny. The new house, number 8 Green Mount Road, was semi-detached with a front and back garden, which was attached to a very overgrown field. Best of all, there were three bedrooms, which meant the girls could have a room of their own and the number of occupants in our bed was halved. We had an inside toilet and bathroom upstairs and another toilet downstairs. For Dad, it was to be much better, he had only half the distance to travel to his place of work, and the journey was along the flat Market Street.

At the top of the road were fields. One in particular was known as the Yokin. There we were to play some of the greatest soccer matches of our lives over the years to come.

From the very first day, our household chores changed a lot, sadly not all for the better. No longer did we have our beautiful range to clean, or the joy of washdays. We did however, have unlimited baths with lots of hot water and, strange as it may seem we kids, loved them. No more trips across the yard to the toilet on cold or wet nights. Mum had a nice gas cooker in the kitchen and she bought a twin-tub washing machine. So, the Peggy tub, posser and giant mangle became redundant and went on the rag and bone man's cart, never to be seen again.

At that time, Thornton village was a vibrant, exciting place. Market Street ran through the centre and was bordered at either side with shops of every kind. The narrow street was cobbled with what we called 'dumplins' (nine inch square blocks of stone) and the pavements were flagstones. Gas lamps were situated equal distances apart, but they could not be lit at night, due to the war and the blackout regulations. They were, however, great climbing and gymnastic apparatus for all the village kids.

Each lamp was about fifteen feet above street level at the top of a cast iron post. Below the lamp head, a three-foot bar protruded horizontally for the lamplighter to rest his ladder when carrying out his regular maintenance. We would climb up the post, swing on the bar and do various tricks, before sliding back to earth. It was great fun, but we had to keep our eyes open for the local 'bobby', Mr Clegg, and hope to get away before he saw us. It was little use running once he had us in his sight because he knew every child in the village by name – but more important he knew all our parents and had their full support to chastise us.

One of our more favoured exercise lampposts was situated at the junction of Corrie Street and Market Street. The post was positioned next to a horse trough, which had a cover in the form of a lovely stone archway. Almost every day on our way home from school we would descend the street, climb on to the roof of the archway and with a short leap grab the bar on the post. After a few swings and an awful lot of showing off, the participant would slide down and let the next budding athlete have their few minutes of glory.

Adjacent to the trough was a narrow passage where the outside toilets for a row of cottages known as Cloggers Row were situated. Within that narrow little passage, PC Clegg would often hide and wait for us to start our gymnastic routine. In his hand would be his police cape, which was made out of a thin rubbery type of material. As soon as we slid down the post and our feet touched the ground, the cape would flash out like a striking snake and sting the back of our legs. That was our punishment for fooling about on the lamppost.

Another regular stop for us young lads on our way home, was to carry out more mischief on Cloggers Row. An old lady by the name of Mrs Topham was our target. When I think about it now, what we used to do must appear very cruel, but I really don't think she was hurt at all. In fact, like so much of our behaviour to other elders at that time, what we kids did was not malicious in any way but a challenge for the grown-ups to take us in hand.

We would do silly things like knock on her door and hide. Sometimes, we fastened her dustbin lid to her door handle then, when she opened the door to chase us, it would be pulled off, and rattle down the yard. And chase us she did, even though at that time she was in her eighties. All through my boyhood and right up to when I joined the forces, she travelled the five miles by trolleybus to work in Bradford's Kirkgate Market selling flowers. No matter how many of us teased her, we never went too far and she always seemed to like us.

Later, on one of my six-monthly leaves from Germany, during my early service life, I visited the market for some shopping and the very first person I met inside the doors was Mrs Topham, who immediately grabbed hold of me and gave me a hug and a kiss before showing me off to her fellow workers. By that time, she was in her nineties and still working.

Mum and Dad were doing extra jobs in order to keep us kids fed and cared for. Dad no longer had his allotment, so that was my opportunity to further my love of animals. We had lost Peggy the cat, but I still had Rip, a fox terrier born the same year as me. Now I wanted more, so I pestered to keep some chickens. Mr Burdin had taught me a great deal about them so, although I was only seven, I was fully confident that I could make a success of such a venture. I pushed my case hard, on the grounds that the eggs would be very useful for the family. Dad seemed to warm to the idea and to my surprise a couple of weeks later a vehicle arrived with a sectional chicken house and pen on board.

It had come all the way from a company in Kent called Halls, how Dad managed to pay for it I never found out. Putting the unit together was no problem, once our neighbours saw it they all wanted to help and within a couple of hours of its arrival, I was looking at my very first poultry hut and pen. The instruction book stated it could accommodate eight adult birds so now I only needed some lodgers.

"That's up to you, young man," were Dad's words. "Save up or earn some money to buy what you want".

That shed was my pride and joy, and for a couple of weeks I drove Mum mad going in and out of the unit. In the end, she gave in and helped me with some cash unbeknown to Dad. Saturday mornings at Kirkgate Market in Bradford had an open section where almost every kind of small livestock was sold. So, my friend, Walter Cummings, and I went at the very first opportunity, we wandered around for hours but could not find anything in my price range.

I was really choked off, having waited for such a long time (only about ten days but one of my weaknesses has always been lack of patience). We were about to leave to catch our bus back home when I happened to notice a cardboard box beneath a table, with six golden chicks inside. They looked so cold and miserable.

"How much?" I asked the stallholder.

"How much have you got?"

When I replied, to my surprise, he let me take them. Fantastic! I wrapped the box inside my coat and off home, we hurried. Once indoors, Mum had a look and seemed a little bit shocked. However, she explained to me that they were no more than a couple of days old and should really be with a broody hen or in an incubator, but we had neither, so we must do the best we possibly could. Most important they had to be kept clean and warm, or they would very quickly die.

Without any hesitation, she set about cutting a cardboard box down to size, so that it would fit inside the airing cupboard next to the hot water cistern. Then she filled a stone water bottle with hot water and wrapped it inside one of Dad's stump socks, used for protecting his stump within his artificial leg. My first attempt at poultry keeping had started. Unfortunately, due to a combination of inconsistent heat control and my lack of knowledge, Mum's prediction came true and five of the chicks died over the next few days. The sixth survived and was eventually moved outside into my luxury apartment. It turned out to be a cockerel, which would normally be killed, as soon as they hatched. Hence, the reason, I was sold them for a pittance.

I learned so much over those few weeks. My first venture grew up to be a magnificent male specimen of a Buff Orpington, which had a crow that could the wake whole village each day at the break of dawn, far better than any air raid siren. A couple of weeks passed and with Mum's help I had managed to purchase a couple of ducklings and four more hens which had started to lay eggs.

Thanks to Mr Burdin's teaching, they cost me almost nothing to feed. I collected potato peelings, old vegetable leaves and stale bread. The veg waste I boiled, then mashed to a pulp with the rolling pin. The bread I toasted and crushed before mixing the lot together with a spoonful of cod liver oil, which had been issued to us kids to make us healthy – but we were only too willing to let the poultry have the horrible stuff. After a short time, Mum talked the council into letting her rent a piece of the field behind the house. Then, once again, with the help of a few friends, more sheds and fencing were quickly built. By selling eggs and the odd bird, I very soon increased the flock to about twenty. Not quite eight, and already a businessman, thanks to a lot of help from Mum and many of the neighbours.

During the previous year, October 1944, there had been another addition to the family, Maureen. Although Mum had a lot to do in the house she always helped me as much as possible with the preparation of the poultry food.

However, one job Mum never did was shopping. That was a job for us children from the day we moved down into the village. Every Friday night, Barbara, Tony, me and even Kath set off along Market Street with our lists and shopping bags for bread, offal and vegetables. By the time we finished we were loaded up like four packhorses, and many was the time PC Clegg helped us to carry our load home. The money for our shopping trip was Dad's wages hence the Friday payday routine. Any cash left over, plus the little earners, was for beer, cigarettes and a few sweets for us kids. Once the money had run out, which was usually by Tuesday, we relied on 'tick' from Mr Robertshaw's corner shop situated some fifty yards from our front door.

We were never refused any item even when the shop was closed, be it night or day. One of us would go to the house door at the side of the shop, and if the request was for cigarettes, we needed a note signed by Mum or Dad. The Springfield Hotel, the local pub, was directly opposite and very often we would be sent to the back door carrying a jug to collect beer. There was as much trade passed through the back doors as through the front.

For many years, I had watched our Dad religiously study his newspaper every Saturday morning and then, as if by magic, withdraw a third of a very old pencil from his shirt pocket, before scribbling the names of his chosen horses for that day's racing on a scrap of paper. By then, I was old enough to be sent on a clandestine mission along Market Street to a certain house. I would knock on the door, which would be opened the very slightest amount by a man (known as a bookies' runner) with the most miserable-looking face, who would look around very furtively before quickly accepting my Dad's bit of paper and his half a crown. Then the door would be slammed in my face.

Very rarely did I go to collect any winnings. I always thought Mum would have been more successful at backing the horses than Dad with her knowledge of animals, though I never knew how that came about.

Now that we lived in the village, Mum was within walking distance of the Catholic Church, so we children were duty bound to attend Mass every Sunday morning and Sunday school in the afternoon, to learn the catechism and all the ways of the religion. Each time we made a mistake, it was like the end of the world and we received immediate retribution from the teacher or one of the nuns. We would have our hair pulled or our ears twisted. If it was of a more serious nature, a rap on the head with a leg from a wooden stool was the normal way to inflict pain. On our return home, Mum would always ask us what we had done, but we never dared to tell her what really took place. She would never hear anything bad about her religion; consequently, we always let her think everything was good.

One Sunday, after the usual questioning, she asked me. "Did you genuflect when you entered?" Before I could answer Dad said, "That little sod gets up to enough in church without you encouraging him".

Another time, we told her the priest had been talking about a suspected unexploded bomb in the field behind the church. Dad said he didn't'" think it was a German bomber that dropped it, but more likely one of our lads who had previously suffered at Sunday school, as we did and tried to have his revenge. He was usually well clear of Mum when he

26

made any such comments about her religion. Unfortunately, that day he wasn't thinking.

She replied; "I don't think that was very funny", and before he could move she picked up one of the girls' pot dolls and bashed him over the head with it.

For years we suffered that weekly torture by the nuns plus their constant threats that "God is everywhere and he knows what you are up to," in order to frighten us into obedience. On my fifteenth birthday, I told Mum, "If God is everywhere I do not need to go to Church to see him or to pray". That resulted in a major Irish flare-up, which lasted for months. In fact, I do not think she ever forgave me, but my mind was made up, and I never went to the Catholic Church from that day.

❛ *The nearer the church the further from God* ❜

LANCELOT ANDREWES

Late 1944 we moved to the bottom of Green Mount Road into a larger house. I continued with my poultry and all was good. It was still wartime and for a couple of years we had been aware of evacuees in the area, most of whom had been taken in by childless couples, or those who were a bit wealthier than others, and in some cases those who thought they themselves were special – as Dad would say, "full of PAI". We did not meet any of those criteria, so we had never had an evacuee until one day, completely unexpectedly, when I arrived home from school a seven-year-old boy called Tony was seated at our table. He was from Surbiton in Surrey.

I have never forgotten his name, or where he came from. Funny how wonderful the memory is because at that time, I had no idea of anywhere except Thornton, Bradford and Park Avenue Football Club. Of course, we all knew about Germany but not where it was. Tony had lived at three homes prior to ours since his arrival in the village. The first family had asked that he be taken away because he wet the bed. God only knows what he must have gone through, being taken away from his home and family and being dropped off in Yorkshire – that alone was good reason to wet the bed. He was removed from the second home, for the same reason and placed with an elderly couple. Mum heard that they beat him because of his habit, so she went to the authorities and asked that he be moved in with us. Tony became another in the band of brothers sleeping in the same bed.

Each morning, when the bed was wet, Mum blamed a different one of us, but there was no punishment of any kind and after a short time, Tony overcame his problem and once again, we slept on dry land. Dad said that was how we all learned to swim. It was many years later I understood what a diplomatic Irish psychologist Mum had been. Tony stayed with us until 1946.

Then one day, a soldier who said he had been in a German prison camp came to collect him. There was no greeting from either father or son; the lad didn't even know his Dad and was very reluctant to leave with him. Handing a young boy over to a complete stranger could never happen today. Off they went, together and we never heard from our southern friend again. I really hope he had a good life because the start of it wasn't very pleasant. How lucky we kids were, to have been spared such an experience.

Tony had not been gone many weeks before a man and his wife came to stay with us. They were also from London, but what they were doing in the area was a complete mystery to us kids. We did know that Mum and Dad had never met or heard of them before their arrival. Thanks to our overactive minds and listening to Dick Barton, we youngsters reached the conclusion that they must be German spies. We all had a terrific pride about our village, and any stranger who entered was watched with great suspicion, so we watched their every move.

After a month, they went back down south and a strange thing happened. The day they left, my little fox terrier, Rip, disappeared and we did not see him again for two years. Then, early one morning, Mum was awakened by a dog barking in the garden. She opened the window to send it on its way only to realise that it was my long-lost pal. We never found out where he had been, but wherever it was he had been well looked after and was wearing a nice new collar.

Winter came that year with a vengeance and was long and horrible, or so the grown–ups incessantly grumbled. However, we kids thought snowdrifts halfway up the windows and being able to see quite clearly all night, was wonderful. People dug pathways from their houses to the gateways then everybody joined in to clear the pavements. The men and older boys cleared half the road to help the delivery horses and carts do their work, knowing full well that come tomorrow they might well have to do it all again. For weeks, we sledged down Green Mount Road on our homemade sledges thanks to our local blacksmith and his free sledge irons.

The ground was still frozen and rock hard, but the snow had almost all disappeared, and Mum had just returned from one of her cleaning jobs. She was carrying a large paper bag, and she called me over to look inside. What I saw made my heart flutter, it was a pair of wellington boots – something we could only dream about, but never afford. Although they were second-hand ones, which Mum had been given, by her wealthy employer, they would find a good home with one of us. Like the ugly sisters, I began to wish to myself that I would be the one they fitted. Then my feet would be warm and dry for the rest of the winter.

When Mum lifted them out of the bag my elation was somewhat deflated. They were ladies' brown knee-high crocodile pattern boots with high heels and pointed toes. However, it turned out that I was the only one they fitted, so – waste not, want not. For the rest of that winter I wore them, and it didn't bother me – after all many other children had to suffer far worse indignities in second-hand outfits. Some had oversize clogs or wellingtons handed down by their dads or bigger siblings; at least mine fitted me. That was a stage of my life when all my dreams were of being the greatest footballer in the world. Part of my preparation for that high position was to dribble a ball of some kind wherever I went. A neighbour once said to Dad, "If Ginger (that was my name or sometimes 'copper knob' because of my red hair) can control a ball like that in yon fancy boots he will be one hell of a footballer". He got that wrong – perhaps I should have kept those boots.

Travelling to and from school daily was one of life's great pleasures, because the boys and many of the girls had steel hoops, as a result of our daily visits to the local blacksmith's forge. Almost every village child would be there at some time of the day. It was a converging place for children going to and from school especially in the winter when we would stand in the doorway and get ourselves warm while marvelling at the skill of Smithy, as he liked us kids to call him, either shoeing one of the Co-op's giant shire horses or repairing carts. The noise made by the huge hammers on the glowing metal and the heavy breathing of the bellows created the sound effects for the magical world we were in at those times of each day. Just to watch him shape a horseshoe followed by the hiss as he cooled it in a bucket of cold water was pure joy. (It was many years after when working on the Blacksmith section of my Artificer Course that I fully understood what great skills we had the privilege of watching). During his slack periods he would make hoops, scythes, axe heads, chains or sledge irons to sell cheaply, but to the poorer kids they cost nothing.

Our hoops were something very special to us. We would run to and from school steering our pride and joy across cobbles and flagstones, and around obstacles with great skill. The cacophony of noise each morning and evening from the hoops and the clatter of clogs on the energetic feet of so many children, was the sound of happiness. We even decorated the hoops each year for the first day of May.

That was always something very special on a par with Christmas Day. For weeks before, preparations took place for a parade. May Day 1944 was really a day I will always remember.

In addition to all the trimmed-up toys, one of our teachers had organised a small fancy dress parade as part of the show. A limited number of pupils were selected and dressed up as nursery rhyme characters. My sister Kath, was dressed as Miss Muffet and she sat on a little tuffet. The tallest, thinnest girl in the class had a large homemade wobbly woollen toy spider hanging from a length of elastic. She was supposed to stand next to Sis and gyrate the elastic at intervals in order to make the spider seem to be alive. But she was terrified of spiders, and as a result of shaking it too much, it accidentally touched her arm, sending her into a fit of screaming, before finally she fainted. I was Boy Blue "Come blow your horn" – not very funny. The Three Bears were children who had bears' heads made out of brown paper bags, which were pulled down over their faces.

May Day disaster. I am in the back row, second from right. Kath is in the centre at the front.

One of the boys wore very special glasses, like milk bottle bottoms, but had to remove them in order to fit his head into the bag. Consequently, when we walked on parade he couldn't see through the eyeholes and he tripped up. The other boy cried because he didn't like being in the dark and the girl wet herself. To top it all, the Humpty Dumpty outfit was completely enclosed, with just eyeholes to see and breathe through. Unfortunately, the boy nominated by the teacher to be squeezed inside the claustrophobic bag suffered badly from asthma. Consequently, he collapsed and had to be rushed away to the doctor. I thought nothing of it at the time, but years later I thought the teacher responsible for the casting of that little pantomime was either very inefficient or had a very sick sense of humour.

Kath had only been at school a very short time, and one afternoon on arriving home, she was in a rather excitable mood and immediately asked Mum, "Where did I come from?"

For a few minutes, Mum was silenced. But, knowing there was no point in referring that subject to Dad, because she knew Kath would only get the comic's view on a very serious subject, she sat her down and in her own way decided to tell her. At that stage, I was all ears and hung around

31

like a morning fog. It was a very difficult subject for Mum to explain, her being a devout Catholic, but she put on a brave face and went into as much detail as she probably knew, continually losing her voice and blushing as all, us redheads are prone to do. None of what she said made any sense to either Kath or me. Once finished and with a sigh of relief she said; "why did you ask Kathleen?"

"Miss asked Billy Earnshaw, a new boy in our class, where he came from and he replied "Bell Deane, Miss" – the next village down the road from ours.

The only way to deal with death is to transform everything that precedes it into art; we have to make sure we make every day as beautiful as we can. 1945 was another year when death came calling. This time it was a boy in my class, a very small boy called Owen. He had a mop of blonde hair and enormous blue eyes and as I remember, was none too clean. But not many kids of eight years are known for being hygienic. The only times I remember seeing him without a balaclava on his head was when he was actually in the classroom, and once school had finished it was firmly back in place.

He wore clogs and, as was normal for most young boys, his clothes were ill fitting and very ragged, especially the rear of his trousers. But most memorable were two things: one was that he had a terrible habit of wiping his nose on his jacket sleeves until the material texture was like glass. Dad used to tease him about it and gave him the soubriquet "Reflective Owen." He told him he should not be allowed out at night if the moon was shining as the sleeves would reflect the light and attract German bombers to our village.

Number two, was that our teacher one day went into great detail about how every part of the human body continues to grow throughout our lives with the exception of the eyeballs. Owen must have gone home and told his Dad because the following morning he was very quick to attract the teacher's attention and tell her that his Dad said what she had told us about the human body wasn't true. In fact, a certain part of the body really did reduce in size, especially in the cold weather. Some of the boys started a nervous type of titter (although I doubt if they knew what Owen's Dad was alluding to). The girls just stood with vacant expressions (today I feel it would be the reverse). "That's enough, Owen", she said. It was a long time after, before I knew what it was all about and I doubt if poor little Owen ever did.

One morning, not long after, when we went into school assembly the headmaster stood before us and in a very quiet shaky voice announced that Owen would not be coming to school again, because the previous night he had been playing around one of the many mill dams in the area. Sadly, he had fallen in and drowned. That was my very first experience of losing someone who had been reasonably close to me on a daily basis. It was made worse by the fact that the week after, we reached the age when we were taken to Thornton Baths for our very first swimming lessons.

This was another small part of my early schooldays never to be forgotten. After teacher's introduction to the shower before proceeding to the poolside, (a much needed visit for many there) we were to be tempted to jump in, at the shallow end of course, where one of the teachers was. There we stood shivering and searching each other's faces to see the fear. Then, all eyes were turned toward one of the girls who had just climbed out of the pool after her very first entry. Her mother had knitted her costume and water on wool has a very strange effect of making it very wet and heavy . Our classmate stood there all innocent wondering why she had suddenly become the centre of attention for the class, especially the boys. Her two shoulder bands were still in place but had stretched until the rest of the costume was snuggled neatly around her ankles. The moment she became aware she started to blush and every one of us knew how far that blush spread. I don't think she ever quite got over her first swimming lesson.

Later that year the war came to an end and celebrations took place all over the country. Our little village was no exception, and there were community parties in almost every street, which lasted late into the night, and for weeks after, groups of children held their own parties in the Anderson shelters we had used as dens for years. The greatest joy of all, was having the gas lamps in the streets lit again, and not being awakened at all hours of the late night or early morning by that wailing siren, before being crammed under the kitchen table for hours on end. It was the very first time we kids could really see Thornton Village with all its shops lit up, and what a beautiful sight that was, just like a wonderland. We had every kind of shop and even though rationing was still in force, it was a place of great activity.

One of our neighbours, decided to have a dinner party in her garden for her children and friends. There was Mum Sally, as we called her (as she objected to being called Aunt Sally) Dad and her children, four boys and two girls. I put Mum first for very good reason; she was most certainly the boss. Like us, she kept chickens and she also kept pigs in the back garden. I think there was some kind of agreement with the council whereby householders were allowed to rear a pig, and when slaughtered a percentage of the meat had to be put into the food chain. I don't think control of the system was very strict because Sally often had more than one pig.

The party that day consisted of about six youngsters plus her family. We all sat around an even larger table than we had at home, eagerly waiting to be fed. First out of the kitchen was the man of the house carrying a huge pan of steaming mashed spuds, closely followed by one of the girls with her arms full of fresh baked bread. Then the highlight of the meal carried out by Sally in person. It was a giant steaming meat and potato pie, which she had cooked in the largest, flowered chamber pot I have ever seen. I must admit that no one that day was put off by her pie dish. Quite the opposite, we were hungry and loved every mouthful of that delicious pie – made with real meat and topped with the most delicious crust – it was a treat never forgotten.

Years later when Sally's boys had grown to working age, she made sure of family security, by ensuring each boy started a different apprenticeship. One was a joiner; another was a painter, then a plumber and finally a builder. I think if Sally and Herbert had only had one more night of passion there may also have been a candlestick maker. When the last one qualified she started a family business buying and renovating properties. A very 'canny' lady was Sally.

All through my childhood and teenage years there had been a most memorable character living in the village, known to everyone as 'Black Harry'. At the end of Market Street where the cobbled road takes a sharp decline and a left turn down to Thornton Road there was a junk shop. There Harry could be found seven days a week and most of the nights. I suppose his name came from his dress, I never saw him in anything other than shirt and tie, suit, boots and overcoat, and on his head a bowler hat, all black. He would purchase anything from anybody as cheap as possible and once the item was acquired, he seemed reluctant to part with it unless the price was so high he could not refuse. Consequently, the shop was piled from floor to ceiling.

As young lads, we would creep up to the shop and peer in through the windows in a game of 'I spy Harry'. We often saw him sitting or lying asleep in the most unusual places. Rumour was that he was a very rich miser, because he was indeed a real-life Fagin. He did not seem to have any family or friends so he spent the majority of his time among his beloved junk. Then late at night when all was quiet, he would wander home to a little back-to-back cottage he had near the shop.

Many years later, when I was serving in the forces, Mum wrote and told me Harry had been found dead among his beloved junk. The house and shop had been sold at auction and it was no surprise to learn that the buyer was none other than Sally. I was told, that for months after the boys stripped every inch of those properties including excavating the garden. One can only guess what they were looking for. To my knowledge, if Harry had a treasure, it was well hidden and nobody ever found it.

Every day we travelled to and from school along a maze of the most wonderful narrow streets and passageways. Part of that journey took us past a small well-hidden paddock of about one acre, in which most times would be one of the many shire horses owned and used for their enormous strength by the Co-operative Society. The plot seemed to be a place where those beautiful beasts had periods of much needed rest after days of pulling carts full of coal, or other heavy goods up the steep cobbled streets of the village.

One particular morning, as we passed one such horse happily grazing, a member of our gang suddenly produced a catapult from his jacket and before anyone noticed his intentions, he had fired a stone at the animal's hindquarters. "Bull's eye!" he screamed. Where the stone actually struck the animal was nowhere near its eye, but the result was just as dramatic. The massive horse screamed out in shock more than pain then it reared up, muscles rippling, and set off on a gallop quickly covering the few yards of field before reaching the four-foot high dry stone boundary wall. Like a Grand National winner, it flew over it, landing in the cobbled street at the other side before galloping off at high speed down the narrow Sapgate Lane towards the village main street. The noise he made on landing and as he went off into the distance, plus the sparks and stone chippings that flew every time his feet hit the floor was frightening. It sounded like a runaway train.

We kids were terrified into giving chase. I don't know why, because we could not have caught that ton of horseflesh in any way. I suppose it was like some kind of guilt complex. One of our members was the cause of the disaster on legs heading for the unsuspecting villagers, so we were drawn along. The horse was finally caught and calmed down, but not before all the people on the street, that morning had dived for cover to save their lives. PC Clegg was very soon at the scene, so we decided it was time we left and made our way, oh so innocently, to school.

During that period of my life, I learned a lot about community spirit, something which is very rare these days. Living in the village was a man in his late thirties, who sadly he had the mind of a ten year old but the physique of a very big man. He was called Akers and he lived with his Mum. None of the villagers seemed to know much about them, I think it was another case of family censorship, which seemed quite common at the time.

Akers was turned out daily, spick and span like a proper gent unlike us urchins and every morning he would join up with one of the groups of children heading to school. The villagers all knew him and treated him just like any other friend. One of his favourite tricks, to try and impress us kids, was to run away from the greengrocers without paying for his penny apple.

Mrs Hollingsworth, who owned the local shop, sorted all the apples brought each morning from the market by Mr Hollingsworth. Any part of any apple bruised or bad was cut off. Then those apples would be lined up on the shop windowsill, each one priced at one penny. To get the best (the one with the least removed) we had to be first at the shop in order to select whichever apple we wanted, then put our penny in a box at the side. Akers would just take one and run with Mrs Hollingsworth in hot pursuit. She knew he would do it and was always waiting, but never caught him. It was a great game to start the day. Then we would continue our journey to school where Akers would play games with the children in the playground until the bell rang for us to attend assembly. Then, with a look of dejection on his face, he would wander off. But, without fail, he was always waiting at the school gates at lunch and tea times.

During all my years at school, I can only remember Akers having to be told off by a parent once. And that was my Mum. He had been coming home back from school with a group, my brother included, when one of them stole his hat and ran off into our garden. Akers grabbed the boy and would not let him go. Mum heard the commotion and came outside. She told Akers to let the boy go but he refused, which was most unlike him. She then called Rip our dog out, he would not normally let any grown up in the yard, as any of the tradesmen would testify. Mum once again told the big fellow to let the boy go or she would tell the dog to bite him. "The dog will not bite me," said Akers and he let go of the boy to approach the dog. So, Mum told Rip to see him off. To our surprise the dog took no notice whatsoever but stood up, cocked his leg on the clothes post and went back in the house without as much as a bark.

Mum told us later that some people believed dogs knew when people were sick, either mentally or physically. Akers continued to be part of our gang on the way to and from school, all the time I was at the junior school, and I have no doubt he did so with our successors. As I write, my thoughts are about what the children and parents of today would have done to our gentle giant of a friend. I have no doubt, he would have been ridiculed or attacked by teenagers. His mother would have been given a very hard time. To us he was a friend and part of our childhood, but most of all a respected member of our community.

It was a fantastic Saturday morning early in 1945 and as always, I was bursting with energy and looking forward to the day ahead. A group of the bigger boys including my brother Tony had planned a trip to what was known as the 'Rabbit Hills'. Why it had that name was always a mystery because we went there, dozens of times over the years and I can never remember seeing any sign of a rabbit. The hills were very steep and to reach them we had to climb up through a very dense wooded area.

On that particular morning, me and a friend, Colin Jaques, had decided to tag along. The place we were going to play was a series of overgrown ruins from days gone by when stone had been removed from the hillside for the building of farms and houses that were now no more than grassy mounds, ideal hiding places for any youngsters to play war games.

As we emerged from the wood, we came face to face with a man carrying a shotgun. "Where are you lot going?" he asked, and one of the bigger boys told him. None of us was worried that we might be trespassing on that man's land because like the Yokin at the top of our road, no one seemed to own the Rabbit Hills. No cattle ever grazed there, nor did agricultural work ever take place.

"You lot can go up to play," he said pointing at the bigger boys "But you should really leave the two little ones with me to look after", pointing at Colin and me. I don't know what went through Colin's head but for my part, I was not very happy. However, before I had the chance to scream out or run like hell, Aiden, one of the biggest boys in the group, said; "No chance, mister, they come with us". At that, the bigger lads seemed to grow in stature and vociferously supported what Aiden had said. They were twelve- and thirteen-year-olds and one or two were footballers from the big school.

The man argued for a short time saying he owned the land and it was too dangerous for us little ones to play on, but it did not sway the older boys, thank goodness. Then the chap simply said, "Bugger off then".

As we climbed the hill and looked back, we saw him running away through the woods like one of the rabbits we had always hoped to see. I have thought many times over the years what could have happened that Saturday morning if it had not been for Aiden's leadership. Unfortunately, however, he lived a short life and died of a heart attack in his early twenties.

With every day that passed my enthusiasm for football was growing stronger, so Dad decided it was time he took me to watch Bradford Park Avenue play. I loved every minute of the journeys over the months and

Dad in 1950's

years that followed. Some were by bus or tram, but the journey I loved the most was when we went by train. Going over Thornton Viaduct was a sight to behold, followed closely by three minutes of very scary smoky darkness as we passed through the Queensbury Railway Tunnel, so exciting for a young boy.

Once at the ground, the entrance fee was not very much but Dad very rarely had to pay for either of us. Once the staff on the turnstiles noticed Dad was handicapped, they seemed to understand the reason why, and let us through for free, with the utmost respect.

When we were inside, the crowd would part like the Red Sea to allow him and any other invalids to pass through to the front of the crowd. Me and any other kids had an aerial trip. We were lifted aloft, and passed hand to hand over the sea of cloth flat caps down to the front to sit on the wall behind the goal net.

After one Saturday game as we left the ground, outside was a donkey harnessed to a portable oven on wheels at the top of which was a sign, which read, 'Hot baked potatoes with butter 1d'.

"Would you like one?" said Dad. As I had never seen anything like it before, my answer was a definite yes. I also wanted the chance to stroke a donkey, something I had only seen in a book previously. When it was our turn to be served, the little old man who I presumed to be owner of business told Dad we were lucky to see him. Normally he should not be there at that time of day because he had a long way to go back home. Unfortunately, his donkey was quite content enjoying all the attention the crowd were giving him and simply refused to move away.

"I don't know how I can get the stubborn little sod back home," the gent said.

"I can move him," Dad said. "Pick up those reins and keep tight hold".

"If tha moves him the spuds are on the house," said the old vendor.

With that, Dad picked up a hot spud lifted the donkey's tail and placed it firmly on its anus. In one swift action, but too late, the animal clamped its tail down tightly in an attempt to protect the sensitive area before letting out the most horrific donkey scream and taking off like a beast possessed with the red, hot spud clamped tight to its nether region and the old chap hanging on for dear life. Potatoes flew in all directions and a trail of firewood littered the road. Very soon, the long-eared equine had disappeared out of sight and the crowd of onlookers were in stitches. We never did see that cart or the vendor again and I never got my hot spud. On the train home, Dad said he had learned that trick during the war when the horses would not move. He never did say where they got the red, hot potatoes.

Although we were only eight years old, a few of us young lads would go on our own to the Avenue at every opportunity, to watch the players training. There was no special area; the running was done around the actual pitch. The technical skills took place on what was the car park but very rarely used.

Every aspect of the game was more or less self-taught; there was no such person as a coach. On those evenings, we would make every effort to join in and listen to all the tips. Some of the players would spend time with us youngsters especially Len Shackleton (Shack) the greatest controller of the football I have ever seen; his skill was pure magic.

All those years ago, the footballs were made out of leather sections stitched together. Inside was an inner tube, which was inflated by a hand pump, before the opening was closed up tight with a leather lace. When the ball got wet and the leather had absorbed water, the weight of the ball could vary considerably and passing became quite difficult. Heading was a very skilful technique requiring extra strong neck muscles and perfect timing. Any mistakes could lead to serious pain, cuts, or even concussion. So, to watch Len make it look so easy, was pure joy to us lads. Sadly, for all the Park Avenue supporters he was transferred to Newcastle United during 1946 and just to highlight his genius, the man scored six goals on his debut for 'The Toon' – a feat that has yet to be beaten.

Walter and I were great friends and probably the very first people in Thornton to have their own private telephone system. We lived about fifty yards apart so to enable us to communicate we decided to set up a system. First, we found two 'Tate and Lyle' empty treacle tins, punched a hole in the bottom of each and threaded fifty yards of string through the holes before tying a knot at each end, to retain the tin in position. I carried the contraption up to my bedroom and one of the tins was dropped out through the window. We walked across all the gardens, watched in amazement by the householders, to Walt's. There he went up to his bedroom, opened the window and I threw the tin through. When I returned home, we pulled the string tight between the two houses, and we had a telephone link – not exactly top class but it worked, better than some I experienced in various parts of the world in later years.

The field behind our house was a mass of nettles and long grass apart from where we had built our mini chicken farm. So, one day Walt and I decided to clear the top off and create our own private sports arena. We built stone piles for goal posts and hammered into the ground a set of permanent wickets. On that tiny piece of scrubland circled by council houses, Walt and I played football for all the home countries on the same day, and during the good weather we played cricket for England and Australia. Many hundreds of hours were enjoyed in that sporting paradise, there we honed our skills from the age of eight up to leaving school at fifteen. As we grew up, our main ambition was to play football in the Yokin with the bigger boys. The field had a twenty-degree slope from top to bottom and all the games were played across the slope.

It was a magnificent arena for many very important matches played at weekends and during school holidays. Our opposition was from the many surrounding villages and the only equipment we needed was a football, usually supplied by one of the lads, who was always guaranteed a place in the team irrespective of his soccer skills, and a number of coats. There was no set age for players; anyone could play if selected. Finding a referee was no problem either. There was always someone who would never be good enough to make the team but wanted to be involved and liked a bit of power. Their decisions as referee were final; no arguments, no fighting, spitting or swearing. We simply played the sport to the best of our ability for the pride of our village.

It will be no surprise to read, my first ever pair of soccer boots were cast-offs from more than one person before Mum got them. As with the footballs of the day, they were manufactured from very hard leather with toecaps like concrete. On the soles were leather bars for gripping. Both the boots had been well and truly used – one more than the other. I say that because they were not a genuine pair, the design of each one was very different. Plus, whoever had worn the left boot suffered badly with a tendency to walk over to the inner on that foot, so when I stood up, my right foot was good but the left leaned inward at a dangerous angle (angles seemed to haunt me during my young life), at least they were left and right and better than nothing. I felt quite proud wearing them with a Dandy comic down one sock and a Beano down the other for shin pads. I had the usual problem with nails, common in all leather-soled footwear, as the sole became worn the nails were pushed up inside the boot or shoe and into the wearer's sock, or worse still into the feet. Many were the time I could not remove those boots after a game, due to the nails being stuck in the flesh. How we, kids never got blood poisoning or worse, was a miracle.

During the summer holidays or weekends, when we were not playing or watching sport we would search for work on the local farms. Anything that would make us some money was always high on our agenda. On one of the farms where we spent a lot of time, there were German prisoners of war, who had been sent there to work the land, in order to earn their keep. We had some great times and they taught us a great deal about farming.

To our gang, the countryside was a place of absolute magic. We learned how to soothe nettle stings by rubbing them with a squashed dock leaf; we drank fresh spring water and chewed vinegar leaves for energy (not that we needed any). We dined on crab apples, bread, and cheese from the hawthorn tree early in the year and we never hesitated to lift a few turnips from the fields or a few apples from any nearby orchard and even squeeze a drop of fresh milk from one of the many cows grazing in the fields nearby. We were indeed the perfect bucolic kids.

On our leisure days or school holidays, we would go as a gang down to the local beck early in the mornings and return home as the light was fading at night. There, we would often fish for rainbow trout by hand. The fish would be hidden away beneath large stones or under partial walls, even beneath the riverbanks. Our technique was to put our hands into those places and feel around slowly, once we made contact with a trout we moved our hand slowly and skilfully up its body until our fingers were on its gills – then we would grab tight and withdraw our hand. Sometimes it was impossible to retreat from the hole, still holding the hapless fish. We would then try to tease it into a more accessible position. It was always a bit scary putting a hand into the unknown, for like all rivers, there were plenty of rats (voles), but we were not deterred. Any trout caught, which were larger than our gang rule of nine inches, was taken home there to be cleaned, cooked and enjoyed for dinner.

A high percentage of the fields were left ungrazed or worked. The grass was allowed to grow and grow to create hay for animal winter feed. Such fields were simply heaven to be near during mid-summer, around cutting time. The vegetation would be three feet high and inter-mixed with every type of wild flower and grass one can imagine, and the smell on a summer's day was unbelievable.

Quite often, the whole gang of us would just lie down in the centre of one such field on the cool ground, chewing a stalk of grass and smelling the fresh hay laced with the scent of wild flowers blown across us, on a warm gentle breeze of a summer's day; completely out of sight from the rest of the world, except the skylarks as they sang their way up to the heavens, or the swallows which constantly flew low across us in curiosity. Probably, it was not curiosity, but more the fact that we were grotty sticky little erks who attracted many flies wherever we went. There, we would talk and plan our mischief or just absorb the sunshine while listening to the sounds of our own little piece of heaven. Life really was beautiful and from those long-gone days, I became an aesthete.

To be down the beck and in the woods was a world of peace where we kids alone existed, and nobody bothered us. During the winter, when the beck was frozen over, and the fields were rock hard and white with ice and snow, we got great pleasure from following animal tracks for miles.

Sometimes Walt's dog, Lassie would lift one of the beautiful brown hares, of which there were so many, and give chase followed by the whole gang of us, for one or two fields. We never caught anything and didn't really want to, but it was great fun and exercise for both us and the dogs. When we did return home after such expeditions, knackered, grotty and very hungry, we quite often got a telling off or the back of Mum's hand, for the state we or the dogs were in. But we never went to bed unwashed or hungry.

> *In youth we learn*
> *In age we understand*

MARIE EBNER VON ESCHENBACH

CHAPTER THREE

1948

A decade had quickly passed since that wonderful day in Hustler Street. During that time, I had seen my share of blood and 'snot and become very friendly with a number of medical staff. I had also taken a massive geographical move to further my education about a mile further up the village at Thornton Secondary School. More important to me, was the fact I was then eligible to wear long trousers. So, once again Mum had managed to find a second-hand pair in time to undergo a major re-design, so they would kind of fit me to start the new term. The bottoms were really wide, because that part of the trouser had originally been the middle of the leg!

My very first trip back home from my new school, was once again a memory worthy of mention. Like all young lads, or perhaps just me and the rest of the idiots I went to school with, we had a never-ending list of strange things to do. That evening, I was to attempt to break the world record for walking a mile in complete darkness. Once again, a piece of clothing became useful for something other than what the manufacturer had in mind.

A couple of my friends fastened my coat around my head, completely blacking out the light. If it hadn't been for the place that they, by chance, left the sleeve. I would also have been without air and would probably have suffocated. I quickly realised that if I held the sleeve out in front of my face, I was able to breathe quite easily. The lads started me off at the school and, by talking to me, intended to guide me the one mile back home. Although I could not see, I suspect the villagers on Market Street that evening, were puzzled at the sight of me with my head covered and my coat sleeve held out in front of my face like an elephant's trunk, as I staggered about, trying to follow the directions of a few undecided idiots. It must have been very entertaining.

To be fair to my guides, we almost made it over the cobbles and uneven paving all the way home, thereby breaking the record. Unfortunately, when well within sight of my house, the team decided to show an interest in a Ringtons Tea delivery horse and completely forgot about me. Suddenly my foot kicked the kerbstone, my head once again, came into contact with some good old Yorkshire stone and lights flashed inside the darkness of my coat. I was immediately unwrapped by a passing villager and given a quick medical before being delivered to my unsurprised mother. Since being picked up, I had been aware of a pain in the centre of my forehead, and it was not easing off at all. Mum took one look and dragged me inside before pushing my head under the cold tap in the kitchen sink. After a few minutes, she brought a mirror so that I could view the result of my daft idea. Absolutely central on my forehead was a lump like a half tennis ball that was soft to the touch. I think Mum's rapid intervention had stopped its growth, but it took a week or more of embarrassment, changing to many different colours, before finally disappearing.

The majority of schools in Bradford and the outlying areas, with the exception of the grammar schools, had at least one football team. The whole city was made up of a number of leagues. Competition was of the highest calibre and the sport was taken very seriously. Soccer fixtures were played every Saturday morning on parks and playing fields all over Bradford. Alas, today most of those fields have gone and the leagues no longer exist.

Every Saturday morning, groups of young boys could be seen on street corners waiting with great anticipation for their sports teachers to escort them to wherever they were due, to play their league match. Most of those lads would not have slept a wink the night before, as a result of the excitement of the challenge to come in the morning. All would be dressed in school football shirts and would have football boots hanging around their necks. The reason for wearing the strip was that not many schools had any changing facilities near the ground. Shoes and jackets would be left at the side of the pitch with no worries about their safety, firstly, because most kids had no clothes worth stealing and secondly because we were proud of living in a community and stealing was frowned upon by the majority of people.

Brother Tony – R.M. early 1950s

As a new arrival at my school, so very young and weighing about five stone, my dreams of playing for the school team were at least two years away, or so I thought. I really got that wrong. The very first Saturday after my arrival at the school, brother Tony and some of his friends, who did not play the game and certainly never watched, said they were going to watch the school team play. I managed to persuade them to take me along, never thinking it would become a day for me to remember for the rest of my life. The area of Bradford where the team was going to play, was called Great Horton – not exactly a good place to go, let alone play football against them.

The weather was atrocious as it had been raining heavily for most of the week and there was still no sign of it stopping. When we arrived, the pitch, like most in those days, was in very poor condition; no grass, lots of potholes full of water, and the whole area one big mud bath. Horton was at top of the league, unbeaten so far that season, and my new school was well and truly at the bottom. One look at the opposition and I knew the top place was not due to their football skill or ability, quite the opposite. I think the other teams let them win because it was much safer. They reminded me of the Bash Street Kids in the comic.

That Saturday morning, one of our school team had not turned up and I heard the teacher saying maybe it was due to weather, or possibly, he was sick. Inwardly, I had a little chuckle, and thought he probably had more sense than the rest. Then I saw the teacher talking to my brother and his pals, after which they headed in my direction.

"The teacher wants you to fill the position; we have told him you are a good player". I bet you have, I thought. What had really taken place was, the teacher had asked which one of them would play and they had all refused but had volunteered me to be the 'patsy'. Inside I was really excited, but I had no kit, only what I had travelled in. They soon managed to search out a shirt for me and a pair of shorts, which would have fitted my Dad. I had to play in my school boots. So that day, I started my school football career way out on the left wing looking like the scarecrow, Worzel Gummidge. The whole match was one of players wallowing in thick mud, except for me stuck out on the wing in the wilderness of Great Horton. Up to the last few minutes of the match, the ball had not once been anywhere in my vicinity, mainly due to the amount of water it had soaked up making It almost immovable. Not that the opposition were really interested in the ball, our team had been kicked off the park. Yet by some miracle there was still no score.

It was just about that time I was having serious trouble just trying to walk about to keep myself warm. My little frame was weakening, as the minutes passed, under a soaked jumper and shorts, and I was seriously contemplating retiring from football altogether. Suddenly, the football was hacked up the field towards me – not a pass by any means, just a last desperate burst of energy from one of our players. It stopped dead, right in front of me with a horrible squelching sound and I came to life and kicked it forward towards the opposition goal. It did not travel very far and for a few seconds I thought my leg was broken, but I limped off in soggy pursuit kicking the ball a few feet at a time. I could hear the Horton players coming after me, grunting and shouting. That was enough to galvanise my body to greater effort. At least three of their players passed me, but could not stop and they slithered by and finished up sprawled in a muddy heap. That gave me the opportunity to move the ball a bit further before finally mustering up every last bit of my energy to kick the soggy, leaden, lump of leather in the general direction of the opposition goal. I still believe to this day, that the goalkeeper had gone to sleep or become numb with hypothermia due to his morning's inactivity. Whatever the reason, he was caught out, and the ball literally trickled over the goal line and into the net. We had won and beaten the top of the league, and I was a hero.

Come Monday morning my name was up on the school notice board and I was given a round of applause in the assembly. I could not have felt prouder if I had been in the World Cup Team. I must admit it was a bit 'hairy' running away from Great Horton that Saturday morning. It's not much fun being a wanted man at the age of ten.

A long time passed before I was chosen to play for the school team again. It was the usual case of being good enough on a wet morning against a team of psychopaths who were leading the league, but as soon as the bigger boy had made his excuses for being absent on that day, I was too young and too small. A few months passed and then I was selected on merit to play at home against Clayton School from the next village.

Our school pitch was at the highest point of Hill Top, where we had lived during the war years. Anyone who has ever made that climb would testify that just to reach the field, is on a par with ascending Mount Everest. On arrival, the first requirement is an oxygen mask, then there is a choice: either enjoy the view or freeze to death before the rescue party arrives. From up there, on top of the world, it is possible to see the whole city of Bradford, some five miles away.

At that stage of the season, Clayton were bottom of the league, as we had been on that historic day at Great Horton. I played centre forward, later to be known as striker, we won the match ten goals to nil. Luckily, I scored five, which I thought was terrific, and we all showed off a bit. We did have a very good team at the time and played very well together; however, our bravado was short lived. Mr Priestly, our sports teacher, gathered us all together and told us that winning by the score we had was great, but not to brag or show off. Sport, more than anything, is the way for youngsters to learn that their competitor on the field is not their adversary, but their partner, and to learn that the object is not just to beat her or him, but to bring out the best in both and grow together with generosity, honesty, loyalty and respect – or words to that effect. Something I have always tried hard to remember and follow.

Come Saturday evenings the young lads of the village would queue up outside the local newsagents, eager to purchase and read the Yorkshire Sports, which contained all the local sports results, professional and otherwise, within its pages. The school results would be there, complete with goal scorer leagues and a short match report on each game. If our names were in the paper it was fantastic. A few years after I left the village, the sports fields were sold off to developers, and the leagues disappeared. Consequently, the young girls and boys lost the very valuable lessons of team spirit and discipline, which help children grow up to be useful members of society.

Not many days had passed after our soccer match, when another great sporting event was organised. Many of my friends were from Irish families and a cousin of one such family had recently moved into the area. It was a lovely evening, albeit a bit cold. We were playing one of our usual games of tin can squat when the self-appointed group leaders, my brother included, decided to organise a boxing match for the 'Championship of the World.

The venue for such a high profile event was to be one of the three disused stone quarries in our village. They were favourite play areas for all of us. Every one of those holes in the ground was a bird-nesting paradise. Over the many years since they became derelict, gorse bushes had grown in abundance and in the spring were home to linnets, bullfinches, hedge sparrows and blackbirds, to name just a few.

A ring was duly marked out with our usual equipment, which means coats were strategically placed (our clothes had a great many uses, especially when it came to sport). A bucket and a sponge were acquired and even a watch for time keeping. Finally, a dustbin lid and a hammer to be used as a bell, were added. We all gathered at the ring at a certain time, eager to see a good scrap. There the bigger boys who were always in charge, got together in a huddle to discuss final plans. After a short time, the self-appointed spokesman made an announcement.

"The boxing match due to take place for the 'Championship of the World' is between ... (long pause) representing Ireland; Patrick, Paddy 'O Kane", he shouted. That was the new kid. I immediately thought, poor sod picked on because he is the new kid on the block. "And representing England; Peter Horn".

That was a hell of a shock, nobody asked me. I found out later that there had been a vote among the older boys. Of course, most of them had appointed themselves to positions such as referee, seconds, trainers and even bell ringer. It was all carried out in secret. I hadn't been party to any of that skulduggery and my own brother was among them.

50

It was quite an occasion, plenty of laughing and friendly shouting especially when they found out it wasn't them who was to be in the ring (a touch of Schadenfreude). After a while, I actually began to warm to the idea and stupidly convinced myself that they really had selected me on merit – one of my many failings as a young boy.

The bell rang for the first round to commence and we danced around each other for a while as we had seen on the Pathe newsreel boxing matches at the cinema, during our Saturday morning visits. Then, we threw a few dummy punches; at least I did, but Paddy had other ideas. Suddenly, one mighty straight left from him hit me smack in the left eye. Immediately the bell rang, so the corner men and all the others who had found themselves cushy jobs could pretend to do their bit. I was soaked with water and given loads of advice. The best advice should have been, get to hell out of there.

The bell for the second round rang out, and the same routine. We pranced about for a short time, then wham! Yet another thunderous left in the same eye. That went on for six rounds, by which time I could not see out of that eye. So, a decision was made by all, especially me, that the Irish kid was the new 'Champion of the World'. (I never found out who the previous champ had been). Home we went, my brother Tony and 'Eye'.

When we entered the house Mum immediately noticed my lovely eye, which was changing colour and closing by the minute and as she bathed it, she wanted all the details. Her face was a picture of pride and smiles as I told her the story. Meanwhile, my brother was trying his very best to disappear. Then I got to the part of naming my opponent.

Suddenly the atmosphere changed dramatically and took a turn for the worse. At that stage, Tony did escape. Mum's expression changed, the smile and the pride vanished, to be replaced with a ghastly look of disbelief, and I received another straight left in the same eye. She knew the family of the recently arrived cousin and was very proud that I had taken part in the fight, but to lose to a Protestant was simply too much for her.

Dad never interfered in anything to do with her Irish friends. She did not expect him to understand their ways, especially the fighting. Mum did say sorry to me later for the smack in the eye. She said it wasn't my fault that I had lost the fight; it was because I was what she called, soft Irish, having been born and reared in England.

Many years ago, I read a quote to the effect, that a leader is a person who has the ability to get other people to do what they don't want to do, and like it. That was Miss Rigg, our new teacher at the secondary school, she was about thirty, very old to us children but by far the youngest teacher in the school at the time. She spoke very nicely and was always impeccably turned out. When she asked questions of me, or any other class member, it was like talking with a big sister. Our knowledge was being constantly tested, and consequently we were doing everything she asked of us, believing that should we have any difficulty, she was always there to help us. I never remember her losing her temper with any one of us, every member of that class was putty in her hands.

Up to that stage of my schooling, I was well below average in every subject and was not really interested in much more than football, cricket, birds nesting and fishing. Then my life changed forever. She had the power to mould thirty-plus sponges to do her bidding, with very little effort. Today, I still believe that young lady had been a very special manager of people, even if they were only four feet tall – a very rare teacher indeed.

Examinations were taken twice a year, in every class at the school, and covered every subject taught during that particular term. On completion of such examinations test papers were marked out of a possible one hundred marks. Afterwards, each child took home to their parents a report, complete with all the results. They included teachers' comments and headmaster's comments. At the bottom of each report was a tear-off slip, which had to be signed by the parents and returned to the school.

Every single result was posted on the notice board along with class positions. Number one, the top of the class would be seated, first left on the rear row and carry on moving to the right as the rows came to the very front of the class. Consequently, all the children needing the most help were directly in front of the teacher, where a close eye could be kept on them and help given if needed. My position in the class that year was, number two and, in the following examination, number three. This was the highlight of my school life and an educational miracle, thanks to Miss Rigg.

I don't know which came first – the horrific cracking sound or the searing pain which started in my mouth then shot up my nose before culminating in an explosion of flashing lights behind my eyes. That day, our after-school dinner play period had started in the same way as every other day. We were playing a very serious game of football with a small ball in the playground, a large area covered by flagstones which had seen hundreds of pupils come and go over the years, and were showing their age. Many were cracked or completely broken; others had sunk, and all were quite well worn. It was a very tricky terrain to play on, but we were never deterred. On that day, the surface of the floor could not be blamed in any way for what happened, only for being there when my face landed.

I was being far too clever for my own good, trying to emulate my hero Len Shackleton by dribbling the ball past a couple of the bigger boys. Unfortunately, one of them was not too pleased and stuck out a leg. The next thing I saw was the uneven floor coming towards me. Then, I was being picked up by a couple of players but left on the yard covered in a very familiar red fluid were what appeared to be parts of teeth. I looked around the faces of my friends who were dusting me down and my now super-agile mind, thanks to Miss Rigg, very quickly knew that all their teeth were intact. Not all in the right places or on the correct level but intact. Then I began to taste the warm salty fluid in my mouth, which had become so familiar to me during my short life, and at that moment I took a sharp intake of breath. Then I really did know whose teeth they were lying there on the yard. It was like two electric shocks starting in my top gum shooting up my nose and making my eye balls spin.

Not for the first time was I escorted home from school, and not for the first time did I hear Mum say, "What's the barmy little devil done now?"

The following day, after a really painful sleepless night and with a face, which, by that time had, swollen at an alarming pace making me look like the Elephant Man, I was at the school dental clinic in Bradford.

The dentist took one look and said to Mum, "What is left of those two front teeth must come out now".

At that stage I had no idea that what was about to happen would change my life forever. I was put to sleep and when I woke up where there used to be two strong healthy teeth was a gap. After a few weeks, I had a very primitive two tooth denture fitted. To hold it in place were a couple of wires, which crudely wrapped around the surrounding teeth. It felt quite loose and the wires were rubbing. I told Mum and she told the dentist who said, "He will get used to them".

As the years passed, I became very aware of how much damage that first plate had done and as a result I had very quickly lost about half my top teeth due to wire movement causing corrosion. Only when I joined the Army did I get any kind of proper dental treatment but too late, the damage had been done. From that fateful morning, I really envied anyone with nice teeth and cursed the many who had good choppers but did not look after them, instead letting them decay or turn colour, giving them bad breath. If only they knew how lucky they were.

My next altercation with the flagstones was not as devastating. Nevertheless, it was very painful and laid me low once again. This time the doctor said I had punctured my kneecap, which swelled up to such an extent that I could not bear to put any weight on that leg. I was sent to bed, there to be burnt to death with hot kaolin poultices, until the swelling had opened and let the poison out.

For almost two weeks, I suffered that treatment day and night, to no avail. Then one night I heard the doc telling Mum that if there was no change in my condition come the morning he would send me into hospital to have it operated on. That night I put to the test what the Catholic priest and his army of nuns had drummed into me. God is everywhere. So, I prayed incessantly to him, I did not want to go to hospital, the last time it took me eight weeks to get back out.

To my delight the following morning, the pain had subsided and when Mum removed the dressing and bathed the knee the poison was pouring out. Needless to say, since that night I have always believed in the power of positive thought and prayer because even though I do not believe in religion, I do believe there is something far superior to us humans, responsible for such a wonderful world. I never told Mum about my praying for she would have taken me straight to Father Moverly at the Catholic Church and they would have used it as a public exercise or some kind of miracle.

At the end of my first year at the big school, I sat my eleven plus examination and was successful which meant I had the choice of going to the grammar school or remaining where I was. Although I knew my Mum and Dad would do everything possible for me to be the first in the family to go down that path, I also knew they would really struggle to afford uniforms, sports kit, books and bus fares. So, I told them I did not want to play rugby, which was the number one sport at the grammar. At that time, I still wanted to be first a footballer and second a fighter pilot. I never understood that I needed that grammar school education to succeed as a pilot.

Mum's relief at my choice was very obvious. Walter, I think, failed his exam but his Mum and Dad sent him to another school in Bradford by the name of Priestmans. They had to pay for the things Mum could not afford; I think they believed Walt would get a better education. So off he went, and our friendship was never the same. I suppose it was only natural; he had new schoolmates and he was playing football for a better school team. However, we still spent lots of time together at the weekends.

Mum, Mo and Danny in the 1950s

55

We had by then started to spend time on Saturdays and Sunday nights in about six different houses. There we played Subbuteo table football or cricket board games. As always, everything was done on a league basis in a very competitive way and all results were recorded and tables kept up to date. Altogether, there were about six of us in the group so with leagues and cup matches we had many enjoyable weekends.

Above: *Walter and me – off to Park Avenue – aged 14*

Left: *Peter Horn, aged fourteen and a half – note lack of teeth – just before leaving school*

CHAPTER FOUR

Leaving School 1952

In 1952 I left school for ever at the age of fifteen years, height; five feet two inches, weight; eight stone, to go out into the big world and earn a living. More important was that I would have an input into the family finances with more than just my chickens, which, by the way, were still doing well. There was no fuss about leaving school. On the Friday night a number of us who were eligible to leave, simply went home never to return. During that last journey from school, my thoughts were spinning around inside my head. Perhaps I could go to Park Avenue and be a footballer or try to be a fighter pilot or ask Dad to teach me how to paint for a living. I had completely forgotten about what Mum might have in store for me.

As I walked into the house she proudly announced, "I have got a job for you, start at seven o'clock on Monday morning, at Mark Dawson's Mill. I have spoken to Jimmy Smith (he was one of the neighbours who had helped me so much with the building of my poultry sheds). He is going to train you to be an Overlooker in the spinning shop".

Sadly, the following day, Saturday, was to be the worst day of my young life. Rip, my little dog who had been a constant companion, with the exception of the two years he was missing, was coming to the end of his life. He had not been himself for a couple of weeks and now was showing obvious signs of pain. "It is only fair you take him to the vets, he has had a good innings", said Dad. He was always considered as mine, so it was my duty to take him to the PDSA.

On that Friday night, I lay downstairs for hours. I had nobody to turn to, so I prayed to God that Rip would get better, knowing in my heart that his life was coming to an end. I kept talking to my little friend, but he was in no mood to pay any attention. By the time I finally went to bed, I had cried so much I ached all over.

On the Saturday morning I travelled the five miles to Bradford on the trolleybus, with my little dog on my lap. He kept raising his eyebrows to look at me and all I could think was, why had he to go? I always knew that the day would come but I always put it to the back of my mind. To this day, I can see him looking at me as if to say thank you; then he licked my hand as the vet inserted the needle, his little eyes glazed over, and my best friend had slipped into an everlasting sleep and my heart was broken. That night I cried until I could cry no more. For weeks after I was inconsolable, and I would often look behind expecting to see him cocking his leg on someone's gatepost. Many people told me he was only a dog. Not so! Every single animal I ever kept has been something special, they give everything and demand nothing in return. But now, all these years after, I know that nothing ever dies if you don't want them to. I will remember all my friends until we meet again.

The following day, another disaster took place. One of my classmates and football team colleagues, by the name of Kenny, was knocked down by a car. That was a very rare happening due to very small number of cars on the roads. His brother worked at a farm near the School Green area of Thornton and Kenny had travelled on the trolleybus that morning from higher up the village. He had jumped off at his stop and, obviously without thinking, run behind the bus across the road into the path of a car. He was taken to hospital unconscious, never came around and died a week later. He was a great little footballer and a tough lad. After my disaster of a fight with the Irish kid, Kenny crossed his path at school and a very good scrap took place. One blow my friend threw, missed and he hit the wall and smashed his hand, and the teachers stopped the fight going any further. We had many schoolyard altercations which boiled over into punch-ups but always on a fair basis, not like today. If one fighter was hurt that was the end of it – no kicking or using bricks or lumps of wood, and certainly very few cowardly attacks with gangs or from ambush. Quite often a fight, which was not settled, because the teachers stopped it or someone was hurt and still wanted to carry on later, took place after school at an agreed place in a proper manner. Most outcomes of such fights were as all sport should be, with respect, shake hands after and be friends.

The whole school went to Kenny's funeral.

Monday arrived and three of us from the secondary school presented ourselves at the mill. There we were met by Jimmy, the spinning room Overlooker, and taken to the ground floor where I was to start my working life. The noise of the machinery was horrendous and the smell from the oil in the wool was quite sickening. It was hot and impossible to converse with each other, I learned very quickly that the workers were experts at lip-reading and sign language. Those two things I would also have to become proficient at. The brief tour was over, and I was put to work on my first task. All apprentices had to learn every job in the department if they ever hoped to be a spinning room Overlooker and one day, be the man in charge of the whole floor, with a staff of twenty women and girls plus six men to operate some twenty spinning looms.

My starting job was that of bobbin ligger. Each loom was some thirty feet long with more than a hundred bobbins, continually being filled with spun wool. The looms were looked after by experienced women operators or girls whose job was to patrol along the front of the bobbins. These were being spun from overhead larger bobbins of thicker wool, which was thinned as it passed through rollers. During the process, the wool often broke; then the operator would find and repair the broken ends.

Once all the bobbins were full, the operator would switch the loom off and very quickly transfer full bobbins to a rack above the loom where empty bobbins were waiting to take their place on the machine. Once they were all changed over, the loom was switched back on and each empty was fed a leader from overhead. The whole task was done very fast in order to keep the machine working to full capacity.

My turn then arrived. I carried a large leather box strapped around my neck as I had to walk the length of the loom, both sides, removing the full bobbins from the overhead rack into the box, before loading them into a waiting cart. Once that task was completed, I filled my box with empty bobbins and put one on each overhead peg. That went on all day; in addition, I took away all the full carts and brought back empty bobbins. By lunchtime, I was absolutely knackered, I was hot and sticky and covered in fine wool, which made me itch like hell, and I was as deaf as a post.

By the time I got home that evening after my first day I had lost all feeling. After a few days, I was used to the heat and the noise and was becoming quite efficient and fast at the art of bobbin ligging. Like most jobs, there was a technical skill even to a job so mundane. One of the older ladies showed me how to use all my fingers on both hands, when filling the racks with empties so that I was able to replace ten bobbins before reaching into the box again. Then she taught me how to run along the rows flicking the full bobbins into the box two at a time. After that first week, I could run up and down the aisles emptying and then filling the racks very quickly.

Unfortunately, after two weeks I hated working there; not the people or the job, simply being locked indoors. I longed to be in the fresh air of my beautiful countryside. I was, however, impressed that the workers were such a good team and worked so hard together. The age range was unbelievable; from youngsters, just out of school like me, to ladies and gents in their late seventies, and even one or two in their eighties. The oldest was a chap called Charlie Smithson who oiled all the machinery; he was ninety-two when I started.

I had many thoughts about leaving to find other employment, but a few more weeks passed and things changed, which delayed the inevitable. That was when my boss started me off as a dinner boy. From that day on, I had to collate a daily list from the floor of my fellow workers' meal requirements. On certain days there were fish and chips, on others pies and peas or just sandwiches. Each day I would go into the village along with lads from the other floors and other mills, because there were three in the village at that time. The job had to be done very quickly because we only had a one-hour break.

When we all arrived at the fish shop or the bakers the staff would be waiting. Speed on the part of all the shop staff was critical, they knew each and everyone of us and from which mill, and they worked like a well-organised military mission. We never failed to be back at the mill in time for the workers to be fed and back to work on time, today such a task would be impossible. I loved the intensity of the work under such pressure and the responsibility of ensuring all the people on my floor were kept working by feeding them on time. But, most of all I liked the teamwork, and the final sense of achievement. Plus, we shop boys got a perk from the bakers and the fish shop, myself and one or two others received a whole small brown loaf, cut in two long ways and spread with butter, we took that to the fish shop where it would be filled with a most beautiful fish – a dinner for a King. Unfortunately, after six months, the longing to be free and outside was too strong, and I finally gave in and found another job.

At that time, I was asked by Dad to go and see a man at Bradford Park Avenue FC. He said they were interested in me, how it came about I never did find out. Talent was found by unpaid scouts or word of mouth, or who you knew. At the same time, Walter had been asked to trial for Huddersfield Town. We both attended as requested, I went two nights a week and Walt went on the odd weekend. Our dreams were the same, we both wanted to make the junior team and work up from there. Unfortunately, most of my time was taken up painting the stands or whitewashing the toilets. After six months, I lost all interest – especially when I never got near the junior team but the manager's son, who we all considered a rubbish player, was in every week. So, my football career came to an end, I was not alone, others left for the same reason. Meanwhile. Walter had broken his arm on his second visit and Huddersfield Town lost interest in him. It was obvious the world wasn't ready for our talent and we were a couple of 'has-beens' at the ripe old age of fifteen.

We both overcame our disappointment quickly because there were so many things for us to do. I still had my poultry and at that time, about forty homing pigeons, which became a great source of revenue for us two lads. Almost every Saturday, Walt and I would take number of cock birds into the market and sell them. All the birds were paired, and their partners were sitting on eggs, so once the new owner let them out they would return with all haste to their good ladies. Every week, we would take different cock birds to sell. Our little business went on for about a year and was a very good little earner.

Our village gang still went down to the beck at every opportunity. On one of those visits we were on a mission for one of the gang. Terry's mum wanted a Christmas tree, I found that a most unusual request because, both our Mums were very strong Irish Catholics and my mum would never have a green plant indoors, she said it was unlucky. That day, we searched the woods for what seemed like an eternity before he finally found one he liked. I was carrying a two-handed axe and once the decision had been made about the one to be felled, the rest of the lads sat or sprawled on the grass to observe. Terry pointed to a spot on the trunk where I should chop, and I took one almighty swing. There was a dull thud as the axe hit the trunk, followed immediately by a horrible scream, which scared the rest of the lads so much they fled in all directions. Meanwhile, Terry was dancing about as if he was on something. Then he held up his hand, blood was pouring down his arm and there was a space where there should have been an index finger.

By then, the gang had returned and grabbed hold of our unfortunate friend. We rushed him home and from there he was taken by ambulance to the hospital. We never did get that tree, or find our pal's finger. Many years later when both Terry and I were grown up and in the forces, we met – and the first greeting I got from him was that he held up his hand, which was lacking half a digit, and shook his other fist at me.

Another time when we were fooling about down at the beck, one of the lads saw a number of water voles popping in and out of holes in the opposite bank. So, like all young boys, we decided to have some fun and see who could hit one with a stone. I know now what a cruel and futile idea it was, but I still had that 'follow the flock' attitude. We were all fairly good at throwing a cricket ball at the wickets, but they never moved at the last moment like our voles.

The throwing went on for a few minutes, during which time I think the rodents were enjoying it more than us. One would run in a hole and another would pop its head out of another hole, they seemed to be goading us. At that stage, we became very tactical. One of the lads had seen a film where the cavalry had formed two ranks front and rear. So, we formed up that way each with a pile of stones at the ready to face the enemy – half a dozen water voles.

I was in the rear rank, which had to bend, pick up a stone then stand up. At that stage, the front rank would bend and pick up a stone and the rear rank would throw. Then the rear rank would bend and pick up and the front rank throw. That was going well for a couple of throws then somehow the timing went wrong. In front of me was David Cullie, I stood up with a half brick and threw it quite forcefully.

In the heat of a battle when the adrenalin is coursing through the veins, the body is like a well-oiled machine. My half a brick flew through the air like David's when he flattened Goliath, it met Cullie's head with a sickening thud, followed by a half-scream which faded away. And then, he was prostrate, face down on the ground, his head in a pool of blood. Not for the first time did we have to cancel our activities to take a casualty home.

On reaching the ripe old age of fifteen years, we lads had been allowed to become members of the local branch of the Mechanics Institute on the village main street. There we learned how to play billiards, snooker, darts and dominoes. But, the greatest benefit was that we mixed with the village elders who taught us so much about the games, and life in general.

Once or twice a week we would go to the cinema inside the Institute; something we had done since we were very small. The manager had one eye and was known as Popeye Thornton – that was his real surname. If the film being shown was suitable for adults only, we needed an adult to take us in. On such occasions, kids would line the staircase to the pay-kiosk, and just ask the first adult to oblige. Not many refused, and Popeye was happy because he had complied with the rules. Once inside, the kids would do their own thing.

Many times, when we were short of cash, one or two of us would pay the entrance fee then once inside, and when the lights had dimmed prior to the start of the show, one of us would lift the lock on the fire escape door which led to a side alley, and let the rest of the gang in for free. Poor old Mr Thornton – we used to drive him mad, but it never went beyond a telling-off from him and a promise from us that we would change our ways.

My next job was one of two years of real hard work but to me it was absolute heaven. I went to be a farm labourer at Hazel Crook End Farm, about four miles from home out in the Yorkshire countryside. My day

Hazel Crook End Farm

started at four thirty each morning and ended at six thirty each night, every day, except Sunday, when I finished at one o'clock. Before I could start the job, I had to make my own transport, as there was no way to get there other than walking.

So, I acquired a bicycle frame from the rubbish tip and with some emery cloth, a bit of paint and some hard work I made it very respectable. The other parts for my steed I got from various places and then worked all hours to complete it in time to start my new job. The first part of my journey to Hazel Crook had to be walked, carrying or pushing the bike up the very steep Yokin, our football field. Once on the road at the top. I could ride the rest of the way to the farm.

The morning trip was always very scary, travelling those dark country roads, especially during the winter when the wind was howling and the rain or snow lashing across the Yorkshire countryside. I also had to pass the scarlet fever hospital, which by that time was almost derelict. It still sent a shiver down my spine as it had done all those years before. That road I travelled every morning and night, whatever the weather and missed the journey only a couple of times in the worst of winter. On those two occasions, the snow was up to the top of the walls and I was asked by the farmer to stay over, not for my benefit but to ensure I was there ready to work the following day. Those two nights I slept on the couch in a lovely warm farmhouse. It was really good because the farmer's wife was the best cook I have ever met. (Sorry, Ma).

After milking we would have a full breakfast of thick slices of home-cured ham; fresh eggs, all from the farm; mushrooms that she had picked from the fields; home baked bread and butter and best of all; her homemade piccalilli; finished off with a pint of tea. Truthfully, I would have worked for nothing just to have such meals every day. Unfortunately, those meals were only provided on those stayovers. Normally, I took my own snack to eat and was given a mug of tea, all to be consumed in the Mistle (cow shed), so that I didn't feel uncomfortable having to watch the three of them enjoy their huge hot meal. At the end of the week, money was deducted from my pay, to cover board and food. Mum had a few choice words to say about that.

My first job every day was to hand milk, along with the owner and his son, the herd of thirty dairy cows. That was a skill I had learned over the many years of helping on local farms where the German prisoners of war were friendly and taught us so much. I loved that part of the job, except when the boss bought a new beast from the market. If it was a bit unruly, I always seemed to be the one who was lumbered. I suppose really it was probably the best way to do things. The farmer was well into his sixties and the son was continually in extreme pain, he suffered from thrombosis in both legs and it was not unusual for him to be laid up in bed for two or three days at a time. A few years later he had both legs amputated; not a nice life for a young man of twenty-eight years.

One such animal was bought from Hellifield cattle market, a young Ayrshire with viciously shaped horns. She was a beautiful little specimen, but flighty and very mischievous. The first trick she would try on me, every time she was having her head secured in the byre, was to try and pin me against the wall with her horns. When that failed, she would move her whole body slowly across the stall in an attempt to try to trap me against the wall. The third trick, if those two were unsuccessful, was to wait until I was almost clear of her stall on the way out when she would try a Kung Fu type kick. Milking her wasn't easy either. She would be nice and calm as I got myself seated on the stool and placed my head against her flank, then she would empty her bladder, deliberately leaving her tail brush in the cascade of urine. Then, after a few minutes, the menace would lash her wet tail around my face. The first few times, when I was not expecting it, I felt as if I had been stock whipped like in the westerns at the pictures. The sting of the wet tail on my face and the urine in my eyes was one hell of a shock, but after a time I learned how to read her muscle movements and prepare myself. Finally, when all else had failed she had one last trick. When I had about half milked her she would casually lift her rear leg on the milking side and deliberately plop it in the bucket; she was indeed a real little character.

Once the herd had been milked and the produce had been passed through the cooler in the dairy, I would fill bottles with the fresh milk using a large enamel jug, before putting cardboard caps in place and loading them into crates, finally loading them on to the back of an Austin pickup. A quick change of clothes and Eddie, the son, and I were off to deliver the milk, fresh eggs and the odd chicken to customers in Shipley near Bradford.

By lunchtime, we were back at the farm where I would have my snack before starting my other daily chores, such as cleaning the cow sheds, pig sties and chicken houses. Once that lot was completed I would go to work on the land, I never had a minute to spare if the boss had his way. Quite often, I was left out in the fields for hours to cut kale or pull turnips in the Winter; in the Spring it would be weeding row after row of seedlings with a hoe. At such times. I would set myself a target to be the best kale-cutter or turnip-puller in the world. Every time I went out my target would be higher than the previous one. That was my way of keeping warm, but I also had a great feeling of achievement.

Alone out there in the fields, I taught myself dry stone walling. During the early days at the farm, I had seen a neighbouring farmer carrying out repairs on one of his walls and he showed me the basics. So, every time I was alone or even on the way to or from work, if I saw a wall in need of repair I simply could not resist stopping and putting a few stones back in place, thereby gradually building it back up. My boss never knew, and I never bothered to tell him or anyone else, he would probably have taken money out of my pay for using his walls for training.

Those little tasks I did all the time I was farming, just doing a bit at a time on a number of different places. I often wondered what the local landowners thought as a broken wall rebuilt itself; no doubt many never even noticed. But, I know at least one did because one day when I was milking I could hear the boss and his wife talking.

He said, "Jonas said wall were reet down to floor and ower a couple o weeks it reeted itsen".

"Don't be daft. How can that be?" she replied.

"Ah don't know. All ah knows is he says nobody's touched it but it's done".

"Well, that's a reet turn up," she said.

I never had any inclination to enlighten them; I simply left them in ignorance. In fact, I made my jobs even more secretive, doing some in the early hours or on the way home in semi-darkness, deliberately to create mystery. The fact was, I love Yorkshire dry-stone walls and to see them in a state of disrepair is against my principles. Perhaps it has something to do with having part of one dropped on my head all those years before.

For two years, I was very happy in my job until an incident took place, which was to change my life forever. One day on returning from the milk round I learned that one of the sows had given birth to seventeen piglets, and the farmer was about to kill the two smallest, the runts.

I talked him into letting me take them home – another of my idiotic brainwaves. It was a hell of a shock to my parents that night when I showed them what was in my saddlebag apart from my lunch tin.

The little animals were less than a day old and would need constant care throughout the day and night, like my first chicks. Once again, Mum came to the rescue. She made up a box and lined it with a baby sheet, then cleared a space in the airing cupboard before producing a baby's feeding bottle and milk. I was then in the pig business. As with the chicks, one died the first night, the other one Mum and I reared by two-hourly feeding, which reduced as the weeks went by. The whole exercise is not recommended to anyone. No matter how hard we tried to keep the box clean and dry it was never hygienic and was very off-putting, especially when someone was having a bath. In addition, pigs have very few manners, and are incapable of doing anything quietly.

For two weeks he lived in the bathroom before I moved him into the chicken shed, how the neighbours put up with it I do not know. Anyone who has never heard a pig scream in anticipation of pain or pleasure has been very lucky, Mum would say he sounded like a banshee. The noise is really frightening, especially during the early hours of the morning. In the chicken shed he continued to grow at a rapid rate and he was becoming a real problem, it was difficult trying to stop a half-hundred weight of bacon on four legs from knocking down the wooden shed built to house chickens. He had an ever-increasing appetite and let the whole estate know when he was hungry, which seemed to be most of the time. And when not eating or sleeping he had a constant urge to escape.

When the pig was about three months old, the farmer casually asked how the pigs were doing. Up to that point he had shown no interest whatsoever, so I had never bothered to tell him.

I told him the situation to which he replied, "That derelict sty at the bottom of yon field – you can use it if tha does it up a bit".

I was delighted and for about a week, I stayed late every night and the Sunday half day off to carry out the repairs. Then the son collected my pig in the pick-up and transported him to his new home. That night a sigh of relief must have been heard all over the Green Mount Estate. I kept him in the sty and cared for his every need until he was huge, then one day he went with a farm litter to the bacon factory. I was very sad, but that is farming.

The factory paid the farmer for all the pigs including mine, and the following Thursday he told me there would be something special in my wage packet the following day. That night I told Mum and she was delighted, after all, she had spent many hours during those early days and nights looking after my animal. On the Friday, I handed Mum my pay packet, unopened as normal. When she counted the money, I had received less than a tenth of what each pig had sold for. To say Mum was mad was an understatement, if the farm had been nearer or if there had been any form of transport to enable her to get there, I fear the farmer and his wife would have spent some time in the hospital. All I could do to pacify her was to promise that I would take him to task the following day.

As soon as I arrived that morning, I asked him why I had received such a small amount of money for my pig. His answer seemed to be very well rehearsed, "Well lad, yer never paid for yon piglets, then there was rent for yon sty plus cost of water, the use of buckets and the transport from yor place to ere".

Nothing he said was justified. I had repaired the sty, and all the pig's food I had brought from home daily and I had been the only one who went near the pig. I had been well and truly cheated and I told him so but he would not listen, I could have given him a good slap and Mum would have been delighted, but he was an old man and his son was crippled so I would have achieved nothing. I told him to stuff his job and left, Mum was fuming when I got back home. I knew he would find it difficult to replace me and no more walls would be repaired by, the 'Phantom Waller', I wondered if they ever realised who it had been. I did hear later that he could not find another worker, and I suspected Mum and her Irish friends had something to do with that.

The following day, I was up and out very early on the job trail, and by lunchtime, I had been accepted by an engineering company to start as an apprentice lathe operator. I was really in two minds about it, I knew that when I reached eighteen I would be required to enter the forces to do National Service, and I rather fancied that. In addition, I did not really want to go back indoors but the family needed the wages and that was the end of it. The following morning, I started life as an apprentice engineer at a company called the United States Metallic Packing Company.

I was met by the charge hand, who said he was to be my mentor. That was a big step from being a farm labourer. Now I was an apprentice engineer for an American Company with a mentor and a charge hand – what a climb up the ladder! He proceeded to show me around the works, then stopped as if he had forgotten something before saying, "I will take you into the lathe shop and introduce you to the trade union rep". Now I had a union rep – as well, things were getting better by the minute.

There I was face to face with a very surly looking chap who had the biggest beer belly I had ever seen. It hung over his waist belt like a snow thaw over the edge of a roof after a really bad winter, making it impossible for him to fasten his overall jacket. After staring a few moments in complete disbelief, I looked around only to find my mentor had disappeared. The union man was gabbling on about lathes, production times and work hours. But, the most important bit of knowledge that came from his speech on a regular basis was, "You listen to me and ignore all the other buggers".

At seventeen and a few months I was gullible, as the farm incident had proven, but things he was telling me seemed wrong and quite disruptive to the company. After that chat, which seemed to go on for hours and was full of the ramblings of a megalomaniac, he ran out of breath and jostled me in front of him up some rather rickety old stairs which led out on to the factory flat roof.

"Have a seat up here, get some sunshine I will be back for you later".

Lunch-time came and went, and I was still up on the roof, bored to tears and catching the full glare of the sun. Finally, I plucked up courage and warily crept back down the stairs into the factory.

On seeing my mentor, I asked him if there was anything I could do. "Nothing now, wait until tomorrow then we will make a nice fresh start", he called back over his shoulder as once more he disappeared into another part of the factory.

The following morning, I was at the factory bright and early raring to go. I wasn't used to such inactivity, so while I was waiting I picked up a sweeping brush and decided to show willing by tidying up around the lathes, not that it looked as if a great deal of action took place in that particular area.

No sooner had the brush touched the floor than Mr Union was by my side, "No call for that, lad, you must learn to pace yourself, off you go up to where I left you yesterday and I will be up in half an hour and get you started". Once again, I was off up those bloody stairs to idle about.

After what seemed like a lifetime and still no sign of Mr Union, I went back down into the lathe room, and there he was. He made a feeble excuse for not coming up for me, before handing me a pile of books. "Sit over there and read all about the company". I don't need to read about it,

I thought, I am learning first hand. It is inefficient and being run by a union idiot and the rest of the workers are too scared to sort him out.

I was left alone, and time passed, and I was by then really fed up and wondering who really did run the factory. I had not witnessed any kind of work taking place during the time I had been on the premises. So off I went and found my mentor and told him I was leaving, he asked me why and I told him; "I have been here almost two days and seen no work done, I am bored out of my skull and sunburned to hell".

"Oh! I am sorry", he replied. "I don't want to lose you".

Then he spoke at great length about me throwing a great opportunity away and how I would not get a better chance to be trained by experts in a worthwhile job. I just could not find words to answer him, so I said goodbye.

Once again, I was out of work and that was the end of my civilian working life and my sad experience with trade unions for many years to come – thank goodness.

CHAPTER FIVE

National Service 1955

Like the majority of young lads in the fifties, I was lined-up to do two years of compulsory National Service on reaching the age of eighteen. I could however, join up as a regular when I was seventeen and a half. So after my very short engineering apprenticeship I decided to visit the recruiting office and save them the trouble of sending me the letter that read; "Come or we will come and get you". A few of my friends had already taken the step and seemed quite happy.

The office was a magnificent large building in the centre of Bradford. Upon entering, I was met by a very elderly lady who simply asked my name and address before directing me into another room which was about the size of a soccer pitch and completely empty, apart from a number of wooden foldaway chairs lined up along one wall.

After a few minutes, one or two more lads were sent in and when there were three of us seated, an Army sergeant entered through yet another door. He asked us our names and then led us into another room. By that time my mind was working on things like what a waste of a huge building and how much time and energy was being wasted, on doing nothing. Once inside the latest room, we were seated behind desks and given a forty-multiple-choice question paper to complete. Once that was completed, we were on the move again, back to the room with all the empty chairs to await our results.

At last, the three of us had the chance to talk and get to know a little about each other. One of the lads said he was not joining up; he had received his papers and would only do his required time if he had to. His girlfriend did not want him to leave her, and he had assured her that he would not pass the medical due to his deafness. He seemed perfectly all right to me and had no difficulty hearing what we were talking about, I suspected he was going to try a fiddle. After a short wait, we were told all our test papers were good and we would be called in for a medical very soon.

I was the first one to be called, into yet another large room, almost empty apart from a desk, a chair and a couple of cubicles similar to those seen at a swimming pool. In one of those, I stripped down to my underwear, as requested by a very elderly gentleman who was seated at the desk. For the first time, I realised just how cold it was and there was no visible sign of any form of heating.

I was called to the desk by the gentleman, who I now presumed was the doctor. He asked me one or two questions before proceeding to carry out the fastest medical examination I have had in my life. The eye test was; "Hand over right eye read three letters from a chart". "Hand over left eye read the same three letters". Then a quick listen to my chest with a stethoscope, a flashing light in my eyes followed by a look down my throat. Then as the doctor walked away from me, I heard him ask my Christian name in the faintest of whispers. I answered him, and he turned and smiled.

Next, I was asked to stand at the desk. That was the embarrassing part as he came up close; "Drop your shorts please", he said as he slipped his frozen hand under my testicles and said; "Cough". Next, he requested I bend over the desk and I felt even more nervous as he came behind me with a torch in his hand to look round my nether regions. Finally, he told me to pull up my shorts and walk across a rubber mat in my bare feet. As I trod on it, water squelched out and once on the other side, I left footprints on the linoleum floor. That was the test for flat feet, hernia and haemorrhoids all in thirty seconds. "Off you go, A1", he called after me.

When I was once more in the waiting room, the sergeant said, "Your test was good and you have passed your medical, so, we are going to offer you a place in the Duke of Wellington's, an infantry regiment". My reply was that I was not interested and would wait to be called for National Service because I wanted to be an engineer. I started to leave but I didn't reach the door before he changed his mind and offered me a place in the REME.

He then went through all the details of where and when I would go, before writing out a rail warrant for me to travel. Finally. I had to swear allegiance to the Queen and sign on the dotted line for three years. Once all the details had been completed, I walked through Bradford with a bit of a swagger knowing that I would be working for at least the next three years.

Before I left the biggest fridge I have ever seen, I had chance to talk to the other two lads.

"How did you go on?" I asked them. The first one, who wanted to be a tradesman, had received the same patter from the sergeant as I had done, about only being able to join the Dukes, and the silly sod did. The other one, who had told his girl he would not pass the medical because he was deaf, said he was doing all right until he got to the hearing test, the part he should have failed.

He said, "The doc thought he was clever and walked away whispering; what's your surname?" I ignored him. After completing all the other tests, he told me to return to the waiting-room and I really believed I had got away with it, but just outside the door he whispered, "Come back in here," and like a bloody fool I did. His last words to me were, "A1", I don't know what I am going to tell my girl."

"Tell her you are not as clever as you think you are," I thought to myself.

Since 1952, the year I left school, a whole gang of us had gone through various stages of growing up. We had all worked at different jobs but every weekend and at night, we got together for some period of time. Walter and myself were the only ones who were in any way sporty, so if we were not going to Park Avenue we would climb the mountain, Hill Top, to support Thornton United who at that time were one of the best amateur football teams in the Bradford area.

Most of the players were former modern school old boys who had spent hours with us youngsters over the years on the Yokin. Walter's elder brother, Harold, was a top player who, during his school days, had captained both the football and cricket teams at the school. He really was something special; one of the best players of a dead ball I have been fortunate enough to see in my lifetime, he could use both feet with equal results.

One particular match has remained with me since those early teenage days. Thornton were playing against a very strong team in a cup match, Walter and I went to stand behind the opposition goal because that was where the most action usually took place. A free kick was awarded to our team about thirty yards out and almost on the touchline. Harold lined the ball up ready to take the kick and my friend decided to tell the opposite team's goalkeeper what his chances were of stopping a shot if his brother played direct. The goalie, of course, laughed and made comments about the distance and the position. Harold took a couple of steps and crack! The ball hit the back of the net and the goalie had not moved. We were laughing, when we became aware the ref wanted the kick taking again.

"He was lucky, he won't do that again", said the keeper. Once again two strides and wallop! The ball hit the net in exactly the same spot as previously and the very same evasive action was taken by the goalie.

Thornton United with Geoffrey Mallinson (back row third from left)
and Harold Cummings (front row second from left.)

Another great star of that team was one Geoff Mallinson, the goalkeeper. The man lived and dreamed only of keeping the ball out of his goal net. He would often arrive at the Yokin when we youngsters were there and have us shoot footballs at him non-stop from anywhere. The sessions seemed to last for hours at a time, he would also stop on his way home from work at night when we were playing in the street with a tennis ball. He would down his lunch haversack and take over in the goal hurling his body in all directions across the cobbles to keep the ball out of his sacred goals. Those were just two players from that really great team, who gave our village so much pleasure for many years.

By the time we were sixteen, we all, with very few exceptions, smoked and drank, if possible. In the village was a very small public house called The Mountain Ash, it was situated directly opposite the ruins of the dreaded Scarlet Fever Hospital. To describe the pub as small, was an understatement. It was the downstairs room of a two-roomed house, the upstairs being the landlord's private accommodation. The floor of the bar room was flagstones which were always covered with a layer of sawdust. It had a very tiny bar with two pumps, one for bitter the other for mild. Behind the bar, on the wall, was a small shelf which contained a very limited amount of spirits and cigarettes, on one wall hung a dartboard and on the opposite side was a hook screwed in about head height and hanging from the ceiling on a string, was a bullring. The length of the cord was such that the ring could be placed on the hook with very little slack. The game was to stand alongside the bullring and swing it like a pendulum in order to get the ring on to the hook. Whoever achieved that in the least number of swings was deemed the winner.

Mine host of that magnificent hostelry was one Harry Kellet, who lived alone except for his chickens and his pig. is attire never changed from the first day I saw him; flat cap, nice shirt and tie, corduroy trousers, brown boots and, finally, a farmer's brown smock. Whether it was due to a lack of trade or his loneliness, he welcomed us young lads into his pub with open arms.

We spent many happy hours playing darts or the ring. Harry would take on all comers for a pint at the bullring; then he would deliberately miss once or twice to up the stakes and then with ease he would hook the ring. All the time the pub was open, the pig would be behind the bar, if it wasn't slurping from the overflow tray it was snoring or farting – it was continually drunk like Harry. Only once did the police visit the pub and I was lucky because that night I had just left, but five of my pals were carted off to the police station and appeared in court later that week to be fined ten shillings, which was about half a weekly wage at that time.

In the winter months, the public baths in the village were closed and the pool emptied before being boarded over to form a dance floor. Events took place every Wednesday and Saturday as well as on the big occasions such as Christmas Eve and New Year. The music was provided by big bands from all parts of the area, they had their own singers, but the bandleaders were not averse to letting any would-be singers show their worth. We had fantastic nights and there were a few fights. At the time, wrestling was very big in the area and most of the top boys used the dance hall. So, a nod from the doorman was enough for one of them to give anyone stepping out of line a slap.

CHAPTER SIX

Leaving Home

On May 5th 1955, I boarded a train at Forster Square Station, Bradford to travel to Blandford in the county of Dorset, the longest journey of my life, there to start my military career. By that time, I had found homes for all my pigeons and Mum wanted to look after the rest of the poultry, so for the first time in many years I did not have to be responsible for anything except myself. The saying good bye to Mum, Dad and the family was very upsetting and uppermost in my mind throughout that trip.

On arrival at my destination, the first thing that struck me was how small Blandford railway station was compared to our own back in Thornton. My thoughts were very soon distracted by the number of military personnel and the activity round the platform and on the road outside. Army green vehicles seemed to be everywhere, each with a driver seated behind the steering wheel; the soldiers on the platform were extremely proactive as we alighted from the train. Some were calling out names and others were dividing recruits into groups before finally ushering us into the back of the vehicles. As each truck filled up, off it went to the camp. Up to that stage, the NCOs had been quite polite, asking us to do things, but once we were inside the perimeter of our new home, and the vehicle tailboards were lowered, the atmosphere changed dramatically, from one of peace and quiet to shouting and ear bashing of every new recruit. We were each designated a platoon number and lined up accordingly, I was allocated to platoon number three, the responsibility of Sergeant Darby and Lance Corporals Donkin and Mooney.

Once more, we were ushered along, this time to the billets. I cannot say we marched because we were really a rabble. We eventually came to a block of single-storey wooden huts, which consisted of one long hut with four extensions either side like legs, we were told later that it was indeed known as a spider. There we left our bags and suitcases before being herded once more along the road to the quartermaster's store. As we entered in single file, we literally had a mattress thrown at each one of us in turn, swiftly followed by two pillowcases, two sheets, three blankets and a bedspread. Those we grabbed the best way possible and, with two lance corporals behind giving every one of us continual abuse, we were rushed back to the billet.

The whole journey had been one continuous pattern of items being dropped and picked up; it had been hilarious. The one good point about that trip was the evening was pleasant and dry, I dread to think what a time we would have had in the rain. I must admit, that day I learned more names to call someone than I knew existed. Back in the billet, we were allocated a bed, a small locker and an upright steel locker all contained in what Donkin gleefully described as "your f.....g bed space". Then we were told to stand down and go to the NAAFI, enjoy some snooker and a beer and we would all meet again in the morning. That first night, after a few beers and some food, we sat in the billet getting to know each other, that was a start of bonding that would be remembered all my life. We all agreed, before retiring for the night that army life wasn't that bad – how innocent we were and what surprises were in store for us.

I was lying in a strange bed staring at the sun glaring through the windows and listening to the snoring and grinding of teeth, still a bit puzzled as to where I was, when I was suddenly brought back to reality by one heck of a noise caused by Mooney and Donkin, walking up and down the centre aisle between the beds banging a dustbin lid with a pace stick. The orders they shouted out were very clear; "Hands off cocks, on with socks, out of bed right away and stand at the foot of the bed". Lesson number one – do not sleep nude unless you are happy to stand to attention in front of twenty plus new friends and a couple of sharp tongued lance corporals. The details of what they required of us were rattled off so quickly, I hoped someone understood because I did not want to be the one to ask for a repeat – then they were gone.

Outside we were met by a young recruit who himself had only been at

Blandford for two weeks. He had been detailed to show us where the cookhouse was. We were served bacon and egg sandwiches and tea, for at that stage we had no eating utensils. Once back at the billet we were met by our duo of corporals, I doubt if any of us thought that particular day was to be one we would never forget. Once again, we were lined up, only this time Donkin gave us a demonstration on coming to attention, stand at ease, right and left turns and how to swing our arms shoulder high and finally how to halt. Then both NCOs put us through half an hour's practice of the movements that we had been shown so elegantly by a five foot robot.

Then once more, we were off to the RQMS Store. The journey that morning should have been filmed, it would without a doubt have been a classic. It was hard to believe that eighteen-year-old lads, when under the slightest bit of pressure, did not know their right foot from their left. Many marched along with right foot and right arm going forward at the same time. Consequently, we were tripping each other up due to that and the variation in strides, we tried to laugh but that was very quickly stopped by the intrepid two.

Once back at the store we were hustled along a narrow corridor with counters at both sides. Behind each, was a stock of military equipment and a store man. At the first counter we had berets issued after being asked, "What size?" Before anyone could answer, we were on the move having had two black discs thrown at each of us. It made little difference anyway because not many of the lads had ever bought a hat so had no idea what size would fit. From the very first counter to the last, the call was, "Size?" followed by a lightning issue where the storeman had simply guessed. The sole aim of the counter staff was to move us through as quickly as possible and by the time we had reached the last counter we were struggling with a massive pile of kit and, just like the night before, we were dropping it everywhere. Finally, we were issued a kit bag! Why the hell was that not issued first? Was it some kind of sheer bloody-mindedness or was it a morale test?

Once all our kit was in the bags we had to pass a table at the exit door; "This is where you pick up your housewife" sneered Donkin. I gave it no thought whatsoever because after almost twelve hours I was beginning to realise there were going to be a lot more psychological games, before the end of our training. However, what thoughts went through the minds of some, I dread to think. The housewife turned out to be a small white cotton bag containing needles, wool, cotton and a thimble so we could repair our kit.

After all that, it was back to the billet practising our marching as we went. All the kit was deposited in our lockers before we were outside again, in order to be crudely marched to the barber's shop. We entered in single file and faced five chairs with an eager young barber at each. The whole operation took no more than ten minutes; no style at all, straight over the top and short all over was the order of the day. That was the first time I saw a young man cry in public, many of our platoon were really 'with-it' Teddy boys from various parts of London, and when they came out of the barber's that afternoon they were without it, and everyone was the same.

Come the following day it was show time. We spent the whole morning trying on our newly acquired kit and clothing, much to the amusement of our tormentors. It did not seem to matter at all to them if our kit fitted or not; that was our problem, but it was one we very quickly overcame by circulating throughout the other billets. We negotiated exchanges with the other platoons until we were all more or less satisfied. Once again, I believe the issue of wrong sizes was deliberate plan to make us confident enough to mix. The stores staff had not issued any wrong kit or equipment; they had simply issued it to the wrong people. It was clever way for the NCOs to make us to solve a problem and start to develop team building.

When we had initially tried on our kit, it was obvious that the stores staff had a great sense of humour. Our corporals said we were all deformed; hence the lack of coordination on the small amount of drill we had done. After our bartering trip, we were left alone for the rest of the day, to iron and clean everything except our working dress and best uniforms – they had to be tailored so that we looked smart.

That one day in the billet to me was unbelievable. I very quickly understood that in every group of people there is almost, always someone who knows something about a particular subject and our platoon was no exception. The very first task was to change the shape and size of our extra-large, Pontefract-cake-like berets. One of the lads had been in the cadets and showed us how, by alternate dunking in boiling water then cold, they could be shrunk down to the size we wanted, before stretching and shaping them across our knees then drying them. After a few hours, almost every platoon member had come up with ideas they had learned from their Dads or Brothers, but never in their wildest dreams thought they would ever use. Ties could be lightened by boiling in a little toothpaste and buckles on webbing could be cut in order to remove them from the kit when blancoing, so that the Brasso used to shine them and did not mark the webbing kit. Soap was used inside the trouser seams when pressing to stick them together and give nice knife sharp creases. We all got stuck in that day and made it a great success.

Donkin had very quickly become known to all members of the platoon as 'Himmler'. The main reason for that was his similarity in build and looks, including the funny little glasses. He was from Sunderland and originally a National Serviceman before signing on the dotted line, no-one could ever call him a bully – everything he demanded of us he could do himself. He was the most smartly turned out soldier I ever saw, and his drill and weapon training lessons were unbelievable. Some of the lads reckoned he really was a robot, every one of his drill sessions was a pleasure to see. However, the little sod could make life unbearable for us and on such occasions, he was having fun.

I witnessed many incidents where he brought tears to the eyes of six-foot-plus miners from the Welsh Valleys. That was the power of the tiny 'Mackem' who seemed to have the wonderful knack of knowing what every member of the platoon was thinking. He certainly knew our weaknesses within a couple of days and made it his mission to eradicate such flaws with all haste, I would think to a man we never forgot what he taught us. Although for eight weeks we hated the sight of him, we had the utmost respect for his abilities. By the time we passed out he was the major factor in us being moulded into a well-disciplined platoon. What a start to a military career!

On the very first Saturday morning at Blandford, Donkin entered the billet and had us all stand by our beds. Then with a grin on his face he announced that the following day Sunday, was to be a church parade. He told us that meant we had to be on parade at eleven, all smart and sparkling, that meant no lie-in but a lot of pressing and polishing that night and early in the morning. "But, I notice there are six Catholics in the platoon who are not compelled to attend, so not to have you buggers feeling left out I have asked the cook sergeant to find you a nice couple of hours cleaning". I was no longer a practising Catholic but thought to myself a couple of hours are far better than being on the parade.

Come the Sunday we reported at seven thirty as per Donkin's instructions and spent the whole day until seven that night scrubbing pans, trays and floors. When we arrived back that night, fed up and completely knackered, I asked the other lads how the parade was. "Didn't go", one or two replied. "After you six had gone off this morning, Herr Himmler came in the billet with a stupid grin on his face and said the parade was cancelled".

They had slept in and prepared their kit for the Monday as well as writing letters home; we still had all that to do. The crafty little sod! He had got six happy volunteers to go willingly to do a whole day of fatigues.

Another time he came into the room, just as we arrived back from evening meal. Outside the wind was howling and the rain lashing down on Dorset. We were all shattered and wet through after a day of square-bashing and physical training, and we still had a night's cleaning and bulling to look forward to in order to be ready to start all over again come the morning. Donkin stood there in the centre aisle, board in one hand, pen in the other, and as usual we stood by our beds. He said the CO wanted to know if there were any sportsmen among us, not uncommon at the time, because even the famous celebrities had to do National Service. The number who spoke up, but had kept the secret from us was a bit of a shock. There were a couple of pro footballers, an amateur boxer and a runner, all those the Mackem seemed to write down with very little enthusiasm.

Then came a voice, "I am a racing cyclist". Himmler's eyes lit up and the pen was immediately replaced in his pocket. Meanwhile the lad by the name of Vaughan, was going to great lengths to let our miniature tormentor know that he had been a really prominent member of a top team. "Good, good, now shut up", said Donkin. "Just what I am looking for", Vaughan's face was a picture of pride. "Outside there is a bike with a front basket full of part one orders, ride round the camp and pin one up on every notice board".

Away went Donkin chuckling to himself, leaving us all in a state of shock especially Vaughan. Another lesson learned – never ever step forward.

Donkin, Mooney and all the other NCOs were very astute and found out in the first few days, as we had done, which recruits were good at certain things and then used those lads to clean their own personal kit. One night during one of many dreaded locker inspections, our little friend from the North East lined us up as part of the inspection to examine our one-pint white china tea mugs for cleanliness. Mooney was sat on one of the beds admiring and smiling at every one of his colleague's antics. Donkin came along the row peering in every mug and especially every crease round the handle, in his search for the slightest stain. He arrived at Vaughan, our intrepid cyclist, one of the corporal's enlisted slave labour team. As he inspected the mug in Vaughan's hand, his whole demeanour changed, and he became the usual ranting lunatic we were becoming used to. He ripped the mug from our roommate's hand shouting, "Filthy, filthy, horrible little sod". Then he hurled the drinking vessel against the wall smashing it to pieces as he bellowed out, "What do you think of that?"

"Not a lot," was Vaughan's reply. "It was your mug that you gave me last night to press your trousers".

The whole billet erupted in laughter; even Mooney, Himmler's number one fan, cracked and quickly left the room with the excuse he needed to visit the toilet. I could have sworn I heard a loud burst of hysterical laughter come from the direction of the corridor as he made his way to the latrine. Needless to say, that night more than the usual number of pieces of kit were thrown out of the window on to the lawn outside, but for once it was well worth it.

Every day was a challenge in some way, PT was a daily morning lesson for almost an hour, when we were really put through the grinder. By the end of each session, we felt muscles aching we never knew we had. One of the recruits in our platoon was doing press ups and after about two he collapsed on the gymnasium floor screaming out, "I think I have pulled a muscle, Corporal". To which the PTI, an Army boxer by the name of Smith, replied, "You only have one muscle, Clarke, and you pull that too much that's the reason you collapsed. Get on with it otherwise you can come and be my sparring partner in the ring".

I don't think Nobby had ever moved so fast in his life, at the end of each lesson we had a shower then about twenty minutes later we were off again.

> **Better to remain silent and be thought a fool**
> **Than to speak out and remove all doubt**
>
> ABRAHAM LINCOLN

A week later, it was my turn to be in the firing line. A group of us were having lunch in the cookhouse when suddenly a very young-looking captain entered with a rather obese cook sergeant and one or two hangers-on. This as recruits, we had never seen before but were to see many more times over the coming years. In fact, during my last seven years in the forces I would carry out the very same duty as the captain many times.

The entourage approached our table then stopped.

"Are there any complaints?" asked the young officer.

"No Sir", we all chorused.

"Good, good", he replied, and they went on their merry way.

Once back in the billet one of the lads who was constantly whingeing about the meals said, we must complain in order to make things improve. Then another said, "Someone has to stand up and speak for all of us".

After a short time, I was asked to be the spokesman. And like an idiot I thought why not, what could possibly happen, it will be a great way to get noticed and that can only be beneficial to my career. Dad always said, "If you want to get anywhere, stand out".

At the next day's lunch, there was a different captain on 'Duty Officer', but he was escorted by the same overweight cook sergeant and the hangers on. Prior to their arrival at our table, our garrulous new friend had decided that the rice pudding should be the object of our complaint for the day.

The group duly arrived at our table and, like a parrot, the officer asked, "Are there any complaints?" He had already pre-empted our answer because he managed to get "Goo ..." out before I said, "Thank you for asking, the rice pudding is burnt, but not cooked".

At that, the officer, sergeant and all the hangers on froze for a few seconds before nervously looking at each other, then the cook sergeant looked at me. I felt as if I had been transported back in time to Charles Dickens' Oliver Twist asking Mr Bumble for more. The officer managed to clear his throat and then stammer out, "Thank you, I will look into it." Then he asked the other lads on the table if they agreed and to a man, the reply was that everything was good.

At that point, it was very obvious that what I had said must have been very upsetting for the sergeant and shattering for the duty officer, who I doubt ever had to say more than his well-rehearsed question and await the usual answers. Somehow. deep down, I had a strange feeling the matter was not ended there.

How right I was. Not many minutes passed before I was being marched along the road escorted by two NCOs to the cookhouse to face a very irate sergeant who called me a whole string of negative words before giving me the afternoon's pan scrubbing. How was I to know that the mealtime charade was simply an exercise in PR, designed to make the hierarchy appear to be concerned about our welfare – but most of all to make them feel good.

I learned that day, that sergeants do not have any sense of humour and cannot accept criticism. I also learned not to be cajoled into doing someone else's dirty work for them, but more important, I learned that my mates, who had set me up and then let me down, felt really guilty and I doubted that they would ever do that to anyone again. Finally, I inwardly thanked Dad. Be noticed indeed! That was on a par with his advice after the incident of the man and the shotgun.

I had been walking with him to his place of work when he said, "Climb up on that wall, son". I was a bit scared because it was quite high.

"Go on you will be all right". When I was on top and shaking like a jelly, he said, "OK, now jump down to me." "No way," I replied. "Come on I will catch you". So, like a prat, I jumped, and he moved out of the way.

Luckily, I was not hurt, or Mum would have clobbered him, it was one hell of a shock. "There is a lesson for you", he said, laughing. "Never trust anyone – not even your Dad".

Back to Blandford and another lifelong memory. One of the never forgotten things about the forces is the service number that every military man has designated, to be put on every piece of equipment, ID Card and our dog tags (small metal discs on string worn round our necks). That number we had to memorise and the NCOs ensured we did, by continually asking us to call out our name and number. Once absorbed into our subconscious minds, it is never forgotten: eight numbers, which I remember very clearly to this day more than fifty years since they were allocated to me.

Unfortunately, those very numbers caught me out after six weeks of military service. It was a beautiful Sunday morning in Dorset and the NCOs told us to press our battle dress, the full khaki army uniform. Up to that stage, we had only been allowed to wear denims for all our training, so to us that was fantastic news – just the thought of being able to look like proper soldiers.

The news got even better. We were then told once we were fully kitted and smart we could report to the guardroom for a quick inspection, then we could all go out for the first time since our arrival. We were ecstatic, but once more, the dark forces of our junior NCOs were at work – one more turn of the knife in an attempt to finally break our spirits. Once ready, off we strutted to the guardroom feeling like a million dollars and all ready to meet the people of Dorset, especially the girls.

On the veranda outside the guardroom was, a full-length mirror and a sign above read, "Check your kit is fit to leave camp and is being worn correctly, if so, knock and wait to be called in".

The first lad knocked and was called in, closing the door behind him. All was quiet for a few minutes then the door burst open and out he came at the double followed by a string of expletives and finally instructions to get back to the billet and clean his belt. That was just the start – every single recruit came out with at least one fault, boots, gaiters or belt, the list went on and on. So, we corrected our faults and went back, only that time less confident. Once again, we were all returned to the billet with different faults to correct, however, we were determined to get out, so we set off again thinking that this time we must be on a winner, at least I did and was really high with expectations of going into the village.

Once I was inside the guardroom, the sergeant checked my kit. Then he said, "Well done, now you can go on your way to the high life". Internally I was bubbling over with excitement and just reached the guardroom door when Himmler spoke; "Shout out your name and number, Private".

For a few seconds my mind, which had been tricked by the sense of euphoria, went blank and nothing would come out of my mouth. The three NCOs had a great time at our expense; "Get back to the billet and practise then next Sunday you may be lucky". That day not one of our platoon managed to escape, what a waste of a whole day, I thought. But, then on reflection, nothing the staff did to us or with us was ever wasted or forgotten.

We had the great pleasure of meeting Corporal Smith. He was one of the PTIs in the gymnasium but was far better known for his fighting in the ring or out. He was built like a tank with a face that looked as if it had been run over by one. During our training we had a weekend pass and a few of us went to Bridgewater Fair, who should be there in the boxing ring taking on all challengers for a prize of a fiver to anyone who could beat him – Smithy, it was a lot of money in 1955. Many tried but none succeeded. Prior to leaving Blandford, a couple of the other lads and I volunteered to go to the Paras and the SAS, only to be told that to be considered we had to go across the Gym for a couple of rounds with guess who? I was five foot four tall and weighed ten stone; I gave that a miss, as did all the other lads.

After nine weeks, our time at Blandford came to an end and we passed out as trained soldiers. From there, we were dispersed to various trade training establishments throughout England. Some went to Malvern to be vehicle electricians, others to Barton Stacey to be trained as drivers and I went off to Taunton in Somerset to become a vehicle mechanic.

The training lasted six months during which time we worked five and a half days every week, learning mainly theory, about every aspect of vehicle technology, with a certain amount of practical work based on faultfinding. The practical side was by no means as comprehensive as a five-year apprenticeship; that was explained to me in detail at my first active service unit. The ASM, artificer sergeant major, pointed out to us that a normal apprentice goes to college one day a week during his training, which taking into account holidays, was less time on theory than we actually did. But the only practical training of any use to a soldier was on the type of vehicle in service at the time and under active service conditions. That is one of the reasons so many military exercises take place every year in various parts of the world, that way we trained on all types of vehicles operating under many different conditions.

Trade Training Camp, Taunton, Somerset 1955

CHAPTER SEVEN

Off to Germany 1956

On completion of training at Taunton, myself and sixteen other newly trained craftsmen vehicle mechanics were posted to BAOR (Germany). The journey was by Army vehicles to Harwich Docks, from there by troopship to the Hook of Holland, and finally by troop train through Holland and Germany to our final destination. The ships had the most wonderful names such as the Parkston Prince, the Vienna and the Wansbeck. All that kit we had struggled with a long time ago on a summer's evening in Blandford, less what we were actually wearing, was packed inside our kitbags and backpacks and carried by us. After a day of travel, we finally arrived at the docks about nine thirty on a very cold December night to find we were not alone by any means. Gathered all around the docks, in groups, were lads on draft from units all over England plus many returning from leave to their units in Germany. In addition, the whole dock was alive with senior officers, dignitaries and cameramen.

We were duly lined up and a number of young officers walked the lines asking us questions and taking notes. About an hour later, when we were all well and truly frozen, the Tannoy system came to life and a list of names was called out, to my surprise, mine was among them. We had to report to the main office on the dock and on arrival, to our amazement, we were promoted to acting corporals and on the spot a tailor sewed stripes on the arms of each ones' jacket. The group then had a briefing on why we had been promoted and exactly what duty we had to carry out during the overnight channel crossing. I was to be responsible for about thirty RAF lads until our arrival at the Hook of Holland. Like me, they were leaving England for the very first time and more than a bit excited, and a few the worse for wear having stopped en route for drinks.

Then we were told about the cameras and the reason for the number of dignitaries and officers. A programme was being televised about British troops travelling to BAOR and the celebrity who would talk to each one of us as we boarded the ship was, Robert Beatty, a famous Canadian film star of the time. That was my first experience of bluff and bullshit better known as PR – Public Relations.

Our kitbags and packs were taken from us and stored below, in the ship's hold, until our arrival at the other side. As we walked up the gangplank, Mr Beatty shook hands with each serviceman and said a few words. The TV programme would later show us travelling in comfort instead of like pack mules.

We settled down in our cabins and prepared ourselves, for what we envisaged being a rather uncomfortable journey because the temperature below decks was even lower than on the dockside. About midnight, our transport started to move, and chains started banging and scraping alongside the hull, then the engines came to life and our vessel began to accelerate. By then, my new RAF friends were beginning to quieten down and, to a man, start a gradual facial colour change. We were in one of the worst parts of the North Sea, on a rough and bitter cold night. What a sight met me at six the following morning, the majority of my draft had been seasick, and the stench was horrible. My job was to ensure the deck was left as we had found it, and to achieve that, we had lots of mops, buckets and disinfectant. To my surprise, everybody got stuck in and we did a good job, the experience was good for me and I learned that night that I was not easily seasick.

Upon my arrival at my new unit in Munsterlager, a little village hidden away in one of Germany's many forests, my first call was at the OC Captain Cockburn's office for my introduction interview. He told me all about the unit and hoped I would like my stay. Then he said the Port Services responsible for troop movements had been in touch and told him that the other acting corporals and I had done a good job on the overnight trip – which was very nice to hear. He said it was a good start but unfortunately, I had to remove the stripes and it was up to me to get them back.

The unit I had joined was an LAD (Light Aid Detachment) to a Royal Artillery Regiment, 94 Locating Regiment. The OC called in the ASM and asked him to inform the Transport Officer that he would like me and two earlier new arrivals to be started on driving lessons immediately. Within only a few minutes of leaving the OC's office, the Transport Officer Lt. Ward, gathered the three of us together and led us to a ten-ton Bedford truck. He climbed in the driving seat with me in the passenger seat and the other two in the rear and off we went out into the beautiful German countryside, arriving after a very short run at a disused German airfield. Once within the perimeter and off the road the young officer and I changed places. When I was settled in the driving seat, I received extremely quick instructions on the working parts and how to start the vehicle, and a quick run through, while static, on clutch operation and gear changing. Then off we went once more, this time with me grinding my way through the gears and jumping the vehicle up and down like a kangaroo, I felt really sorry for my new colleagues in the rear.

In the fifties, gearboxes were of the crash type with no synchromesh to help smooth gear changes. One had to get the engine revs correct before double-declutching. After a while, like all beginners at anything, I began to gain confidence and the MTO said, "OK, out, and send one of the others in".

Once we had all spent a short time on the airfield I was once more reinstated in the driver's seat. "Right, off we go to town", said Mr Ward. Munsterlager was a small village and not many people or vehicles were on the road, thank goodness. My trip that day was dramatic to say the least. I mounted the pavement numerous times and scraped along a number of walls before finally knocking a lamppost down. Not once did my instructor show any sign of emotion, he simply said, "Carry on" at each incident. The other two lads did an equal amount of damage before we returned to base, with a rather battered Bedford vehicle, just in time for lunch.

As we alighted from our transport, the OC was coming out of his office.

"How did they do, Mr Ward?" he asked.

"All passed sir", was the reply.

Passed what, I thought to myself. After lunch, we found out when the

Lt. came into the workshop, gave each of us a pink slip and told us to send it to a certain government department in England to get our driving licence. We were now classed as fully qualified drivers and from then on it was a case of teaching ourselves.

Less than a week later, we had the opportunity to undertake some serious driving practice and really test ourselves. The LAD had to go on a night drive through the woods in the area that involved support vehicles of all shapes and sizes, fully loaded, being taken out and driven over a specific route in convoy. That type of driving on the roads is not too bad because there are lights in villages and from houses or factories, which help to light the way. But convoy driving in the woods entails, one small light on the vehicle being lit and that is directly over the differential on the rear axle. Apart from that, the lead vehicle in the convoy has headlights behind covers with a tiny slit, and the rear vehicle shows taillights and each vehicle travels about twenty yards behind the one in front.

That night I was allocated a Thames Trader stores vehicle to drive with a young storeman as my co-driver. That was really my first opportunity to practise my driving skills, learnt in all of one hour on my very first morning. Before we set off, I took the opportunity to familiarise myself with all the bits and pieces in the cab. Luckily, I had struck gold because the Trader was the most up-to-date vehicle in the workshop and the gearbox was semi-synchromesh, which would make life a little bit easier for me.

So, I took off into a pitch-black night, concentrating on the small light beneath the vehicle in front, and with the help of my passenger, was able to stay in convoy. It was quite difficult and a terrible strain on the eyes even though the roads were reasonably straight, then the fun really started. We turned off the road into the woods to follow our planned route. Whoever had planned it gave little thought to what happens when there are too many bends in the track; even with the help of my hawk-eyed co-driver, we kept losing the light on the vehicle in front. Every time that happened, I was in complete darkness and feared I was being left behind so I automatically put my foot down on the accelerator. That was working out all right, with the exception of a few hairy moments when the light ahead suddenly appeared right in front of me and required me to brake quickly. Not easy when experience is very limited, and one has to think where the brake is.

Once again, just like on my lesson, the confidence started to build up inside me, and I was speeding up and slowing down each time the light disappeared and then reappeared. Then one time it didn't reappear and suddenly my truck started to lean over at a very precarious angle so that I slid across the engine cover into my co-driver's lap. He immediately started to squeal and shout, but it didn't stop there. The next thing I knew, I was upside down on top of my passenger who by then had stopped the horrible noise he had been making and was now jabbering away like an idiot.

When the vehicle stopped moving I said to him, "Come on, let's get out before it catches fire" and out I climbed into the pitch-black of a German forest. I struggled to drag myself up what felt to me like a hill, all the time talking and trying to encourage my passenger to follow me. Within minutes I felt alone – then I realised I was, all I could hear was the faint drone of vehicles nearby. Twice more, I called out to my passenger but to no avail and by that time I was becoming extremely worried, what could I do if he was injured? I didn't even have a torch and the location of my truck was a complete mystery. After what seemed like a long time, lights appeared and our workshop recovery vehicle, specifically tasked to follow the convoy and pick up any idiot casualties like me, pulled up alongside and two of my new friends in the workshop climbed out. I explained what I thought had happened and lights were produced and then a search began for my Thames Trader.

Although there had been no noise from anywhere in the near vicinity, even when I called out, the vehicle was indeed very close by and the first things we saw were four wheels pointing up to the sky. My truck was completely upside down, but where was my passenger? Then we heard a very faint mumbling coming from near the crippled vehicle, he was still in the same position as I had left him, upside down and somehow wedged in the seat mumbling away quite unbelievable things. He did not recognise me or either of the two lads with me, Medics were called, and he was taken away. It was a few weeks before he returned to the unit, but he was never the same again and needless to say, he never again wanted to be my co-driver.

A couple of days had passed when the workshop personnel were given a talk by ASM White, (Chalkie to us lads when he could not hear us), about SOXMIS cars. These were Russian military cars, always black, that were not supposed to be inside our zone. None of us lads had ever heard of them before and it was all so secretive and vague that even after the talk, I had the feeling the bosses knew little more than we did. We were told to keep our eyes open for them and report anything suspicious.

The next day I was on the disused airfield, for the very first time alone, road testing an Austin Champ, which I had repaired. T the far side of the runway I noticed a black car and a soldier carrying out some kind of work on it. Being a young soldier and a nosey sod, as well as being a vehicle expert, having carried out a few repairs, I decided to drive across and offer my services. When I got there, I noted that the soldier was not English, to be honest I had no idea what his nationality was, apart from knowing, he wasn't a German. It did not help much being unable to speak to each other, but it was easy to diagnose the problem. He had a punctured tyre and was trying to change the wheel, unfortunately, his jack was defective. I offered him the jack off the Champ, then I noticed, sitting in the rear seat behind darkened windows, three huge military officers – their uniforms adorned with medals and red bits. By using my sign language learned at the mill, I tried to communicate with the soldier and make him understand it would help if he could get those three lumps out of the vehicle, he tried but to no avail. The three fat sods were not for moving. After fifteen minutes, we had changed the wheel. I think he thanked me, which was more than his passengers did. We shook hands and he went off on his way.

I returned to the workshop and never thought any more about the incident until a couple of days later. There seemed to be bit of panic and excitement among the officers and senior ranks, the story eventually filtered out to us young soldiers on the vehicle shop floor. It appeared that the Garrison HQ had been asking if anyone had reported seeing a SOXMIS car in the area, they believed the occupants had been up to no good and all the top brass were a bit tetchy. So, I told the ASM what had happened on the airfield a couple of days before, he went very quiet and his face turned a funny shade of grey. Then he seemed lost for words before walking away from me as if I had not spoken, so, I returned to my work and never heard any more about it. Anyway, I did not think anything suspicious about a driver changing a wheel because it was punctured; in my naivety, I also thought we were supposed to be allies of the Russians.

About a mile away from our living accommodation and the Administration block and hidden deep in the forest was the workshop store and fuel depot, obviously built by the Germans to make it very difficult to see from the air. We young lads carried out guard duties on all those areas except the perimeter fencing which was patrolled by a uniformed German security organisation (GSO) employed by the War Office. Each GSO member had a huge dog, either a German Shepherd, a Doberman Pinscher or a Rottweiler. We had a pick handle.

On one of those scary duties at about 3am, the loneliest time to be out alone in the forest, when the nerves are really on edge, I had the urgent need to go to the toilet. I made my way to the toilet block with the help of the smallest torch the military could supply, I opened the outer door and my light picked out two eyes directly in front of me. There I was, face to face with a very large black German Shepherd dog, it was sat rigidly upright outside one of the cubicle doors, its security lead fastened to its collar but nothing at the most important end.

Upon seeing me, its eyes narrowed, and its lips rolled back to show me a magnificent set of teeth. For a few seconds I was transfixed as the drool from its mouth found its way to the floor, and then I was off, stupidly forgetting to shut the door behind me. As I took my first step, I heard its claws grip the floor to propel it forward in pursuit of me, at the very same time as a very dominant German voice called out "Nein, nein, nein". The dog was obviously very well trained because it never landed on my back and when I had the courage to look back there was nothing in sight. Afterwards I thought to myself I should have been calling out "Nein, nein, nein".

During my early years in the forces, young lads were still being conscripted and that continued up to the early sixties. Consequently, a good percentage of the LAD and the parent unit were National Service lads. Prior to enlisting, I had been told many horrific stories from ex-servicemen of how much the conscripts hated the forces and being forced away from their homes. Any truth in that I found to be the rare exception, the majority got stuck in and seemed to enjoy the time they served. Their age groups ranged from eighteen to twenty-five due to it being possible to be deferred, if they were serving an apprenticeship, until it was completed. The mixture of young men from all over the UK with various standards of education and technical abilities was phenomenal and rewarding for the whole unit.

One such soldier I met on my arrival was known as 'Gladys', a nickname he brought with him and he was more than happy for us to use it. He was a member of a very rich furniture dynasty in London and was very happy doing his two years as an instrument mechanic. It was something he had studied and more or less taught himself because he had a passion for watches and mechanical toys and, as he often told me, he didn't have to work. H e was a real up-market speaker with a vast vocabulary, but no frills – a real nice lad. However, he was one of those youngsters mentioned earlier who had to be taught the general basics of body hygiene, he was, however, a very willing learner albeit rather slow.

He had one habit, which never ceased to fascinate anyone who went to NAAFI break with him. That was a must for every soldier wherever they are in the world to replenish the energy used up square-bashing. The counter display was always a joy to behold; cream buns, scones and cakes of every shape and size plus a variety of sandwiches; bacon, sausage, egg and many more delights. Gladys would always purchase one large currant bun and a glass of milk, most of the other lads would gorge themselves with sandwiches followed by cakes, yet we always had to wait for him to finish. He would very carefully break his bun into equal-sized pieces then eat it one piece at a time. When the last one had disappeared, he would continually wet his index finger and very carefully pick up every single crumb until his plate was completely clean. I witnessed that ritual scores of times during our service together, and not once did he change his routine.

On completion of six months service, all soldiers could apply to their

OC for a pass to allow them to wear civilian clothes when off duty. To get the pass we had to have our civilian clothes inspected by the OC or one of his representatives before he would sign a pass giving his authority. The requirements were very strict. All clothes must be, as the rule said, "of a sober nature, clean and in good condition." A smart shirt and tie, a nice suit or jacket and trousers, nice clean shoes and clean underwear. When the time came for Gladys to apply, a large parcel arrived for him, inside was a complete set of the finest clothing to meet the military requirements. Most of it was handmade and such a parcel arrived every two weeks until he left on demob. He never washed anything, just wore it for two weeks then threw it all in the bin and started on the new set. Needless to say, when the parcel arrived there were always a few young lads hanging around the bin area like vultures, ready to pick out his two-week-old clothing.

There was a lance corporal, also from London, but the other side of the track to Gladys. He was a cockney character who had been captured in the East End to do his National Service. He was a real wide boy whose military trade was recovery mechanic, that allowed him a lot of time away from the camp collecting damaged or broken down vehicles, which was ideal for his little tricks. He was the Arfur Daley of the fifties. Every week on payday, each soldier collected coupons allowing us to purchase two hundred duty-free cigarettes. This lance corporal would purchase the coupons from the non-smokers, then buy the cigarettes and sell them downtown to the Germans for good money. He would also empty petrol from all the casualty vehicles he recovered, before bringing them back to the LAD that was also sold to the locals. Even when he went on his six-monthly two weeks leave, back to the UK, he had a scam. The four brushes for boots, Brasso and clothing we were issued way back at the RQMS store in Blandford came in very handy, he had them modified by one of the local carpenters to accommodate two watches in the wooden back of each brush.

He loved every minute of his conscription up to the day of his release and then he was off back to his beloved London. I once asked him what he had done before he was called up and he gave me a really colourful life story, which covered almost every job one could think of. I remember him saying he once drove a hearse and after about six months, he became bored, so he became a taxi driver.

"That must have been a hell of a change", I said.

"Sure was, me old luv, I had to change me trousers three times in the first week, cos it was a real old shock when some geezer started rabbiting to me from behind".

My first major military exercise took place on the Soltau training area of Germany in January 1956, during the coldest weather I had ever experienced. The temperature dropped to minus twenty degrees most days, and the nights were far worse. My God, it was cold. The biggest problem was the powers-that-be had not foreseen what was coming and we were totally unprepared.

Our clothing was inadequate, and the vehicles not properly protected. Batteries were simply wrapped in felt, a special type of grease and engine oil had been used and that was about the limit of preparation for terrible conditions. Consequently, the majority of our time was taken up trying to stop vehicles from freezing up and keeping all our fingers and toes.

Worst exercise ever – Soltau, West Germany 1956

We slept very little, deliberately keeping ourselves awake by walking about and stamping our feet in order to keep the blood circulating, for fear of not waking up or of getting frostbite. We had simply not been correctly trained for the conditions. Within a very short time, of no more than two days, a number of soldiers had been evacuated back to units with serious cold problems because they had fallen asleep in vehicles, covering themselves with anything they could find but to no avail. I was quite lucky that one of the lads with me was a bit of a survival freak, thank goodness, and knew about the buddy system whereby one guy looks after another. It even went as far as warming our buddy's hands or feet under our arms or even in the crotch. It worked for us and I thanked that guy for all my little bits over the years.

The exercise itself was achieving nothing at all and the word was it was going to be cancelled if the weather didn't improve. However, it still took another twenty-four hours before a decision was made and we packed up and returned to camp. Back at base, we were ordered to hand our weapons into the armoury then park our vehicles, still loaded, and return to our billets as quickly as possible, where medical staff were waiting for us. We had a quick check over and into a warm, not hot, shower then into bed. I remember how I felt and from the moans and groans emanating from all areas of the billets, I was not the only soldier suffering the agony of hot-aches caused by the pain of blood circulation in my feet and legs – they were really bad, and it took a long time before any of us started drifting off to sleep. It seemed like many hours after before the medical staff were moving among us carrying out more checks, but they seemed quite helpless to do anything. It must have been twenty-four hours before we were eating and drinking, myself and many other soldiers were still feeling the pains many months after. That was the worst military exercise in which I was ever involved.

From the day I left home in 1955, Mum wrote me a weekly letter. Although her education was very limited it did not deter her from filling a page with Irish Tinker language and English in her well-meant attempt to keep me updated on the latest news from home. Every sentence she wrote ended TG – thank God.

The letters usually read; "Dear Son what are you doing. Today Father Moverly (the Catholic priest) visited the people in the street but not me maybe next time (TG) Your dad is alright (TG) don't know why he didn't visit, could be your fault for not going to mass. Mrs Clancy said she heard a banshee the other night and tonight we are going to have a Guinness or two (TG). Mr Gath who is 93 had a stroke the other night and the doctor said he will never walk again but just before closing time at the spring in, he walks with Mrs Gath and orders a beer, well he didn't really walk, he dragged his half-paralysed body along the floor. By closing time and after a couple he was standing up a bit unsteady but that could have been the beer (TG). Then Mrs Gath who is ninety-four said cheerio to a young soldier on leave, I suppose, when are you coming home? Well when he got her outside, Mr Gath hit her over the head with his stick, flat out in the road she was. That will teach her to flirt with any old soldier the tart, he said. Write soon Mum, oh by the way I fed your chickens again."

Before leaving Taunton to go to BAOR I had written to Mum telling her that I would send my new address as soon as I could. The very first night at Munsterlager I did just that, a week later I got a letter from her in which she said; "Thank God you have written I was so worried about you, I told Father Moverly but he wasn't bothered. Maybe it's because you stopped going to mass (TG). I have sent you three letters without reply love Mum ps. Dads ok and I have fed your chickens again."

On my very first leave home I asked her how she had sent three letters when she did not know my address; "Oh that was easy", she replied. "You told me it was Germany, so I wrote on the envelope Cfn P Horn and underneath in very large letters Germany so that it wouldn't get lost". My dear old Irish mum.

Three months after I joined them, the regiment moved into the town of Celle. Our new barracks were a magnificent ex-German Infantry Headquarters, built for what they considered the best army in the world at the time. The accommodation building was four-storeys high and made from very hard grey granite blocks, with a very wide central stairway, which climbed to every level.

At the start of the stairs on the bottom floor was a miniature self-help medical room. On returning from the town every soldier who had been up to something that might incapacitate him in the future had to take immediate action. It meant washing whatever part could be infected then treating such parts with ointment provided, before finally printing one's name, rank and number in a book. We all used to give that book a good looking through and make sure we were mentioned in dispatches, as much as all the other guys.

Herring-bone design, rooms protruded from each side for twenty-man sleeping rooms on every floor of the building which overlooked a magnificent parade square to the rear and to the front a tree lined road running alongside a football pitch. At the ends of the building, from the second floor up, were single NCO rooms and in the centre, built around each stair head, were the toilets and ablutions. The whole bottom floor consisted of cookhouse, dining rooms and rest rooms. That was what we inherited by occupying Germany. Situated in the grounds were NCOs' messes, gymnasiums and a workshop. In addition, there were a number of small buildings which were very quickly taken over by the NAAFI and the WVS; both of which really looked after us young soldiers.

The town was a mere ten-minute walk away and because only ten years had passed since the war, there were lots of derelict buildings and great shortages for the German people. Nevertheless, we had two, favourite but completely different, bars to go to for entertainment. The better known and most up-market of the two was the 'Kronen Schanker', great for dancing and socialising with the local population. Unfortunately, the Americans were stationed nearby and I never found the two armies to be a good combination for many reasons. The first was, the pay differential between the two armies and then there was the fancy equipment and flashy dress of the American forces. I have seen American soldiers with more medals than Field Marshal Montgomery although they were just out of basic training. All those things made them believe they were better than us and the majority of them were quick to let us know.

A few of our lads didn't help by constantly telling them they had seven Brit Presidents before they finally had an American. It was a perfect recipe for a punch-up and most nights that is what would happen. It would last until either the local police, who were armed broke it up, or the US Military Police backed a vehicle up to the door and then lifted every Yank involved and threw them in the back of the truck before taking them back to their camp.

The other bar was a large wooden hut known as Smokey Joe's. It was the complete opposite side of the coin, where we could really let our hair down and the law, very rarely took any notice. That was usually our last resort on the way back to our billets in the early hours of the morning.

It was at that time in Celle that I started getting back to fitness and started playing football once again. It wasn't very long before me and a friend John Milson, a Newcastle lad, had the privilege of being selected to play for the Artillery regimental team. We had been noticed when playing compulsory sport every Wednesday against various local forces' sides. It was great to be part of a squad, which had at least half of each working day training or playing, and even more pleasing was the fact that with the exception of John and me, all the other members were pro footballers, albeit from Scottish League teams. All of them were doing their National Service. I was playing a sport I loved and living a good life but I did not progress a lot as a footballer or a soldier mechanic, we had special meals and were excused guard duties – in fact, we were completely spoiled.

Every six months, we were allowed to return to England on two weeks leave. The travel arrangements were almost the same as when we travelled to Germany, the difference being we had a train from Harwich to King's Cross Station in London. Once there, we had the tricky task of avoiding the Red Caps (Military Police) and the Snow Drops (RAF Police) who patrolled the station platforms in pairs, trying to be as disruptive as possible. Like Donkin many moons before, they were never satisfied, but it was all good fun and once we got away from them and were on our homeward train, leave had really started and for the rest of the journey we felt free.

On one such leave when travelling through Holland, I headed to the buffet carriage on the train for lunch. Two young WRAC ladies were blocking the corridor by leaning across the aisle and looking out of the train window, as if saying farewells to somebody. Both were dressed in uniform including full-length raincoats. As a young soldier, and full of it because I was going home, I patted one of them on the buttocks and said something like, "Move this", she did, and I went on my way. On my return journey both ladies were still in the same place but without raincoats, one was a major and the one I had patted, a colonel. That time they moved without being asked and never said a word, simply watched my facial expression then smiled at me.

I had some wonderful times with the Royal Artillery and made some never-to-be-forgotten friends. One such lad was a member of the LAD, a tall skinny red-haired gawky youth by the name of Knight but known to us all as Lulu. He was a really intelligent National Service kid from

Lulu from Greenford

Greenford in London, his trade was that of radar mechanic. The proverbial square peg in the round hole, nothing and nobody could upset him, and God knows many tried because of his nature and his trade.

Chalkie, the ASM, would protect Lulu from certain duties so that he could use him as his own private lackey on exercises. Our red-haired friend would fetch and carry for Chalkie and clean his kit, he was a real dog's body but didn't seem to mind at all. On one exercise, the ASM told Lulu to dig the latrine for the LAD senior ranks and officers that he did diligently in accordance with his training; four feet deep, eighteen inches wide and four feet long. On top, he placed the two-seater toilet box, finally surrounding it with a six-foot-high hessian cover supported by poles. The exercise was to last two weeks, covering various types of training in the woods of Germany.

As LADs, we more or less remained static, carrying out repairs on all kinds of equipment required by our parent regiment. A common drill on all exercises was to practise "standing to" in the event of attack, especially at night. They were usually announced by siren or by the guard shouting, "Stand to".

After a week, Chalkie instructed Lulu to fill in the latrine and make a new one in a new location. Off went my red-haired friend to carry out the ASM's wishes. During that night, or to be more precise four o'clock the following morning, all hell broke loose, and the siren came to life. It was a dreaded 'stand to' – every soldier's worst nightmare, which usually means climbing out of sleeping bags in the early hours of the morning to be shot at.

The camp was in chaos, no lights allowed. We had to find clothes and weapons in the dark before making our way to designated firing positions on the perimeter of the camp that was by no means an easy task. Everything was going as every such practice before until there was a blood-curdling scream followed by a string of expletives, which were obviously aimed specifically for the ears of Lulu. There were a number of death threats and then comments about his parentage, his standard of education and finally his life expectancy – then complete silence. After breakfast the following morning Lulu told us he had been given a real old rifting from the ASM. The day before, when he had been told to relocate the toilet, then fill the hole and dig a new one, he had dug the new one and relocated everything. Then evening meal had been called and he had forgotten to return and fill in the old hole. In the early hours during the 'stand to', in the panic and darkness, poor 'Chalkie' had jumped out of his tent, run a few yards then disappeared down a hole full of s..t.

Time passed, and the exercise was going quite well, apart from the pitch-black nights. which always created problems because everything had to be done with the minimum of noise and light. One such night and I was working on a Ford Willy's Jeep, down a very narrow track alongside the camp. It had broken down and had to be made mobile, without calling for a recovery vehicle. The track was barely wide enough for two vehicles alongside each other.

The job was taking longer than I had anticipated and I was in almost complete darkness. Then Lulu arrived with a hot drink and sandwiches, he took out a small torch and directed the beam at my work. He sat alongside me on the vehicle wing and we were chatting away quietly, then I had a problem. I needed a very small socket which was not part of my kit, my friend immediately jumped from the wing and disappeared with the words, "I will get one" trailing behind him. After a short time, he returned, and I could hear him rattling about at the side of the vehicle. Then he was back in his seat on the wing handing me the piece of kit I required.

Unless you have been in a forest late at night, it is very hard to imagine how dark and disorientating it can be, and how noises of any kind are so difficult to locate. We were chatting away, and I had almost completed the job, when we heard the sound of another vehicle in the vicinity. Suddenly I saw the slits from the headlight covers; it was coming directly toward us down the track. We knew if we stayed where we were on top of the broken-down vehicle we should be safe and it would hopefully pass us by, depending on how good the driver was. As it passed we heard it scraping alongside the Jeep, then there was a horrible crunching and crushing sound before the vehicle moved off into the night.

"What the hell was that?" I asked Lulu who failed to answer for a time, then he lowered himself back to the ground and said, "Shit, it's the tool box I borrowed".

"Whose box?" I asked.

"Chalkie's", was his reply.

We dragged the flat toolbox into the workshop area where we could have a better look. It was the most fantastic set of tools – or had been before a half-track, as we found out later, had run over it. Lulu put the box back where it had been, come the morning the whole of Germany knew all about my friend from Greenford. What a guy! Never a dull moment when he was around.

Another friend and great character from London was one Dave Scribens who was from the Fulham area, and, I believe, brought up in a care home. Like me, he was a three-year regular, a real pint-sized eight stone human dynamo. Unlike Lulu however, he played sport but was by no means as intelligent, Scribens could get into trouble at the drop of a

Dave Scribens, the Fulham menace

hat. We always said he could start a fight in an empty room. The problem was he was good at starting something but did not know how to stop. He reminded me of my fox terrier Rip, if he got an idea in his head, it was immovable.

The time was 4 a.m. and five of us were returning to barracks after a very heavy night out in Celle. We had all drunk far too much and were acting the fool a bit, as we trudged through pouring rain, which made no difference to us because of the state we were in. Coming toward us was a young German chap, sheltering as best he could from the wind and the rain beneath an umbrella. Dave was on the outside of the group nearest the road, the young man moved to step into the gutter to allow us to pass. Suddenly, out went the Terrier's leg and the unsuspecting German went flying over it and landed face down in the flowing water. Scribens was elated, but unbeknown to us we had been followed from our last port of call, none other than Smokey Joe's, by a German police car. Obviously, they had been reading the mind of the idiot from Fulham.

As soon as their countryman finished up trying to swim and save his brolly in the surging waters of a Celle back street, they were alongside us. The car doors flew open and out jumped a couple of very large well-armed policemen. It got worse. The third one to climb out had with him a huge German Shepherd dog secured by a chain. We were lined up and told to walk in front of them to the police station which was not far away. That however, was against the thinking of Scribens and he had the temerity to argue. At once, the handler released the animal's lead just enough for it to reach its target, the buttocks of good old Dave, there it sank its teeth before the handler pulled it back. Scribens must have felt the bite even in his drunken stupor but it did not deter him at all. He continued to stop and argue and each time the reaction from the dog and handler was the same, all the way to the police station.

Once there, we were put into a cell to await the RMPs collecting us and taking us back to our camp. So, while we were waiting we inspected the rear end of the London prat and found the whole of his buttocks were covered in puncture wounds and a beautiful pattern of different colours was starting to emerge. When our police finally arrived Dave started arguing again, telling the RMPs that he was going to claim for the damage done to his 'April' by the police dog – so they left him behind to spend what was left of the night in the company of the Germans.

His wounds had not healed before he was in trouble again. We were all in Smokey Joe's where almost all the girls were 'ladies of the night. It was a one-star pub, but we enjoyed our sessions and really let our hair down. That particular night was no different, and we were having great fun, a young driver called Jeffries had just completed a dance to a record of

Elvis Presley's 'Don't be cruel' on the top of a round table, followed by a strip down to his army boots and his green military issue underpants. The place was buzzing with an equal number of Brits and Yanks. It was not a very good mixture really, but that night things were going unusually well. Then our London friend started mumbling away about someone chatting his bird up, we took no notice of him, so he sat there in deep cogitation. We all knew the situation in that bar between girls and soldiers, but Scribens had the blinkers on.

As the night progressed and the beers flowed, he constantly pointed out to us a girl he said was to be the future Mrs Scribens. It so happened she was sitting with a huge American soldier. The Fulham idiot commented about his bird being taken advantage of and no matter how many times we told him she was just earning a living, he took no notice. Finally, he stood up and stretched himself to his five foot plus a little bit more and said, "That's enough, I am going to sort him out", but not quite in those words.

The American was seated on a chair the wrong way around, he was leaning with his chest against the back and for a few moments, I was worried what our friend would do with the back of the unsuspecting American as his target. But, he had obviously noticed his enemy was wearing a sporty type jacket with a centre split at the bottom of the back, which was quite fashionable at that time. Scribens approached our ally from across the Atlantic quietly from behind, he grabbed his jacket firmly either side of the split and with all his anger ripped the jacket from bottom to collar.

"What the hell", roared the GI and stood up and turned in one swift movement, grabbing our London friend by the lapels and lifting him clear off his feet, before carrying the wriggling idiot outside. The door closed behind them and there was a lot of noise, then it went silent. After a few seconds more, the door opened and in walked the American, he removed both halves of his jacket and threw them under the table before seating himself once more and carrying on his conversation, as if nothing had happened. A further two minutes must have passed before the door opened again and in staggered Dave, his face covered in blood. He made his way back to our table with a huge grin on his face and a gap where one of his front teeth had been a few moments before. He sat down and announced very proudly, "That'll teach the bugger not to chat up my bird".

Early in 1958 I was coming to the end of my three-year contract with the Army and I had been told I could make sergeant if I studied for another level of 'Education and Trade' as well as signing on again. My mind was made up to leave; there was no logical reason for my decision except I enjoyed my leaves back to the UK, boozing, dancing and sleeping until the pubs opened the day after. Not once did it enter my head that I would have to work in a completely different environment, where there would be no sport three times each week or regular meals in a ready-made community. I simply wanted to follow the others into civilian life.

So, in April 1958 I left the Army with the rank of corporal thinking I had done really well. However, on reflection later, three years of my life had been wasted. Lulu was discharged on the same day and we travelled back to the UK together. Our first port of call once back in Blighty was the depot in Woking where we were issued our demob clothes ready for our return to civilian life.

Once again, we went down the stores' aisles but this time it was far more civilised than the visit three years before. We were measured for our demob suits prior to being given the choice of grey or brown. Then a gentleman packed the suit nicely in a box and we moved along to receive shirts, ties, underwear and shoes – once again a choice of black or brown. Finally, we were issued a trilby hat and a raincoat; we had a great laugh at the thought of being togged out in that gear.

We had been put wise on what would happen when we emerged from within the store. So, before we went outside, Lulu and I went to the toilet where we carefully opened the boxes and removed the good stuff such as shoes, socks and underwear and put them in our suitcases, prior to resealing the boxes. Outside, ready to meet the both of us were a number of spivs and, just as we had been told, they offered us a fiver for each of our boxes. We accepted and very furtively, they threw them in the back of a van without checking the contents. The fiver paid for lunch and a few beers for Lulu and me, then we went for a walk in Green Park while I waited for my train time. When that time finally came, my red-haired friend and I shook hands, said our farewells and never saw or heard from each other from that day on. I really hope he did well in his life because we had many happy hours together.

CHAPTER EIGHT

Back to Civilian Life 1958

Back home in Bradford, living with Mum and Dad once again, I started two years of absolute stupidity. Every spare moment when I wasn't working I was in one public house or another. I had managed to get myself a job of sorts within a few days of my return from Germany, at Thornton Swimming Baths as an attendant lifeguard. The only thing I achieved in the year I was there, was passing my life-saving certificate but that was no great thing. However, I did see a dear old friend from my childhood; unfortunately, he was in a world where he could not see me.

One of my jobs at the baths every Friday night was to look after the Slipper Baths. There were six cubicles, each fitted out with a bath and a chair. The bath could only be filled by me, with the use of a T-key, people who did not have the luxury of a bath at home or those who had dirty jobs and preferred to leave all the filth for me to clean up were the customers, and would start arriving from about five in the evening until nine. They would pay at the desk and be issued with a towel and a small bar of soap, I would run them a bath to their satisfaction and they were allowed half an hour to bathe. After they had finished I would clean ready for the next customer.

On one such night who should arrive, but dear old Billy Gill, but he was a shadow of the man I knew as a child. I found out later that he was still employed by the Co-op but no longer with his beloved horses, he was filling coal sacks in the depot. His brain was a complete blank and he had no idea who I was, I don't think he really knew who he was. From the moment he arrived until he left, he was in constant conversation with his horse.

I was told, by another member of the staff that he had been that way for years and he talked the same way in the local pub. All I could hear from Billy that night was, "whoa boy, back up old lad, steady now, that's a good boy, you can do it". He was in a world with his old horse, I felt so sorry, here was a man who probably carried a ton of coal in hundred weight sacks on his back every day in all weathers across terrible terrain to make a very basic living, now reduced to a shell.

Once again, the indoor life was of no use to me. Then a friend of mine, who I spent far too much time with drinking, gambling and being a general waster, offered me a job. He was the owner of a very unsuccessful painting and decorating business, at least I would be outside in the fresh air, or so I thought. Walter, who took me on, was an alcoholic and a philanderer – hence the state of the business. He had a heart of gold and to me, at that stage of my life, a ticket for me to carry on being a waste of time. A few men were employed by him, but really, he was being ripped off. Once I started working for him I did very little except accompany him everywhere he wanted to go, day or night, he paid my wages and we got on really well together.

Every day, after I arrived at whichever site his men were supposed to be working, he would arrive and pick me up and off we would go to the nearest betting shop, race course, dog meeting or working men's club. It was all about betting or drinking when he was not chasing some woman or another. I always had the impression I was on the books as a companion minder, rather than a worker, I was really no better than the rest of his staff, after something for nothing.

It was because of one of his many night trips with different women that my life took a dramatic turn. He had met a young girl who had two children and her husband had done a runner. One night he asked her to go out with him to a pub in the country and she turned him down because her sister was due to visit.

Not to be deterred, Walter right away, unbeknown to me at the time, said that I would make up a foursome. The girl I met that night was my present wife, Moira.

She was the most beautiful girl I had ever seen. Her turnout was immaculate and there was I, looking as if I had just jumped out of a dustbin. At that moment, I realised just how much I had let myself go, not that I could have been any better dressed – I simply had no clothes. All my money was being wasted on booze, cigarettes and gambling. I pushed all those thoughts to the back of my mind in the belief that it was a one-off night and tomorrow all would be back to normal.

The four of us went to a really nice public house on Baildon Moor by the name of The Cricketers. Everybody in the crowded room made us most welcome, they even found seats for us because of the girls – especially Moira, who stood out from the rest.

Seated at our table were an elderly couple, who at a guess must have been well into their eighties. As the drinks flowed so did the conversation and there were no barriers between tables. The elderly couple seemed very curious about me and Moira – were we married? or courting? plus many more questions.

At that stage, I realised just how shy Moira was, every question caused her to blush. The interrogation was incessant and Cyril, the old chap, was warming up after a couple of milk stouts and the feedback he was receiving from the blushes. Martha, his wife, kept trying to quieten him without success; one could sense the whole roomful of people were hanging on his every word.

Then! to his wife's embarrassment he announced that they had to get married as teenagers – the honourable thing to do in those days if the girl became pregnant. It was a bit of a sensitive subject for Moira and me, having just met. "It all happened," he went on, "due to being in the very pub we were now in and the sheep that roamed the moor".

By then he had the full attention of everybody, including bar staff and people trying to get in from other rooms. One night when he and Martha were courting and walking back across the moor in the moonlight after having a few in The Cricketers, they both became rather amorous and one thing led to another. By then poor Martha was trying her very best to become invisible and the crowd were closing in not to miss a word. The old boy looked at me and Walt with a cheeky smile on his face, as if remembering fondly.

"We got down on the grass and everything was good, in fact, it was bloody marvellous. Tha knows when it's time to withdraw, well; I was just about to make that move when one o' yon bloody sheep jumped on me back". The whole room erupted in laughter and poor Moira almost burst a blood vessel. I didn't think I would be seeing her again – but after that,

Moira – when we first met

there would be no chance at all! Fortunately, we all agreed it was a good night and I took her out at every opportunity for the next six months.

She came from a family who lived at Thornbury, a village at the opposite side of Bradford to where I was living. Her father was an ex-coal miner from the Newcastle area, unfortunately, he had lost a leg in a mining accident and by what I was led to believe, it changed him into very bitter man who used to beat her mother for almost anything. What I saw of him, which was not a lot as Moira moved in with her sister shortly after we met, was that he was just a nasty bully, who made his wife and children's existence unbearable and it soon became very obvious she had a terrible childhood and moving to her sister's, was the best move she ever made.

> **❛ I don't know who my Grandfather was. I am much more concerned to know what his Grandson will be ❜**
>
> ABRAHAM LINCOLN

Up to then I had been living in a black and white world, but I was reborn in the spring of 1960 when we married on the 26th of March. The wedding took place at Bradford Registry Office; we had two witnesses, my best friend from the army Peter Knott from Woolwich and Moira's best friend from work, Joan Taylor. After the ceremony, we had a chicken dinner provided by mum at home and in the evening, drinks and music at the local pub until closing time at eleven o'clock, then we really spent much needed money on a taxi into Bradford to a single room mum had acquired from a friend, by the name of Miss Wood. There we started our honeymoon. We had a key, so we let ourselves into the house and proceeded to climb the stairs very quietly in order not to wake our new landlady. At that stage Moira started the giggles due to the copious amount of Babychams she had consumed. We entered our small room complete with double bed a chest of drawers and a carpet.

We never made it to the bed before the honeymoon started. Like Cyril and Martha in the pub, we settled for the first flat space, on the carpet and as Cyril said, it was good, without the sheep. Then, the room door opened, I could not turn to see who it was, our feet were in the wrong direction, then a voice; "I have made you a cup of tea my darlings, oh, so sorry I will leave it on the chest of drawers", followed by the closing of the door. What a finish to the day my darling was blushing from top to toe!

On the 13th of December that same year, our first daughter, Tracey, was born at 13 Mary Street Thornton, a little back-to-back house we managed to save £40 deposit to purchase. The rest was a loan from a local businessman.

What Moira had seen in an impecunious little jerk like me, I will never know. Throughout the night of December 13th my boss and I sat on the doorstep, while Moira was inside in labour. What a night that was, when my daughter finally came into the world I knew that my life really did have to change. What I had thrown away by leaving the security of the forces was emphasised the following day, by Dad.

He said to me; "You are married and now have a little girl, she and Moira are your responsibility, make sure you do it right – go and make something of yourself".

Very soon after that, I stopped working for my painter friend and started odd jobbing for myself. For almost two years I cleaned windows, painted houses or rooms, replaced roof tiles; in fact, anything I could find, to make money in order to keep my two ladies. I must have carried ladders hundreds of miles around the village. But I was reasonably happy because I was managing to provide for my family, which had by that time increased. Cheryl had come along during June 1962, and the following year Linda was on the way.

Things were starting to become harder by the day. Money was scarce, mainly due to my work ethic, which was not right by any means. For such a long time I had lived a very selfish life and was finding it hard to change the drinking and gambling. It was much less, but still unacceptable to me. All that time Moira had been terrific with the girls, although we had little money, she always ensured they were immaculately turned out; she was a first-class mum in every way.

The worst winter for freezing temperatures making outdoor work impossible I can ever remember in England, was that of 1962/3 and seemed to last forever. That became the final straw. It and that was no use at all, I needed to change everything and give my family a better life. Moira and I came to a decision – I should join the Police Force. So, off I went to their recruiting office and sat the examination. On completion, I was told they would be in touch within a few days. Unfortunately, the police suffered from the good old English disease of "attend and we will action it next year"!

By nature, I cannot sit around once my mind is made up to do something, so after waiting about a month and receiving no reply, Moira and I decided I should try to get back in the Army. Off I went to the recruiting office once again and after passing the various tests and the medical, the recruiting Sergeant promised me that on my return I should be able take up my qualifications and rank from where I left off. (From that day, I have hated the word "should" and every time I hear it or see it written, a shiver goes down my spine). That was great news, so I signed on the dotted line for the full term of twenty-two years. I was informed that I would be contacted within the week, and off to the depot within the month. A couple of days later, I received a letter informing me that I had been accepted for the police, too late, so I had to turn them down, but I have always wondered what our life would have been like, if that letter had arrived a couple of days earlier.

We sold the house, paid off our loan, and parted with most of what few belongings we had. We prepared to move out the day before I would report to the forces. That day duly arrived, and Moira and the girls moved in with my parents, to live in their front room. I knew it would be very hard for Moira, because my mum was not the easiest person to get along with. In fact, she exceeded all our worst expectations with a typical mother-in-law attitude. In her eyes, my wife was incapable of looking after our children. It was also her fault that I had joined the King's Army. (The King had been dead for more than a decade). It was one almighty clash of personalities. Every time I received a letter from home, I wished I had not taken the step to put Moira in such a situation.

CHAPTER NINE

Back in The Forces 1963

On my arrival at the REME depot, I had an interview with the CO who told me that the recruiting office had made a mistake, I would not get my rank, and qualifications back. However, he was willing to let me go to the Trade School at Bordon prior to starting my basic training. There I could sit a trade test but if I failed after completing my basic training, I would have to go and do the basic trade training again. That would take almost a year and there would be no chance of the family being with me. I decided against telling Moira, at least until after I had sat the Trade Test. that was arranged for me to take, one week later.

Alas, it was not the end of my problems. I had not worked on a vehicle for five years, plus all the time I had been absent from my previous workshop in Germany, playing football. My world literally fell apart for a few hours that day until I put my mind to what I could do about it. I had to find all the old test papers and books on vehicle mechanics. I could then study day and night and pray that my mind could find from somewhere, all my previous knowledge. The mere thought of failing made me physically sick.

A week later, I went to Bordon and everything seemed to go reasonably well. By some miracle, at the end of that week I was told I had passed with second-class marks. That alone would increase my weekly pay. On my return to the depot the CO seemed upset that I had passed; no congratulations or well done, he simply informed me that I would start the next square-bashing course. However, once the sergeant and the corporals knew that I had been a corporal and served three years in Germany, I was allowed to be a mentor to the recruits.

During that training, I went home on a forty-eight hour pass and witnessed what poor Moira was suffering at the hands of my mother. I promised I would have her with me at the earliest opportunity. I also

Moira – Colchester 1964

told her about the CO's decision because I firmly believed he had a lot to do with the reversal of the recruiting sergeant's promise to me. I learned not long after, while still at the depot, that the CO had volunteered for the Special Services during his early army days, but during the training had seriously injured himself. As a result, he still walked with a limp. He had therefore been sent back to his parent unit. It would appear it was a case of bitterness he carried about with him. Moira accepted the situation and promised to bite her tongue as long as needed.

What that major did for me that day was the greatest incentive I could ever have imagined. I was more than ever determined to reach for the skies, for the sake of my family. In April 1963 Moira and the girls finally joined me at my first posting after completing my basic training – 8 Infantry Workshop REME based in Goojerat Barracks, Colchester. The accommodation was a caravan on a small park a few hundred yards from the camp. It was heaven, at least we were together and not before time, poor Moira had been put through the mangle by my mum.

On August 8 1963, Linda was born in the Colchester Military Hospital at 1.20 am – exactly the same time as the Great Train Robbery was taking place. After that, everything started in earnest.

I was fanatical about regaining my rank and qualifications as quickly as possible. It really was very selfish of me because, it meant my wife would have to spend lots of time alone when I was away on courses and even when I was at home I would have to study constantly. In addition, there were also the regular military activities such as sport or guard duties to contend with. But most time-consuming was to be the number of military exercises we had to do. I had a good posting but at the wrong time. The unit was part of a rapid response brigade, which meant any regiment or battalion within our brigade could be called to a problem anywhere in the world and the workshop, or part of it, could be sent in support.

During the next eighteen months, I passed nine major examinations toward my qualifications. I also took part in two very big exercises, one in Libya and the other inside the Arctic Circle in Norway. One of the courses I went on, back at Bordon, was for a period of four weeks to gain my A class vehicle training – Track vehicles. There, I was lucky enough to meet a genuinely good man by the name of Ray Scovell, a rarity in life. He was an instructor on vehicle hydraulics. During the Second World War, he had served with the Eighth Army in North Africa, he was an expert on Centurion tanks, APCs and Ferret scout cars. It did not take him long to see that I was struggling on the hydraulics, once again due to my lack of education, so he seemed to make it his business to drive me along from day one. Consequently, I was very successful on that part of the course.

Many years later, when we met again, and he was retired, he told me that he could see that I had my heart set on achieving something good from the Army, and he wanted to be able to say he had been part of it. Ray died of a heart attack during the seventies, his wife Kitty graciously wrote me a letter, which said how proud he was of me, and she included his eulogy, something I will always treasure.

Every weekend we were allowed to return home at our own expense, which meant hitchhiking, as there was no way I could have been able to pay my fare. On one horrible, wet and windy Friday, I was on such a journey; I had managed to get as far as the A303 near Blackstock on my way to London. That night I was really lucky, because I had been standing at the roadside, no more than a few minutes, before a car pulled up and the driver asked me where I was heading. I told him Colchester and he said "Hop in, I am going to Brentwood".

What luck! That was the longest part of my journey taken care of. I climbed into the passenger seat just as another vehicle came up behind and for a few seconds, as its headlights lit up the car through the rear window, I was able to catch a glimpse of my good Samaritan's face. It looked very familiar but no matter how much I thought, I could not place it. We talked a lot as we travelled or at least Ron did – or was it Don? I didn't know, because he introduced himself so quickly. He wanted to know what I was doing, and I told him I was a soldier on my way home. His reply was that he had done a bit. All the time his face was preying on my mind. Who was he?

The more we talked, the more I got the impression my driver was acting a part, and I was his truly mesmerised audience, willing to let him go through his routine without me talking. Every question and answer, was very eloquently asked or answered, and when I could see his face, the expressions were quite unforgettable. As we arrived in the centre of London, the rain was lashing down and the wind was howling and buffeting the little car about. Suddenly there was a terrific bang; then it went dark for a few seconds.

When it cleared, my knight of the road suddenly lost his refined accent and changed to a more cockney voice and said, "Bugger it" plus a string of expletives. He then stopped the car and we jumped out just in time to witness the bonnet of Ron's car being blown away down the road behind us, like a newspaper in the wind. Then things got worse. The bonnet crunched into the front of a car before disappearing underneath, with the most horrible scraping screeching sound.

"Quick, get in". His accent had changed again, to now sounding like a real country gent. "Must not be involved", he said, and he drove off at speed, the subject not being mentioned again.

Where had I seen him before? I kept asking myself. He had the most unusual face with a variety of expressions that had to be seen to be believed. It was no good – I could not place him. We shook hands and parted at Brentwood.

On arriving home that night I told Moira the story of what had been the most manic, yet wonderful, car journey I had ever experienced. For weeks, his face haunted me and I was determined to know the identity of my mysterious driver on that wet Friday night.

I very rarely read the papers or visited the cinema, and the tv was very limited due to my constant studies. Many weeks later, I was looking through a magazine in the hairdresser's while waiting my turn. I turned a page and there looking at me was Ron, the face I could not forget. He was a tv and film star by the name of Ronald Lacey.

From that day on, whenever I saw that face on the small or large screen I had to smile. The memory he left me with was one of admiration for a very fine actor with whom I had been very fortunate to spend a few hours. The man could make me smile or scare the hell out of me. Years later, I saw him in "Raiders of The Lost Ark" with Harrison Ford; about the same time as I found out, he had died. Rest in peace, Ron, I enjoyed your company for one stormy night in the sixties. I still believe it was criminal of the director of that film to destroy such a wonderful face the way he did, albeit just a film.

We left Colchester by military vehicles, destination Brize Norton RAF Camp in Oxfordshire for yet another exercise. This time it was a really big one in Libya, North Africa, to support the brigade. We flew out in a Britannia four-propeller troop carrier and it took eight hours, with two short fuel stops. The desert was a wonderful sight as we flew into El Adem, RAF Base near Tobruk. Once we landed and the aircraft doors were opened, the heat, which entered the plane, was unbearable and when outside, every breath burned the inside of my throat and lungs. But there was no time to dwell on that, and we were very soon on our way along the northern coast road to a spot about twenty miles from Tobruk where our advance party had already laid out a campsite. There we would stay for a month.

At that time, there was minimum concern about the sun and skin cancer had yet to be recognised as dangerous. Consequently, the majority of us were burned within a very short time, some quite badly because we were working from dawn to dusk in shorts, boots and hats only. We did, however, learn very quickly how long to stay uncovered and the best times of the day to carry out certain tasks. We had instruction on fluid intake and the essential use of salt tablets, and most important we learned how to slow down. (As the union man had said in a previous life, "Pace yourself lad".)

In a short time, we became experts on the wildlife, which was everywhere. Scorpions were the worst and could give a nasty sting, not life threatening but one that could lay a man low for a few days with violent headaches and flu-like symptoms. A few of the lads were bitten during the night while sleeping and the culprit was thought to be the camel spider, but we were told it was not the case. Whatever, the following morning there were small holes in one lad's hand and another's forearm. The wounds would not heal – in fact the very opposite, the skin rotted away in those areas and both soldiers received treatment for weeks, after returning home.

That month in the desert taught me a lot about British soldiers who had trained there before us. Tortoises were everywhere, and I did not come across one that didn't have a regimental badge painted on its shell. So strange how British soldiers seem to have the desire to let the world know we have been there, especially that guy Kilroy.

The vast area of the Libyan Desert was, and more than likely still is, littered with burned-out tanks and guns as well as an enormous variety of other vehicles from the Second World War, left like reminders to the world that many lives were lost on those burning sands. Everywhere one looked, fox holes could be seen still surrounded by sandbags, and near each group was a dump of old fuel cans and other discarded military kit. Almost every vehicle and piece of equipment had been signed by Kilroy and many other people, even Erwin Rommel. Battered minefield signs and barbed wire were a common sight; unfortunately, the signs were not very reliable because of the sands moving with the passing of time. Consequently, many Arabs, especially children, were killed or injured each year as a result of their curiosity.

Our camp was twenty miles from the nearest civilization at Tobruk and many tens of miles more, in other directions. It was completely flat as far as the eye could see, and the road we camped alongside stretched for miles like a straight silver ribbon, and all the time we were there I never saw any vehicles other than ours. But, right out of the blue on our second morning, a group of Libyan women and children appeared outside the camp asking for medical treatment and medicine. How they got there and where from, remained a mystery. Our doctor examined them all and gave various medications, after which they all set off into the desert in the opposite direction to Tobruk. We could see them for the whole of the day as they travelled away into the distance.

On another burning hot day, when all we wanted to do was hide away in the shade, in a pointless attempt to keep cool, the shout "Fall In" shattered the silence of the Libyan Desert. A none-too-bright young subaltern had decided to take a small convoy to a place called Dherna up near the north coast for water supplies. Up to then, we had collected water from the nearby El Adem Air Base or Tobruk, who were we to question his urge to go sightseeing? The convoy consisted of three water-carrying vehicles with two men in each cab, and two goods vehicles with two men up front and two in the rear of each. En-route we stopped off at the Brigade HQ to fill the two goods vehicles with rations for all the workshop personnel.

We arrived at the village after a rather sweaty journey and a great deal of cursing about why our leader had decided to waste time travelling so far, for no good reason. We had no sooner started filling the water trucks when the village children began to appear. There were just a few in the beginning then more and more; the ages ranged from toddlers to teenagers. Like all kids, the tiny ones started asking for sweets and chocolate while the older ones wanted cigarettes. Once again, our young Rupert showed his lack of experience and decided we should open a few boxes of our compo rations and take out the sweets, and he would play the generous Brit by giving out the goodies.

One moment the kids were on the desert floor begging, but as soon as the boxes were, open they were up and over the sides of the vehicle like an army of ants, to see what was actually in the boxes. The constant chattering in their own language soon attracted the teenagers and the grown-ups who started asking for food and cigarettes. The little ones by then, were getting their hands into the boxes and starting to throw the goods over the vehicle sides. It was only a very short time before we had adults on the back of the vehicles alongside us tossing complete boxes off, by then we had a real problem trying to stop them opening more boxes and removing them from the vehicle.

The situation was becoming ugly and we were having to physically throw them off. It was starting to be quite hopeless and, as our young Rupert was a bit undecided about what to do, the junior NCO took charge. The drivers were instructed to start their vehicles and move out while the rest of us got rid of all the unwanted Libyans as quickly as possible, we really had to be aggressive. As soon as the vehicles started to move, the bricks started to come showering down. Thank God, that day the vehicles did not let us down and we managed to get away with a few cut heads and many bruises.

Once again, British soldiers had been placed in a situation where the outcome could have been far more serious. That day, those Libyans were not playing games. Dherna would not be one of my places to spend a holiday and our young subaltern was removed from our Christmas card list.

On one of our many trips away into the desert on recovery missions a colleague, Ron, and I were searching for a broken down vehicle many miles south of Tobruk, fighting our way through the sand dunes in our Scammel recovery vehicle. We reached the top of a small ridge and there, gathered before, us were a number of camels tethered in a circle and not far away, preparing refreshments, a group of the much-heard-about but very rarely seen "Blue People" – Tuaregs. That was the first experience for both of us, meeting real Arabs in their own environment. They numbered about a dozen and were dressed almost exactly as we had been told. Some of them wore dark clothes but the majority were in faded pale blue and almost to a man, they were veiled. The most worrying aspect of our meeting was how well they were armed.

"What now Ron?" I asked. We were less than twenty yards from them so any thought of trying to turn and run was out of the question.

"Let's just play it cool and see what happens", was his reply.

We had a common problem experienced by many soldiers when training in various parts of the world. Some of the indigenous people did not always take kindly to intruders, as we had found out at Dherna, and we were never armed. So, on that particular morning a few thoughts were bouncing about inside our heads. The desert wanderers standing before us could quite easily get rid of us and bury our remains in the sands and no one would ever know. Suddenly, a couple of them waved and started to approach our vehicle so we dismounted.

The only way we could converse with them was by using sign

language. (I always knew my mill training would come in useful some day). We had been told that body language was all-important when facing Arabs, so we stayed cool and smiled a lot. Thankfully, it seemed to work, and they were friendly and curious. Very soon, most of them were swarming all over our recovery vehicle, searching every nook and cranny. Then they came across our weapons, issued to us simply for training purposes, and they started jabbering and laughing, not at the type of weapon I suspected, but rather at the fact that there was no ammunition anywhere to be seen. They continued to laugh, and we worried a lot more, but tried our best not to let it show.

Once their curiosity had been satisfied, they made it clear we could join them for their break and my partner and I sighed with relief at overcoming that stage of our meeting, yet still fully aware that the situation could very quickly change as the Blue people did not have a very good reputation of being friendly – even with other Libyans. We still had a vehicle to find and a journey back to base, but both Ron and I thought it might not be a wise move to refuse their hospitality, so we joined the circle around the fire and made every effort to enjoy their company.

A huge teapot was being passed round the circle, we sat patiently watching our new friends who by that time, with few exceptions, had removed their veils, and what was revealed was not a pretty sight. If a film company had gone out to recruit for a film a group of scary rough-looking renegades, they could not have done better than hire the band sat with us that day. Some of them had whole or part fingers missing and almost a half had one or more nasty facial scars or defective eyes, and all of them without exception, were seriously in need of dental treatment. They really were an evil-looking bunch, but they continued to be friendly. My thoughts were interrupted by the sound of the teapot in the near vicinity. The etiquette seemed to be, that a man received the pot from the man on his right and then he poured a copious amount of tea into that man's glass before moving the pot along to his left, and that continued round the circle. I received the pot and filled the man's glass to my right before passing it along to Ron who duly filled my glass . . . and then!

Unfortunately, the Arab on Ron's left was the one you certainly would not have taken home to tea. Not only did he have the most scars, but he had a mouthful of rotten teeth and one white eyeball. Finally, his body hygiene, or lack of, was beginning to emanate due to the heat of the fire and I could smell him from the other side of my colleague. He took the pot from Ron and smiled. That alone was enough to put anyone off sitting down to tea. He commenced filling Ron's glass. Almost immediately, the flow of hot liquid slowed to a dribble, our host shook the pot vigorously and tried again. There was no change, so once more my friend got the full Colgate smile followed by a full blast of laughter, the wind of which could have melted the paint on our Scammel. Poor Ron looked at me and I could see that the face of my tough rugby-playing friend, who had also completed some hundred freefall jumps, was rapidly changing colour.

"Pick yourself up", I whispered. Then the Taureg turned the pot around stuck the spout in his mouth and blew. Ron turned to me and said, "I'm not drinking that".

"You bloody well are, your friend may get annoyed and we don't want that".

During the sitting, we had a few eats. What they were, we dare not think – every mouthful made us choke. After that, they waved us goodbye and we could not get away quickly enough, our appetites were non-existent for almost a week. I did find out later, that the tea they drink is made from a very strong infusion mixed with mint, herbs and crushed dates that would almost certainly have had something to do with their dental problems.

On the way back to base, we decided to stop at a position along the coast and have a stroll along the beach while enjoying a cigarette. As we approached a small rocky mound we heard someone singing in Arabic, at least I think it was singing more like wailing to us young lads, who had been brought up on Elvis, the Everly Brothers and many more. This time, we thought it wiser to peep over the top to find who was on the other side, rather than just show ourselves. Anyway, I don't think Ron could have managed another tea party. To our surprise there was one Arab standing by a huge boulder, which he was using as his washing machine, he took each item of clothing to the sea and gave it a good soaking. Then, to our amusement, from behind the rock he took a large packet of "Tide" Washing Powder, covered the item, then bashed the hell out of it on the rock before heading once more to the sea to rinse off. That little incident cheered us both up after our stomach-churning day.

Once back in the UK, we were kept very busy repairing military equipment in order to be prepared to move out at short notice should the need arise. Colchester was a very strong Army town with numerous barracks and vast areas of lush green sports fields plus a very substantial military hospital. So, it was only to be expected that at certain times various military events should take place, such as tattoos and inter-services sporting championships.

On such occasions, the junior ranks from all units in the brigade were used to carry out various tasks such as selling tickets, organizing the seating or putting up tents and many other general fatigues. The very first Military Tattoo I was involved in took place in Colchester central park during the wettest week in Essex for many years. Myself and another volunteer, as the senior ranks liked to call us, were put on arena gate duty for the week. When each new act was due in the arena the announcement was called out over the tannoy system to inform the paying public what spectacular act they were about to see. That was the cue for my colleague and me to be ready to open one large gate each, the only way into the showground. Then the spotlights would illuminate the ring and we would open the gates and allow whichever act to enter, before closing the gates once more – nothing to it. The first two nights went well, then on the third night, which was still wet and very windy, lined up waiting to enter the ring was the band of the Welsh Guards and standing in front, ready to lead them out, was a colour sergeant with the band's mascot, a giant of a ram on a rope. It was indeed the largest, most beautifully turned out animal I had ever seen.

Suddenly the Colour tapped me on the shoulder, "Hold on to that while I go for a Jimmy, boyo" he said as he thrust the rope into my hand and disappeared.

Within a couple of minutes, the tannoy burst into life and then the area was ablaze with light. My partner, seeing my predicament, thought he would do me a favour and open both gates. That was the trigger for the band to strike up. I was at a loss for a few seconds about what to do but the bloody ram had made his mind up. After all he must have gone through the routine many times before – only then he had been kept in check by a giant of a colour sergeant.

That night half a ton of mutton (it seemed like that) took full advantage of my wimpy grip and took off like a greyhound out of a trap, with me trying to keep up like something out of a comic film. I shouted at him but that only seemed to spur him on, I don't think he understood English. The crowd was in stitches, which stirred the ram to even greater efforts. Thank goodness, after only a short time the handler calmly made his way through the ranks of the bandsmen and took over, while I, sheepishly, sneaked back out the way he had come to my post on the gates to the cheers and clapping of the crowd. That night after the show, as the spectators were leaving, I heard a small boy telling his parents that the best part of the show was when the sheep ran away with the clown. How right he was, and then to top it all the following morning back in camp the sergeant major sent for me.

"Yes Sir", I snapped as I entered his office.

"Craftsman, don't you ever again take on a comedy roll with the Taffies without first asking my permission. Is that clear?"

"Yes Sir". Dozy prat, I thought, I wasn't that good

The following day the tattoo organisers had come up with a bright idea. A Ferret scout car would set off from the far corner of the arena. At the same time, a Land Rover would enter through the gates and drive straight across the ring and into the side of the Ferret, creating an accident. A request would go out over the tannoy system for a REME recovery vehicle, an ambulance and the RMPs to show the public how various services deal with such a concatenation in operational conditions.

I didn't know about the plan until reporting for gate duty that night and being told I was to be the Land Rover driver. At the meeting earlier in the day, our CSM had put my name forward with the tag line, "He thinks he is a bloody star – let's see what he can do".

One small point had been overlooked. How could I and the armoured car driver guarantee to be in a collision position at exactly the same time without at least one practice session? How, could we possibly judge the braking distance, especially in such a muddy arena? Alas, we had our orders and were told we would be given a signal when it was time to move.

There I sat in my Land Rover waiting to go into the unknown. The gate opened, signal received and off I went. I must admit both the Ferret driver and I worked strictly to our orders and braked when our signal was shown. We were like two bars of soap being thrown across a tiled floor and consequently we missed each other, much to the amusement of the audience, I was praying they didn't recognise me as the dope on the rope from the previous night. When we did finally stop, we were berated by the CSM, who I doubted had ever been behind the wheel of a vehicle. His final words to us, after many unspeakable ones, were that we must judge vehicle speed and react accordingly to ensure contact. My partner in crime and I, tried to explain to him that we did not think that was correct. Unfortunately, I would have got more sense from the ram. So, off we went once more to do as we were told while the MC told the crowd the weather had been the problem, but he assured them the next time would be good.

Working to our leader's orders, once more we set off. The MC was right about it being good, what was supposed to have been a fifteen-mile-an-hour side shunt became a forty-mile-an-hour crash due to the mud and my need to accelerate more and more – thanks to the Ferret driver taking the CSM''s orders on acceleration to heart, and streaking off across the arena like a bat out of hell. I had to put my foot down in order to make contact before he left the field and disappeared into the Essex countryside. The outcome was most enjoyable for the crowd, but we finished up with two very battered vehicles and a ringing in the ears for the next hour. After that, I thought, that's one thing they will not ask us to repeat. I was so wrong; the stunt was the highlight of the show for the rest of the week and the workshop got more than its fair share of body repairs.

A month had passed since our return from North Africa and the other half of the workshop, who had gone off to Borneo on an emergency prior to our desert frolic, returned to base, minus one man. He was a young lad named James. He hadn't been with us long, but he had babysat for Moira and me on the two rare occasions when we had a night out. He had been on perimeter guard in the jungle and simply disappeared, never to be seen or heard of again. Another one of the lads who returned from the trip was a friend by the name of Dave who I played a lot of cricket with. I spoke to him the night before he went to spend two weeks back home with his family in Tyneside. He complained to me that he felt grim and was suffering from bad headaches and thought he might be starting with flu, I said cheerio to him and off he went the following morning. No more than three days later we were informed our young colleague had died from cerebral malaria.

Once again, we were lumbered as gophers to put up tents for the Army Athletics Championships. A Fijian friend by the name of Joe and I were working away with a number of other fatigue men when Joe wandered off to watch one of the athletes going through, what I presumed to be, his final training session before the afternoon's activities. I don't know if Joe was really interested or found it easier than putting tents up. Once or twice, I glanced across the field to where he was standing behind a discus thrower.

"I can't understand why that guy is in the competition".

I looked up and my Fijian friend was talking to me, at the very same time as a young subaltern was walking past, and he heard Joe's comments.

"Because, Soldier, he is the Army Champion", snapped the young officer. Silence for a few seconds and the officer carried on walking.

"I can throw it further than him", blurted out my friend.

Oh hell, I thought, in trouble again. The young officer stopped and returned with a smile on his face. "Have a go and show me".

At that invitation, my colleague ambled back across the field with me in close attendance. That morning, for some reason known only to Joe, he was dressed in the usual denims for fatigues plus a greatcoat and gloves, even though the weather did not warrant the latter two garments. We stopped where the discus thrower was still hard at practice, the officer said something to him and he stood to one side. There was my giant friend dressed in his very flat-shaped beret, denims, gaiters and army

131

boots and fully covered in his huge greatcoat. "Strip off, Joe", I half whispered to him as he bent down and picked up a discus in a huge gloved hand. He bent down once more and placed the discus back on the floor. I thought for one foolish moment I had got through to him and he was going to strip – no chance, he simply removed his gloves and picked up the discus again. He stood on the circle, took one quick look at the direction of throw, then two lazy turns and away went the object. It carried on going for what seemed like an eternity before landing way down the field, the officer and the athlete stood transfixed with a look of complete disbelief on their faces. I had been fortunate enough to have spent a fair amount of time with Joe and some more of his countrymen on the rugby fields so, nothing about their athleticism surprised me. Joe just said, "OK Pete, let's put up tents", and we left.

Later that day the subaltern once again found us and informed Joe that the distance he had thrown that morning was further than the Army Champion could throw, and would he like to join the training squad with them? A great pity that the young lad with the pips did not know anything about Fijian psychology. The word "train" to Joe and all his countrymen meant physical exercise and discipline. They were great performers, but under their own terms and at their own speed. The answer that day from Joe to the young officer was an emphatic, "no".

Once again, I was off leaving Moira and the girls behind. We were going to Tromsø, inside the Arctic Circle, for winter warfare training. This time we had the proper kit such as snow cat vehicles and skis as well as all the correct clothing, unlike the debacle on Soltau training area during another life. We landed on a very snowy day in Narvik, Norway and from there we were transported to Tromsø where we would live for a month.

Our accommodation consisted of twelve-man tents. The centre pole of the tents was also the chimney for our only source of heat – a wood-burning stove that was constantly supplied with silver birch logs cut from the nearby forest. From the moment we arrived until we left, the fire was alight and tended full time. It was critical; failure to do so would almost certainly have meant freezing to death for anyone static within, especially with wind chill factors in excess of minus 40c, which was quite a common temperature reading during our stay.

Each day we had a programme of working on equipment in such severe temperatures. We also carried out acclimatisation and a lot of time was spent on ski training with Norwegian army instructors. They taught us the basics and we carried out a number of trekking exercises carrying heavy packs and at intervals shooting at targets. We learned how to build igloos and survive in such extreme conditions. Most important we operated the buddy system far more extensively than on our previous winter farce.

At night, we slept in the circular tent, feet toward the centre. The ground was covered with a full size ground sheet upon which each man had a reindeer skin and then on top our sleeping bags. Before turning in for the night we stripped off our outermost garments and they joined us in the bag. Fastened on the tent wall above each man's position was a very sharp knife that was our means of escape in the event of a tent fire during the night. The routine once awakened was slash the tent open and roll out with whatever kit as quickly as possible. We knew it could be a very dangerous situation, having witnessed one of the tents catch fire during the day when only the man on fire watch was inside. From start to finish it took no more than thirty seconds to complete the burnout. To ensure the fire never went out at night or to raise the alarm if any problem occurred we had a tent duty roster, which started with the first man on the left inside the door. He would stay awake for one hour of duty feeding the fire, then wakes the next man on his left for the same period of time. This carried on throughout the night.

The eating, drinking and limited ablutions were very different especially going to the loo for either. It was a rush job and one executed with great care. The cookhouse was only a road's width away from the tent but we were not allowed to hang about in the warmth. We had to quickly collect our food and return to our tents before it froze solid – all part of our training. We had great fun throwing a cup of tea in the air and watching it crystallise before hitting the ground. The sight of the Aurora Borealis was mystical and worth being on the exercise for that alone; it made all the hardship worthwhile.

Finally, when our month was completed and before our return to the UK, every man was made most welcome in the Norwegian army camp. There, I had the most pleasurable bath ever, it was heaven after a month without being able to strip and completely immerse oneself in hot water. Afterwards, we changed into clean clothes for the journey home, followed by a welcome hot meal in warm surroundings among very friendly people.

In late August, we were, fully occupied with helicopter training around the Colchester and Stanford training areas. Annual refresher training it is called; abseiling fifty feet from a Wessex or jumping out as the chopper hovered a metre above boggy ground or landing then disembarking to cover a patch of land quickly. It was most exciting, but very time consuming as far as I was concerned, when all I wanted to do was study. Finally, we went to Pool Harbour, Dorset to carry out beach landings with the Royal Marines Commandos, once more returning knackered to our home base.

The final exercise for the season, which we knew about, was to Otterburn in the north of England. Everyone was pleased and really looking forward to having a break, back at base with our families, where we could enjoy some camp entertainment and sport. I would be able to get my head down and do some serious work towards my goal.

Just one week had passed on the cold wet moors of northern England, when the news arrived. I can't really say bad news because I was a soldier who had signed up to do a job, but it was not what I wanted to hear, with my heart so set on improving my career. The unit had been called back to base. From there, we were going to Cyprus to support the United Nations troops who were already on their way to the island because trouble had flared up between the Greek and Turkish Cypriots.

We drove all through that night reaching home in time for breakfast. Then we received the really bad news that we had to move out at three that afternoon. Unfortunately, that was the penalty we had to pay for being part of the, rapid response brigade. By the time, we had cleared our vehicles and stored all the kit away we barely had time for a bath, change of clothes and a meal, before packing and being ready to move out. Once more, I was leaving Moira and the girls for an unknown period of time.

That evening we flew out of Gatwick, loaded up like packhorses, in an RAF transport plane on a long and arduous journey. There are no seats in such aircraft, only what we called 'onion bags' which hung on the side of the fuselage. Positioned down the centre, was a Land Rover and a stack of kit including fuel, so smoking was out of the question. We had two fuel stops en route during which time we were allowed out on to the runway to stretch our legs and breathe in some much needed fresh air.

Throughout the whole of that journey, I could think only of my Moira and the girls. Not many months before, we had been allocated married quarters inside the barracks. It was a large property usually reserved for the RQMS but he had one, somewhere else. It meant that my family was isolated from the rest of the military wives and children. Moira was alone in the midst of a very active military establishment with a very young family surrounded by soldiers and military vehicles. She had no form of transport and the nearest shop was almost a mile away on the outskirts of the town. She would have to go everywhere with three children on the pushchair or tagging along behind.

It would have been some help to her if one of them had been at school, there, she would have met some of the other wives. The only form of heating for the house was an open fire with a back boiler, which required coal. The nearest supplier was the one small shop, which sold small bags, she would have to push the pushchair and control the girls. All these things were going through my head, what had I let her in for? She had already suffered at the hands of Mum and through loneliness because of exercises and my study, as well as the numerous courses. There were no friends for her to talk to due to us being away from the other married quarters, when we were living on the caravan site, and we had done little or no socialising, due to my study at every single opportunity.

Then there was also the problem of money. I was a craftsman on the lowest of wages and now we had two homes to run. Please let this trip be a short one, I thought to myself.

Cyprus in the sixties was an island of heartbreaking conflict between the majority Greek Cypriots and the minority Turkish Cypriots. It is the most beautiful of islands in the Mediterranean Sea. When the climate

Me – Cyprus 1964

was hot and dry, the landscape turned a magnificent shade of brown, then all that was needed was a good rainstorm and a couple of days sunshine and within that short time the scenery changed dramatically into a mass of flowers, blossoms and grasses. Wild garlic covered the areas with beautiful white flowers. Anemones, with their beautiful white, tinged with pink, were a delight to see on the shorelines and the elephant garlic's huge pom pom purple heads seemed to be everywhere. I took every opportunity when travelling to study nature, but the top of the list was always the bird life, especially the swallows which swooped around the graveyard in Dhekelia.

Since that time, whenever those marvellous little birds have gone on their migration flight from the UK to southern Africa, I say to myself, I want to see you return. Each time that happens it is as if life starts all over again and I know how lucky I am to be here. On two occasions during that Cyprus tour, I could have lost my life but it was not my time. However, there is a very fine line between life and death.

Early one morning, a Swedish driver and I took a ferret scout car out on road test. I was one of two Brits who had been attached to the Swedish Battalion serving with the UN to maintain their English vehicles. Our base was a tented camp at Skouriotissa Mine near Xeros on the northern coast of the island; a couple of miles along the coast road was, the most fantastic little café overlooking the Mediterranean Sea. There, we would often stop to have fresh eggs and the tastiest chips ever, made from the finest potatoes in the world, accompanied by a beautiful side salad washed down with an ice cold beer.

As we were travelling along one of the roads between the hills, I heard a few shots but took no notice because it was quite normal for the two sides to have the odd pot shot toward the villages of their enemies. On our return to camp, the guard on the gate was very quick to point out to us that the bins on one side of the vehicle had been hit with four shots. We had not been aware at the time, and throughout that journey, I had been sat on top of the turret, like a coconut at the fair.

The second incident was far worse. One evening I had to travel about twenty miles to my parent unit, the workshop in the Nicosia area, to collect a spare part. I was alone in a Land Rover and on the passenger seat was my LMG, light machine gun. Having picked up my vehicle part, I was on my way back along the same route, a bit later than I really wanted to be travelling alone. As I negotiated the winding road, I became aware of how quickly the light was fading. My mind was telling me, you are alone in the wrong place at the wrong time. When suddenly, without noticing, I rounded a bend and to my surprise, I was faced with an ineluctable situation. There before me, stood a Greek Cypriot roadblock. It was not unusual for the two sides to do such a thing outside their own village, but we usually knew where to expect them.

The windows at both sides of the cab were slid open before I had time to fully stop and a light was flashed in my eyes, blinding me. When my vision returned, I could see the block was manned by three, so-called Greek Cypriot soldiers, no more than early teenagers. However, they were mentally quite smart teenagers because the position of the roadblock was such, that I had no time to do anything about it after negotiating the blind bend. They really were like Dad's Army, but terrified, which meant the situation could become very volatile.

They gave me the once-over and looked all around the vehicle, which again was unusual. Normally, whichever villagers we met would have a few words, a joke and cadge a cigarette then, we would be on our way. Those lads must have been fully aware of who I was. My vehicle was white with the UN logo on the side and I was wearing a UN uniform, albeit a Swedish one, complete with blue beret. But for some reason unbeknown to me, they seemed to be agitated and were talking amongst themselves and pointing at my gun on the seat beside me. Then one of them, who seemed to be the leader, asked why I had it, when they must have known that even UN soldiers have weapons. They chose to go down a route that I was smuggling weapons to the Turkish Cypriots.

The discussion between us went on for a few minutes then, the one who seemed to be the so-called leader told me to get out of the Land Rover and go with them. All around was nothing but dark woodland, so I declined. There was no telling what they might do to me all alone on that dark Cyprus road. I was quickly becoming very aware that the main speaker seemed to have his own ideas and if anything were going to happen, it would be him who would instigate it. I was in a very precarious position because one of the lads to my left was right alongside me, and my gun was nearer to him, than me.

But, I had noticed in the light from one of the torches, that the young so-called soldier did not have a bolt in his old Enfield rifle and another of the youths was right in front of the vehicle in the full beam of my headlights, so I doubted if he would be able to see a lot. I was just contemplating having a go at the most vociferous one on my right and reaching for my gun, when headlights from behind lit up my vehicle. It was another UN vehicle and one of the passengers was out and alongside me in no time at all. He asked what the problem was and I told him. He immediately shouted something in his own language and I heard the vehicle doors opening and three more fully-armed Finnish soldiers were alongside him.

The first one spoke to the Greek Cypriots in a very clear, concise way – the United Nations have instructed us not to shoot any of the people on this island but they have not said anything about this. At that moment, as each one of the lads from Finland removed a large knife from within their boots; that was enough. The sheer panic and reaction had to be seen to be believed and within seconds, the barrier was raised and both our vehicles were waved on through.

To this day, I thank those four lads and I am unashamedly very biased whenever it comes to anything involving the people of Finland. My journey back to base that night, although only thirty minutes in reality, seemed like thirty hours. My mind was in a complete turmoil. I don't know if it was caused by the adrenalin, but for whatever reason I could not concentrate in any way. I was aware that at no stage of that encounter was I fearful for my own personal safety, even though my mind kept telling me I was in real danger had I alighted from the vehicle, as requested to do. By that time, I could have been lying dead in some ditch, shot by some young Greek Cypriots who were really frightened and being spurred on by an idiot. I had indeed been scared for those lads, yet at the time, I had not been aware of such thoughts.

When we first moved onto the island we had been issued with our personal weapons and a limited number of rounds, but as always we were under strict instructions that we were not allowed to shoot, unless we, or our colleagues were being shot at – not very good really. What it means is, either you or some of your friends lose their lives before action can be taken, because soldiers or terrorists have usually practised and know how to shoot in most instances.

The predicament that night before the Finns baled me out, was binary. If they had not appeared on the scene, and I had managed to get my gun, there was every probability that I would have come out of any skirmish the winner – not that there are any winners in such situations – simply because my weapon was loaded and in good working order and I knew at least one of the Greek Cypriots' weapons was defective and maybe, even more. Secondly I was fully trained and the young lads were frightened. If that scenario had taken place what would have happened to me and my family? Would I have been supported or would the politicians have turned their backs on me?

On the other hand, if that night a politician had been sat alongside me and I had managed to get my gun and either kill or wound the young lads, I have no doubt I would have been hailed a hero and received a medal of some kind. But if, as it was, just me, with the same outcome, I have no doubt I would have been charged with murder or manslaughter. Then all my plans for Moira and the girls would have ended on that road to Xeros. That was my greatest fear that night, and on a number of occasions before and after.

Just prior to entering camp when I had overcome the scary bit and my heart had finally stopped pumping adrenalin, I stopped the Land Rover and sat in complete silence, yet a lot was said during that period of time. The silence thing I discussed with many of my colleagues, and all were in agreement, that after any kind of serious incident, even groups have silent periods when a lot is said to themselves. It appears to be a military phenomenon.

The artificer sergeant major of my parent unit took it upon himself to inform the Swedish military hierarchy based on the island that I played football. The result was, that with very little notice I was selected unseen to play for the Swedish Army against the Danish Army at Nicosia Stadium. It was a great honour but one I most certainly should have declined. By the time the match took place, we had been in Cyprus for almost three months and because we had been fully occupied repairing vehicles, our fitness had suffered. We had in fact played no sport at all during that time. The infantry battalions consisting of Swedes, Danes and a few others were on continual fitness training for their job.

To make the matter worse, the non-sporty members of the battalion such as the clerks and store men, the ones we lived among, loved to party at every opportunity, especially when the drink was free, the situation was just so. Tuborg Brewery supplied them non-stop with canned beer, so we two Brits were involved far too much in their social lives.

The day of the match arrived and for some reason, unknown to me, I was treated like the first 'million-pound player', I could only assume my ASM had given them a load of bullshit. From the very first moment I stepped on to the pitch, I knew it was a very big mistake to accept their offer. The Swedes lost by one goal and I felt awful. I was at least two yards off the pace throughout the whole game and apologised profusely to the officer in charge, and although he said he didn't mind, I did. I let them down and myself. That day I have never forgotten, but for all the wrong reasons. The ASM who put my name forward made it up to me later in my career.

I returned home from Cyprus in May 1965 on the very day my beloved football team, Leeds United lost the Cup Final 2-1 to Liverpool. We had to sit on Swindon railway station platform listening to that sad news while waiting for a train back to Colchester. Another thing our Government was very good at, when we had been called out to Cyprus we went with all haste, no expense spared but returning to our families after a long and arduous tour, we had to carry our kit and catch trains. Once more, certain military bosses had been a bit economical with the truth, they had told us we would be on the island a very short time. In the end we had been away for seven months, by which time I was really frustrated about my career and even more determined to be an Artificer, for what Moira and the kids had suffered.

Within hours of being back in the unit, I made it my first goal to find out what I had to do to get to Bordon School of Electrical and Mechanical Engineering to be that Artificer. The outcome of my enquiries painted a very daunting picture I needed to pass three major theory papers in Mathematics, English and Physics. The Mathematics was a far higher standard than I had ever heard of, let alone done, and Physics just never came into my school curriculum so I would have to learn from scratch. But, before I could sit the papers, I would have to be first class in Military Training, Vehicle Mechanical Training and Military Education. When I finally passed all those tests, I would be invited to Bordon to undertake fitness tests and command tasks before appearing before three interview panels. Last of all, I would have to attend an interview board consisting of a number of very senior officers. If successful on all counts, I might, be invited to take a place on a course, which would last for twenty months at the school.

Before starting, I would be promoted to acting sergeant and if I completed the course successfully, I would be a substantive staff sergeant. My pay for the first step would be unbelievable but the second step would be a complete life-changer for all my family. The very thought of that chance for my family was all I needed. Bring it on; nothing can stop me, I thought to myself. Three months later, with a lot of help from friends, especially my wife who was a rock – always alone because of my constant study, even when I was in the house, and the education officer, who literally went grey while I feared for his sanity in his efforts to teach me Mathematics and physics, I had passed my three first class subjects and hopefully had the knowledge to apply to sit the three theory papers at Bordon.

That I did some three or four months later, and for two weeks after, I was impossible for my family to live with. Finally one morning the OC sent for me, I had never been as nervous in my life as when I entered his office. He immediately congratulated me on passing the three papers, not brilliant marks but all passes which, considering my education standard when I left school, was a miracle – one of those Mum always dreamed of telling Father Moverly about.

Once he had managed to calm me down, he told me that if I were agreeable, he would inform the school at Bordon that I wanted to be considered for the course. That may take a few months, he stated, before being called forward for the next stage. Meanwhile he would speak to the CO about the possibility of me spending time with the weapons instructors and tactics advisors at one or more of the infantry battalions in the area. The result was, I had two weeks with them and was able to gain a higher qualification on weapons than my first class military certificate, which would benefit me greatly, should I ever get to Artificer training.

It was late 1965 and I was back in the workshop. The CO sent for me and said how pleased he was with my progress and how he wished he could promote me. Unfortunately, that was not possible because there was no vacancy for a paid lance corporal. However, he was going to promote me to the rank, acting unpaid, so that I could regain some management experience and Moira and I could use the NCO's club – always providing we could get a babysitter. In the meantime, he would telephone the school and try to pull a few strings in order to move things along.

I thanked him, saluted, and was about to leave the office when he said, "But there is one thing I want you to do for the unit."

"Whatever, sir," I replied.

"I want you to spend a week training some of the workshop senior ranks who have not reached your standard of weapon training and may never do so, but whatever they learn from you can only benefit the workshop personnel in general."

Then I was on my way.

That night, I gave Moira all the great news including the last bit, even though I was very apprehensive. I could not see them taking any notice of me when they were by far the senior. Moira pointed out that the CO was a bit of a crafty basket. It really didn't have a lot to do with training senior ranks, but more to do with me gaining experience of teaching what indeed could be a difficult class, before going cold to the school. I hadn't seen it that way. Monday morning arrived and I had been assigned a classroom, and sent a programme of the CO's requirements, over the course of the next week.

Attached was a list of those attending the course; three sergeants, two staff sergeants from another unit and, unbelievably, a warrant officer class two. At the sight of the strangers on the list and the last mentioned, I felt very nervous. I wasn't worried about the teaching, I had done quite a lot on my qualifying courses, it was more about how I could get them to do my bidding. I need not have worried; within seconds of the last man to arrive, the CO walked into the room.

He asked them all to be seated then he introduced me, and then he told them, "I know this is an unusual situation but this lance corporal (me) – anything he asks you to do for the remainder of this week you will do without question, as if I were present. Is that perfectly clear?" "Yes, Sir," all answered.

For the first day, I felt very strange about the situation. The only time I knew of a similar situation in the forces was senior ranks training young would-be officers at Sandhurst. Many years later I watched an old movie "The Guns of Navarone" and saw Gregory Peck as the senior officer instruct his men that they would all obey David Niven, their junior, on the subject of explosives. Perhaps that is where the CO got the idea from.

A short time later, I passed the rest of my tests and interviews and was put on a waiting list for a course date, which I was told could be up to six months. Not good news for me because once I make my mind up to do something I have no patience.

Within a few days, I had really overstepped the mark in my eagerness to get started on my Artificer training. I happened to be working on a vehicle in the workshop right outside the office door of the workshop OC, who was no other than the ASM who had volunteered me for that fateful football match back in Cyprus. He had been given a short-term commission on his return from Cyprus and given the post, when his predecessor left.

On that particular day, he had a sergeant in his office, the door was partly open and I could hear them talking. The NCO, like me, had passed his exams to do Artificer training and had been waiting a long time to be called forward. From what I heard of the conversation, the officer was telling him that he had received his date and it was two weeks from the day. "Lucky sod," I thought.

Then I heard the sergeant say he would like a delay, I did not catch the reason. Then the OC's voice was raised so I was able to hear him more easily. "Why?" he asked and the sergeant told him it was a family problem which he went on to explain. The OC was far from happy and told him so, and that he might have to wait a long time before the school asked him again. He also said he did not know what the reaction would be from the powers-that-be at the school, because they would have to find a replacement at such short notice. However, he would let them know and the NCO was dismissed and left the office.

Once he was out of sight I plucked up courage and knocked on the OC's door and he called me in. By that time, I was shaking like a jelly. He asked me what I wanted. Then I had the audacity to tell him that I had overheard the conversation, which had taken place a short time before. He just sat there staring at me in disbelief, I really thought by that time I would have been in the middle of a real telling-off or even worse. But no! he just sat there transfixed, so I took the opportunity to go the whole hog.

"Can I take his place on the course? It will save Bordon a lot of man hours and money finding a replacement." It seemed like hours before his expression changed. Then he just said, "Good. I will try to fix that up and talk to you in the morning."

He told me to get back to work and as I reached the door he called out, "And don't listen to any more private conversations, Corporal."

As I looked back, I could have sworn he had a grin on his face. Later, when I said my farewells to the unit, and he shook my hand, he told me he had been in two minds that day about having me put in the nick but, on thinking very carefully, what I had done that day took guts and was a bit different to the guy who turned down such a chance. In addition, he owed me for the football incident in Cyprus.

CHAPTER TEN

Bordon, Hampshire 1966

After two weeks of living in a daze, I was in Hampshire, at the school, starting my Artificer course. I could quite easily have been in the middle of twenty-eight days in the slammer, for approaching the adjutant in the manner I had, but he was a good soldier and officer and true to his word.

Once again, Moira was to be alone with the girls for six weeks until I had completed the military and physical part of the course; anyone who failed that was a non-starter. Those weeks were very hard, doing drill and assault courses every day and regular ten-mile runs carrying a telegraph pole between ten of us. There were a number of failures due to injuries or because they simply did not have the stamina. On the completion of that stage, I was the fittest I had ever been in my life.

The family came to join me in our first real army quarters, among other personnel from the same unit and their families. We knew where we would be for the next twenty months and we had good money now that I was on a sergeant's pay. But, more important, Moira was within shopping distance of the NAAFI and the village. She had neighbours and friends, the girls were able to attend a good school, and Moira and I could have a social life in the Mess. At last, I was achieving something. I still had a lot of study to look forward to but there were no more exercises and very limited duties, due to the number of sergeants on the courses.

Stage two of the course was really hard for me and cost me many nights with little sleep. I had passed Mathematics to a standard beyond my wildest dreams just to be where I was, but now I had to go far higher. Thank goodness, my overtime paid off and I managed to scrape through. On that part of my course, I learned a very valuable lesson, which has remained with me throughout my life.

During one of the many Mathematics lessons, we were briefly dealing with the subject of revenue and capital. The teacher stood before us and said, "You may find it hard to believe, but on the previous course one of the lads did not know the difference between the two."

First, one of my classmates started to laugh rather weakly, and then the rest followed. Suddenly the teacher turned to one of the lads and said;"please explain to the rest of the class what the difference is." You could have heard a pin drop. Thank God, he didn't ask me because I didn't know either and I found out later, nobody else did. The lesson learned that day was; don't be a prat, if you do not know, ask.

Our next stage was four weeks of metalwork and blacksmithing. Up to then, we had understood that we had to pass each end-of-section examination by the minimum of 65% to progress to the next stage of training. Should any student fail, by the odd few marks, they would re-sit and should they still fail, they would be put back a course.

Unfortunately, at that time, a new brigadier had taken command of the training school and the policy had changed – new broom. The new policy was, that any student who failed by even one mark would be interviewed personally by the new boss. What would happen then, we had to wait for the first failure and see. One of the tasks in that section was to make a bowl from a small sheet of copper, by hand, to specific measurements, using only a wooden mallet, tin-snips and polishing material. After two weeks of hammering, shaping and finally polishing, every member of the course seemed well pleased with their finished bowls.

When the marks were published, three of us had failed the bowl test, me and another young sergeant by two marks, the third by five marks. The very sight of those results made my heart sink and I literally shook all over and felt physically sick. After a couple of days of torture and sleepless nights, we got the call to be interviewed by the brigadier himself and the three of us feared the worst because the rumours were that he was going to return all failures back to their units – which would be the end of my Artificer dreams. In my case, I would have to revert back to being a Craftsman. The loss of pay would be devastating and my chances of being anything for the rest of my contract, very bleak.

First in the brigadier's office, that morning was the guy who had failed by five marks. After a very short time he was back outside, his face pure white. True to what we had heard, he was to be sent back to his unit. He was more fortunate than the two of us. Having been a sergeant before he started the course, he would just have to overcome the stigma of being a failure. Many years later, I met him in Cyprus and he was still a sergeant.

Next, the two of us went in together, I suppose that was because we had the same marks. There we stood, or should I say trembled, while the commandant tore us off a strip before reaching his decision. We were both expecting the worst but TG, as Mum would say he gave us the strongest warning before sending us back one course, and telling us that was our final chance and we would be very carefully watched. It is impossible to describe the relief on hearing that statement. Once more, back outside the office, there was no cheering or smiles, it took the rest of that day for what had happened to sink in and even today, I know how near I was to losing my career.

Some weeks later, when we had cleared that section, a young sergeant from two courses behind me, whom I knew only by sight, came to the house one night and asked me to do him a favour. He said he had made a complete mess of the copper bowl exercise and was really worried. After my experience, he had good reason to be. His effort, he said, would certainly fail and would I loan him mine, which I had thrown to one side in the spare room in disgust. At that stage, I could not contain myself any longer and burst into laughter.

I told him what had happened to mine and suggested he go somewhere else. He told me he had a young family like ours and he had really tried many places before coming to me, almost a stranger to him. He was desperate because it had to be handed in the following day, so I loaned the bowl with the comment of; "don't blame me." And off he went with my feeble effort.

A week later, he was on the doorstep again. When I saw him, I was ready to duck. "I have brought your bowl back," he said. Then his face broke into a huge grin from ear to ear, he had received top marks of 79% in the class and all he had done was give it a bit of a shine with Brasso. Not long after, I had another request for the same thing, no doubt my new friend had told someone. Once again, the young sergeant gained top marks.

Many times I have asked myself if it was a subjective opinion taken by the markers, rather than working to specific parameters, or was it a deliberate ploy to give the brigadier a chance to make his mark very quickly. Whichever it was, it almost cost me my career. It was very strange how my copper bowl, which I had so lovingly made, went from being my pride and joy, before leaving it to the markers, to almost being the wrecker of my life and how it was thrown in a cupboard rather than the dustbin – then finally became a life saver for two future Artificers.

That was to be the first of many instances where a teacher or senior officer was to give a subjective opinion, which changed my life in some small way. The case of the bowl was different because it had been marked three times by the same markers resulting in three different marks. I felt then and still do that such tests should be marked to fixed parameters and guidelines, especially when someone's whole life is at stake. That lesson I took with me through my whole military career and into civilian engineering management. I always ensured that any test papers were marked by more than one person and to very specific guidelines, and every interview was carried out by more than one person.

Rugby Team SEME Bordon 1967–68 PH back row – second from left

During those very happy days at the school, I was fortunate to play a lot of rugby for the unit and to be in two winning teams of the major unit's cup; one against the Paras at Aldershot stadium winning 15-7 and the other against the Royal Signals Regiment at Bulford winning 26-3. They were fantastic games and I was proud to take part.

I remember we paid for our win at Aldershot with a lot of pain. In the first five minutes, I was put out cold with a hammer blow to the kidneys, which was seen very clearly by our captain, six feet six and almost seventeen stone of very mobile muscle. We went into a ruck and the Para, our captain had seen clobber me, came out in need of a few stitches to his eyebrow. Nevertheless, the whole game was most enjoyable. Afterwards, when we had showered and those in need of stitches or medical repair had been dealt with, we went at the invitation of the opposition to their NAAFI for a celebration.

The first two hours went really well, then things got slightly out of hand for the NAAFI girls. Our young Irish standoff half decided to do a tabletop dance. That was going well and the lads were all cheering and having a really good time when he decided to liven it up by dropping his trousers. That was OK until the girls took a closer look and noticed his underwear was shot to pieces and what little remained was not too clean or hygienic and no form of cover at all. So, we were given a roasting by the manager.

Then came the final straw. One of the Para lads had a flight-type boot laced tight up to the top and filled with beer, he was filling glasses or offering drinks direct from the boot. He arrived at one of our younger lads, who by that time had consumed far more alcohol than he was used to and was looking the worse for wear. The Para poured a drop into the lad's glass then said, "Wait a minute" before dipping his hand inside the boot and withdrawing a sock which he wrung out into our teammate's glass. That was enough; our pal immediately started projectile vomiting. The NAAFI manager lost his sense of humour and told us to leave. We left carrying our trophies and singing, "We have been thrown out of better places than this".

At the close of the 1967 season, six of us were awarded; REME Corps Colours for Rugby, a great honour. Our names were entered in gold on the honours board inside the gymnasium entrance at SEME, School of Electrical Mechanical Engineering, Bordon. Unfortunately, part of the building, including the entrance, burned down not long after and I don't believe the board was ever replaced. Nevertheless, I was proud of the achievement and I left with many happy memories of a great bunch of lads.

Now, as I write my book, suffering with a hip that needs replacing and a knee that has no cartilage, both feet suffering and misshapen fingers, I can remember quite clearly, each and every tackle, which caused such damage. The fingers were a result of having them dislocated or trodden on and my right foot was as a result of going over sideways with a couple of bodies on top of me.

Many years later when I was diagnosed with arthritis in that foot, the surgeon said, "If they had done a better job of setting that ankle when you broke it, you might not have had this problem." Fact is, when I visited the physio and the docs after that particular match, they both agreed that my ligaments were damaged, and I was sidelined for months. The hip was the worst damage I ever felt.

We were playing against the Royal Marines with a spattering of Navy chaps thrown in. I had the ball, saw a tackle coming in on my right, and took appropriate action to hand him off. Then, I thought I had been hit by a truck on my left side, I actually thought my hip was broken or at least dislocated. As it was near the end of the game, I retired swathed in ice packs. After that, the hip never again felt safe but it did not shorten my playing career in any way.

Apart from the Monday morning session, every week after the matches the only other nasty injury was to my mouth. In those days, gum-shields were non-existent and, as stated, many moons before, I had lost my two front teeth. By that time I had lost a few more so, without dentures in, there was no protection for the inside of the lips against the edges of the remaining teeth. I saw the opposition coming and, as I went in to tackle him, instead of a hand off, I received a full-blooded bunch of five, wrapped up in a huge fist. Luckily, or so they told me, one of the opposition was a doctor and he had his bag in the car. I was quickly stitched up on the touchline with no anaesthetic. Every time I winced, all

I got from the doc was, "Don't be so soft, a few weeks ago I was operating on children in Africa and when we ran out of anaesthetic, rather than miss out on their treatment, they had all kinds of operations done and never said a word."

July 10th 1968 was one of the best days in my life and I have had so many. I had finally passed my Artificer course and been promoted to substantive staff sergeant and I was so proud. From 1963 to 1968, I had worked and studied like a fanatic, and to reach that rank in such a short time was quite unique. The journey had been far from easy with all the major obstacles along the way. But knowing that all Moira's efforts had not been in vain was my reward. We now had security for our four children – yes, Clive had been born the month before – so we had a double celebration.

I could not get to the camp tailors fast enough to have my badges of rank sewn on to all my uniforms and for months after I would stop at every mirror to admire them, and let a great feeling of pride flow over me. Now all I had to do was be good at my job for the next six years and I would have automatic promotion to warrant officer too. From then, to the very top non-commissioned officer would be fully dependent on my annual reports and recommendations. My first job in my new rank was at SEME Bordon for a month instructing on APCs, armoured personnel carriers.

CHAPTER ELEVEN

Celle, West Germany 1968

September 1968 and I was off to Celle in West Germany once again; this time to join up with 3 Royal Green Jackets, one of the best Infantry battalions in the British Army. My position was to be one of three similar ranked vehicle artificers in the LAD. The bulk of the work was on APCs, the main transport for the Jackets.

I was immediately attached to B Company and my new OC was Major Mike Tarleton, one of the finest officers I was lucky enough to serve with – even though he was fanatical about long-distance route marches, especially across the sands of the Libyan Desert. Such marches we did on two occasions, thirty miles each time in the scorching African sun. He often told me his men were not dependent on the transport; they could walk anywhere.

One fond memory of Major Mike was when we were on exercise on the Soltau training ground once more, but this time it was quite warm. He was sat with me and a group of my lads; he had come to see us at the end of the training and brought with him his customary few crates of beer as a thank you for a job well done. The CQMS truck returned from HQ with a few supplies and the mail, also on board was a young subaltern, a new arrival from UK to join B Company.

He arrived at the entrance to the tent, jumped smartly to attention at the sight of the Major and threw up a salute before introducing himself as "Second Lieutenant Melling-Ward reporting for duty, Sir."

"OK Ward, pull up a chair and sit down," replied the OC.

"My name is Melling-Ward, Sir," said our new boy.

"OK, pull up two chairs and sit down," said Major Mike.

I felt that the Major was saying, in the nicest possible way, "I am with my lads who have just completed a hard week and you can wait. Double-barrelled names mean little you will become another member of the team." He had a wonderful way of chastising someone in the most courteous way, which left no doubt in their mind not to cross him again.

1969 arrived and once more, we were in the Libyan Desert, only this time we were a lot further south of Tobruk than on our previous visit. One of the lads was a corporal clerk who I became quite friendly with; we both had a passion for birds and other animals so from our very first meeting we hit it off. Every moment off duty was spent scouring the sky and the desert for wildlife. We were lucky to be there at the same time as my favourite little birds, the swallows, which were passing through on their migration to southern parts of Africa. The path they flew across the Libyan sand was no wider than a two-lane road and, quite contrary to what I had always thought; they were not in large groups but in a constant stream of ones and twos, quite often no higher than a foot from the desert floor. As we walked the imaginary road, we came across dozens of the tiny masters of the skies down on the sand, in need of rest or water. Many of those we forced to drink and hopefully they took off again and completed their amazing journey.

Roy, the clerk, and I spent a lot of time discussing how such little birds did that trip twice each year. Their experience and determination strengthened my belief in the little creatures. My thoughts always return to how lucky I am each time I see them return.

I really loved the desert. Just to sit on the top of a small hill and see nothing, but sand and shrubs as far as the eye could see in any direction, may not be ideal for the majority of people, yet there was something about Libya that made me feel I belonged – that I had been there before, long before my first trip from Colchester. I simply loved the heat and the harshness. To this day, I often think about it; the feeling of being there was so surreal.

Many years later I read an article in a magazine by a psychologist called Abraham Maslow who had studied such happenings, he called them peak experiences. Apparently they happen to only very few people and cannot be self-induced. They happen completely out of the blue.

I digress – back to bird watching. Roy was scanning the desert when he said he had seen a small group of pigeons rise up from the sand before settling again, and nothing since. Off we went in the direction they were last seen. As we walked, we talked about why would there be pigeons so far out in the desert away from water and roosting sites. On arrival at the spot, where the birds had last been seen, there was no sign of any birds. We walked around expecting at any moment to see some pigeons lift, but no such luck. We started making a noise on the off chance that we might be in the wrong area. Suddenly, one rose up from a clump of shrub, on inspecting the area we found a small hole, which went down into the sand. After a bit of scraping and clearing we came across a large flat stone buried beneath shrub and earth.

Between us, we managed to lift the stone to reveal a hole, large enough for us to enter and descend beneath the desert floor. By using a lighter, we could see ledges like steps, which we were able to negotiate downwards to find ourselves in a cavern about the size of a house. Half of the space was taken up by a raised pool with ledges at frequent intervals. Looking up, we could see chinks of light entering the chamber through various holes, which were obviously very well hidden because we had only managed to find the one. Once our eyes were fully accustomed to the light within, it became quite easy to see.

Some of the ledges were like seats; others like beds. On those, a colony of about a dozen rock doves lived. They had eggs or young and by the look of things, many generations had lived there. We just sat in awe at what we had found; a man-made place, developed around an underground spring where people had spent time bathing or living beneath the African desert. How many people had seen it? Had there been anybody at all in hundreds of years? We left the place as we had found it, even wiping away all footprints and traces of disturbance in the hope that we would not attract any predators to the home of those beautiful birds who had found a paradise in such a barren place. Later Roy told me that what we had found that day was a Byzantine well.

One of the never-forgotten memories of a very bad time in Libya was a visit to Knightsbridge Second World War Cemetery. On entering the gateway to the last resting place of so many young people who gave their lives for freedom, one could not avoid being overwhelmed by an enormous feelings of pride and sorrow. The white headstones standing like soldiers in row after row as far as the eye could see really made me think. What if?

We returned to Celle, but there was to be no peace. Within a few weeks three quarters of the Battalion along with half the LAD was sent to Northern Ireland because trouble over there was really getting out of hand. The OC rear party was an ex-Green Jacket RSM who had been commissioned and given the post of RQMS. He was well known to all, as being a bit of an eccentric.

It was my turn to take the morning muster parade of the rear party, a daily duty for one of the senior ranks. I became aware of the OC standing at the side of the drill square taking everything in, which was not the normal practice. Suddenly a young rifleman crept into the rear rank of the parade, a little bit late, and before I had the chance to take any kind of action the OC's voice boomed out.

"Take that man's name, Staff, charge him and bring him before me on orders this morning."

After the parade, I tried to explain to the captain that one or two of the younger lads were trying very hard to come to terms with the idea of being left behind, while their mates were in a trouble zone and that I would give him a good talking to, but it was to no avail.

At the appointed time, I marched the young soldier and his two-soldier escort in front of the OC who read out the charge of being late for parade. his was something I can never remember a soldier being charged for. Normally they would be given a dirty job for a couple of hours. He then asked the rifleman, "Do you accept my punishment or do you wish to go for court martial?"

Nobody ever asked for the latter; they simply took their punishment – end of story. A court martial for this kind of charge in the military world is the equivalent of going to the Old Bailey for a parking offence, but military rules state he had to be offered the choice. What happened next was certainly unexpected.

"I will take the court martial, Sir," said the soldier.

The silence in that room was unbelievable. Finally, after a bit of spluttering by the OC and gasps of shock by all those present, the OC managed to regain his voice. "Get him out of here, Staff, and report back to me."

That I did and by the time, I returned the ex-RSM was a lovely shade of purple. "What is wrong with the bloody man?" he asked me.

"I don't know but if I had some idea what punishment you intend to give him I might be able to make him see some sense."

"I will fine him 10DM," – Deutsch marks.

Back outside, I told the soldier, who said his reason for such drastic action was he thought it was very unfair to be charged for such a trivial offence. I told him not to be a silly sod and to let me take him back in so he could accept the fine and let us all get away from the nut house. He agreed and once more, I marched the three of them into the office.

This time when the captain got to the choice of punishment the soldier accepted the OC's punishment which resulted in the OC almost exploding with rage and shouting out, "Fined 50DM."

That time there was no silence, only gasps of astonishment because that was a ridiculous fine for what the lad had done.

"Now get rid of him, Staff!" screamed the OC. I turned the lad and escorts and proceeded to march them out. Suddenly, I don't know what made me anticipate danger and so stepped sideways. It was similar to a boxer whose instinct makes him avoid a punch, he does not always see it coming but knows it is about to happen. By stepping to one side, I stumbled and went halfway to the floor – a lucky break for me. I felt the turbulence in the air, then heard a sickening thud of something very hard hitting something also very hard. Then my young soldier was flat on the floor face down. At the same time a solid glass ashtray was spinning to a halt on the floor at my feet, closely followed by the words, "And don't f—k me about again!" screamed out by the OC.

I was now thirty-two and for the first time in my life, I could say I had security for my family, and I was able to purchase our very first car. I ordered a white Ford Cortina Estate 1600 from the NAAFI, it was duly sent as an export model from UK to Bremerhaven near Hamburg. The day of collection was one to remember. It was our very first luxury item, the real proof that I was moving in the right direction. The vehicle stood there alone in a compound, all nicely cleaned and polished by the

Germans and ready for me to drive away, once I had signed receipt documents. I stood outside that compound for maybe five minutes just looking and thinking what Moira and I had achieved in five years. The fifty-mile drive back to Celle was like a dream come true; I was floating on air. The beautiful smell of newness and knowing it was ours was a great feeling that would take a long time to sink in. Moira, the family and myself were now reaping the rewards for years of hard work for me, and loneliness and financial hardship for her. We had made it and the only way was up.

Less than three months had passed when, returning home one night from the cinema, just as dusk was falling, out of a side street and straight across our path came a Mercedes. I could not avoid it and like my Land Rover years before at the Military Tattoo, my beautiful Cortina hit it full in the side. Moira flew under the dashboard, injuring her knee quite badly, and the driver of the other vehicle broke his arm. The speed of the German's car and the angle of impact had bent the whole front end of our car like a banana, and it was in need of major front-end repair. Within minutes, the very efficient German emergency services were on the scene. A doctor dealt with Moira's knee and very kind people in a nearby property looked her after. The driver of the Mercedes was checked to ascertain if he had drunk too much and he was deemed to be unfit to be on the road, and fined on the spot by the Police before being sent off to hospital for treatment. Both cars were removed from the scene and in no time at all the police told me they had sent my car to the nearest Ford dealers with instructions to start repairs immediately because the German driver was fully to blame. Then they took us both to our home.

The morning after, I visited the Ford dealers to find my car was already stripped down and ready for repairs to start. I was given a two-week completion time, which I found very impressive. A couple of days later I received confirmation by post from the police that I was in no way to blame for the accident and all costs would be met by the other driver. Two weeks later as promised, my car was ready and as good as new. The body repairer who had carried out the work told me because it was English-built he had travelled many miles to find another similar car to measure, to enable him to rebuild the front end. I was even more impressed.

Six months had flown by since the car crash and we were really settled in to life in Germany. I was enjoying my job in the LAD where I had two German gentlemen clerks working in my office, Walter and Fritz. They were chalk and cheese. Walter was by far the fitter of the two. he was in his late sixties and Fritz in his late seventies, or maybe early eighties, and far from fit. He found it very difficult to walk even with a stick however; he was always cheerful and most helpful without a hint of sycophancy. On the other hand, Walter had a chip on both shoulders about the war and always gave the impression that had the roles of our two countries been reversed we would not have been around very long. He continually parked his battered old Volkswagen in my parking spot no matter how many times I asked him not to. Finally, I told one of the Green Jacket APC drivers that if he saw the vehicle there again he had my permission to run his vehicle over the top of it, knowing full well that Walter was listening to my conversation. It was never ever parked there again.

One morning completely out of the blue, a very official letter arrived. After trying to read the letter, I showed it to Fritz, who after reading it said he knew the name of his fellow countryman who had driven his car across my path six months before and was now blaming me for the accident. He was what the two clerks called a 'Blue Blood', from a very wealthy family. The letter was a summons for me to attend a court in Uelzen to answer a charge of dangerous driving.

Within the letter, his legal expert had clearly laid out in detail what his client was aiming to claim from me. The whole list came to thousands of Deutschmarks and that did not include a figure, which he hoped to receive for his personal injuries. I was clearly taken aback and Fritz took control.

"I may be able to help you," he said. "I have a good friend who knows a bit about the law; I will talk to him if you want me to."

I had no choice, not knowing of an alternative, and fearing that our recently acquired financial comfort could come to an abrupt end, I accepted. The following day Fritz told me he had arranged for me to see his friend, a Mr Bloomberg, and he wrote out the address and directions for me to find him in the town. Complete with summons in hand, I was off as quickly as I possibly could to take advantage of the man's offer.

The address was that of a very large four-storey block of offices in the heart of Celle. On the door of the number my clerk had written, was 'D Bloomberg' followed by a washing line of letters, which meant nothing at all to me. I knocked and waited until a voice called out what I hoped, was permission to enter. As I stated before, my first visit to Germany in another life was completely wasted. The only German language learned was how to order beer and not much more.

Once inside I literally took a step back in time to the Dickens era, it was so surreal. The single room office, although very large, was made very small by the columns of files, which were piled from floor to ceiling around three sides. What could be seen of the internal decorations was deep orange from years of smoking. Amidst all the paperwork was a monster wooden desk absolutely littered with more files and loose papers among which I could see a large ashtray full to overflowing with cigarette ends. There was a half-full glass of what looked like whisky, and a bottle, which I suspected, was the same.

Seated centrally behind the desk was a gentleman who I presumed was Mr Bloomberg. I stood there for what seemed like an eternity while he was deeply engrossed in a document. Then he lifted an arm and beckoned me, without shifting his gaze from the paper, to sit in a chair to his front. He appeared to be in his forties but somehow looked much older. His hair was long and very unkempt, I could see his clothes had been quality at the time of purchase, but had not been looked after since, and dandruff was freely scattered all over his shoulders. The word 'sloven' came quickly to my mind.

Finally he put the document to one side and reached out a bony hand with nicotine stained fingers and long untidy nails, quickly introduced himself, not making any eye contact, and shook hands. Then without any questions or hesitation, he went on to explain my letter fully as it must have been told to him by Fritz. He then asked two questions only – time and place of court appearance – which I duly told him. His final words to me were that he would be at the court on the day. Our meeting came to an abrupt end and he went back to his papers.

On the day of my court appearance, Herr Bloomberg and I came face to face again, only that time he was standing up. He looked even older than at our first meeting, and much smaller. Even though he was in his robes and about to appear in court, his appearance was no better than at our first meeting and dandruff still lay like fine snow on his stooped shoulders. He told me where to sit in the courtroom and said if they wanted me, I would be called. The proceedings were carried out in German.

I was asked if I wanted an interpreter but I declined, because I was sanguine about my one and only hope, Mr Bloomberg, and knowing what was going on would be of little use to me. I took it to be the lawyer of the person who was claiming against me who spoke first. He went on for quite a time, then up stepped my hope. At that moment, the whole of the courtroom went deathly silent except for a bit of furtive muttering among some of the seated. He talked with the other lawyer and the judge had the occasional input.

Then from the other side of the courtroom, the driver of the Mercedes was beckoned to stand in the dock. His own lawyer first addressed him and then it was Bloomberg's turn. Once again, when he stood up there was mumbling and whispering. He seemed to ask questions of the driver, received replies and asked more questions for about fifteen minutes. I could understand very little but it was quite obvious from the body language that my man was making the Mercedes driver feel very uneasy.

After a few more minutes, it all came to an abrupt end and I had not been involved in any way. The judge gave a very short speech and then left the court. My 'legal eagle' put his file under his arm and came over to me. The outcome was, the German driver had failed in his effort to receive remuneration from me. In fact, he had been held fully responsible for everything that happened that night and had to pay all the costs including 500DM for Moira's leg injury, as well as items in my car, which I was not aware had been damaged, I had been happy just to have my car repaired. Mr Bloomberg said his farewells, shook my hand, and was gone and I never saw him again.

The following day my first call was to thank Fritz for his help and he wanted to know all the details. All the time I talked, he had a smile on his face. Finally, I had to satisfy my curiosity and asked him how he came to know such a lawyer. The story was, that prior to being retired and working part time in my office, he had worked for more than forty years for Bloomberg's father. He had been like another parent to my hero from the previous day, and as a result, Bloomberg would do anything for my old clerk. It also turned out that he was not the normal, everyday 'legal eagle' but in fact, one of Germany's best criminal lawyers. Hence, the mutterings in the court and the easy way he seemed to sort the situation out.

I once again thanked Fritz and asked him to tell Mr Bloomberg where to send his bill, dreading what that might be, now knowing the true facts. My old clerk just smiled and said, "There is no bill. Just call it a gift from me and Dietrich to you and your family."

During that period of my military career, I gained invaluable experience from being with top class infantry battalions of the Royal Green Jackets. I actually served first with the 3rd Battalion, then the 2nd followed by the 1st and finally the 4th TA Battalion on an exercise.

Shortly before my departure from Germany in 1972 to take up a posting at SEME, School of Electrical Mechanical Engineers, at Bordon, Hampshire to teach the Rolls Royce engine as used in various armoured vehicles, I was interviewed by the CO RGJ. He told me he had put my name forward to the regular officer selection board at Westbury in order for me to undertake officer training at the Sandhurst Military College and he very strongly advised me to go and do it. I asked him if that was possible because I was, thirty-five and thirty was the limit to apply. I also knew short-term commissions were possible on reaching WO2.

"Don't worry, you have some good support behind my recommendation," he replied.

That was a fantastic thing to hear, and a few days later, I swept my family up and returned to Hampshire.

CHAPTER TWELVE

Back to The UK – Seme 1972

All the time the children had been growing up and like most other kids, had a yearning to own a pet dog. Moira and I had always managed to put them off; we didn't think it was a good idea because of our nomadic way of life. But, on hearing the news that we were returning to UK for an indefinite period of time, the subject was brought up once again. Once again, we tried to put them off the idea, but we did say that once back home we would give it some thought, rather hoping they would forget. No such luck. On our car journey from Harwich to Bradford where we were going to spend a couple of weeks with Moira's parents, before moving south to the school, we passed a sign on the grass verge outside a smallholding, which read: 'Cocker Spaniels for sale.' We had discussed settling in, before thinking about their request, so fingers and legs crossed, we hoped the kids had not noticed and I drove straight past. They had seen the sign and tormented us to return just for a look.

Inside a rather large shed were a few litters of pups with their mums, they were the most beautiful little dogs I had ever seen. Almost each litter was a different colour; there were blue roans, orange roans, reds and blacks. However, someone up there was on my side because the owner informed us that none of the pups would be ready to leave mum for another three weeks. I gave a huge sigh of relief, the girls were very understanding, so we said our goodbyes and carried on our way up north. That reprieve was short lived. Quite honestly, when we all saw those little pups we were of one thought, that chance visit in Essex had been the persuader. Anyone who can look in the face of a cocker and does not have the longing to own one cannot appreciate true beauty. So, Moira and I succumbed and the very next litter we saw advertised we went and purchased a little red bitch, which the kids duly christened Candy.

After our short but most enjoyable holiday with the in-laws, we arrived in Bordon with the four children and one very lively canine. This time the posting promised to be more family-orientated than our previous tour, there was to be no study or exercises and very few duties. My job was strictly nine to five Monday to Friday only, teaching the B Series Engine. The family very quickly settled in, the kids went to nice schools and Moira got herself a little job at the Cheshire Nursing home for people with life terminal illnesses.

True to his word, my last CO had indeed put my name forward for a regular commission and had obviously overcome the age limit. Within a couple of weeks, I had received a letter asking me to attend a selection board at Westbury in Wiltshire.

On my arrival, I booked in as requested and was immediately issued with a set of overalls with a number displayed above the left breast pocket. That, we were told, was to be our only form of identification to the adjudicators throughout our period of testing until the final interview. That way it would be an impartial board. The course was made up of twelve graduates not long out of university and another serving NCO like me, except a few years younger.

The first day was very difficult. Again, I was to struggle with three written papers on Mathematics, English and Science. The following morning, after sitting those three theory papers, we were all sent to the mess for coffee prior to being told the rest of the programme for that day. Suddenly the tannoy system in the room came to life.

"Will the bearers of the following numbers leave the mess and report to reception now please."

The rest of us finished our break and a Captain came in and informed us that the six people who had been called, had failed the education papers sat the previous day and had now left the course. No doubt, that was to save embarrassment or any form of discussion.

I was elated at having passed when six graduates had failed. To this day, I do not know how it happened. As I stated earlier, my education was very limited and I had passed my education standard for the artificer course by constant study. But since then, I had done nothing at all. Somebody up there really liked me or the papers got mixed up. The

English paper especially, was a complete mystery to me. I had to write five hundred words about the late Prince of Wales and Mrs Simpson.

When I saw that question, I almost died. My knowledge of the couple consisted of little more than knowing their names. I honestly wrote a lot of bullshit with lots about how the nation really loved him and how much he would be missed now that he had died. I could only think the marker was simply too lazy to be bothered to try decipher all my crap and gave me the benefit of the doubt.

On day two we split up into two groups in order to carry out command tasks. At first sight to the unprepared, the tasks looked impossible and the equipment issued to carry them out useless. However, they could all be carried out quite successfully with a bit of thought and teamwork. The supervisors started the groups off and once under way, they were continually checking and listening for who took control, or came up with practical ideas and so on.

That kind of test I had done so many times before, prior to my artificer course and in practice at Bordon before travelling to Westbury. So I was fully aware of what to do and found it very easy to take control and more or less show the young lads how to do it; consequently, my group finished all the tasks put to us in very quick time. The graduates, although intelligent, willing young lads, were followers rather than leaders.

Our next task was to give a fifteen-minute talk to the rest of the group on any subject of our choice. We were given one hour to prepare. Once again, I had done that type of thing many times over and was now actually teaching at the school. One or two of the graduates froze in front of the small class or had no prepared talk. I made my subject the three methods of chicken farming, a subject I could have talked about all day.

Finally, we had to complete a rather tough assault course. It was physically hard but I was probably at my fittest ever, since I was a young boy, due to playing rugby two or three times a week, so I completed every task without any problems.

Once the practical fitness and education had been completed, all that was left was a series of very searching interviews with various officers before a final interview in front of a panel of five senior officers. During that final stage the bubble burst. On my very first interview in front of a colonel he told me straight out that, I might be offered a short-term commission when I reached WO2 if I failed the board. Obviously, he knew all about me, contrary to what we had been led to believe on day one.

The next officer asked me a number of searching questions about my brothers. I knew I had been vetted but although my record was good, that of my two brothers was not. They had both spent time as 'guests' of Her Majesty so I had no option but to confirm what he already knew. The third officer was most insistent, that should I fail I must go forward and take up a short-term commission. Before I left Westbury, I had the distinct feeling that the outcome was inevitable, due to my brothers' records, my age and knowing that a certain number of graduates must pass come what may.

The following morning the mail arrived and true to what I expected, I had not been accepted for a regular commission. In my heart I blamed my brothers and – to misquote a brief but well-known epigram – because of their today's, I lost my tomorrows.

For about a week, I thought bad thoughts about them and stuck pins in dolls, but then I thought that if I had not met my darling wife and started a great family I could quite easily have been with them. However, the letter strongly recommended that I take up a short-term commission

once promoted to warrant officer. I was devastated because I knew in my heart that I had not failed. Not many soldiers ever reach the rank I had achieved and certainly not in such a short time. I would have been very proud to have progressed further. What a result that would have been for a working-class lad from Bradford, with such limited education on leaving school!

Unfortunately, Dad never lived to see any of it. He died a month after I qualified as staff sergeant but during

Mum and Dad in his last months 1968

his last few months, he knew little of

165

what was happening around him. I never did take up the short-term commission, although both Moira and I were constantly badgered to do so, right up to my leaving the forces.

Many nights and weekends, we spent as a family walking around the beautiful Hampshire countryside. It was mainly to exercise the pup but it also gave me the opportunity to further my interest in wildlife and at the same time teach our children all about the woodlands, fields and rivers.

On one such walk Candy sensed something in the woods and started barking, and was almost immediately answered by a number of other canines. On investigation, we found ourselves standing before a most beautiful old cottage with lawns that stretched down to the River Wey in Lindford. We later found out that it was actually five hundred years old. We walked around the perimeter until we arrived at the gate and came face to face with a number of geriatric dogs, four Springer spaniels and a very poor specimen of a griffon.

I remember thinking about what an old farmer once said to me way back in another life at Hazel Crook End Farm. He had among his herd of cows a real old bony beast and one day I made a rather derogatory remark about it. "That beast is older than you, young man, best cow, missus and I ever bought. Now she is just an old pet. Tha should never look at a tree in winter when it has no leaves. Better in spring or summer when it's in its full bloom and showing its true beauty," he snapped.

The excitement and barking very quickly brought a very tiny figure outside to see what all the noise was about. Of what gender at that time I had no idea. One thing was for sure; using the calculation that if, as often said, a dog's life equates as seven years to one of ours, the person approaching us was probably the oldest of the whole group. We introduced ourselves to the person before us and became aware that the lady or gent was even more diminutive than at first sight. After she introduced herself as Miss Tony Eland, we knew which gender. She was about four feet ten inches tall and at a guess no more than five stone in weight. Her hair was cropped, short back and sides like my National Service days and her features weathered with years of outdoor work.

The diminutive Miss E – 1972

She invited us into her fantastic garden, which she told us was three quarters of an acre, lovingly cared for and all expertly laid out with fruit trees, shrubs and flowerbeds, surrounded by magnificent lawns. As we walked and talked, we learned that her real name was Esmee, a vicar's daughter from Liverpool. She was a spinster who, for a great many years, had been companion to an elderly lady. The two of them and the dogs had moved into the cottage about ten years before.

The lady had died and left the property in trust to our new friend. The dogs, with the exception of the one eyed one toothed griffon, were all ex-champion show dogs – the last of a long line the two ladies had bred and shown throughout a lifetime all over the country. They were the founders of the Whadden Chase line of English Springer spaniels, and the Lymbourne beagles. Miss E, as she was always known to us from that very first meeting, looked after the kennel welfare and took the dogs into the show-ring.

Miss E's home in Hampshire

167

After quite a long time talking about gardening, which Moira just loved, we had tea with her and then said our farewells. As we walked home, we discussed how lucky we were to have met someone so knowledgeable about gardening and dogs. From that day, we visited her at least twice a week. Moira and Miss E would work and talk in the garden; the children and myself would take the healthiest of the old dogs plus our pup for walks in the woods and at the same time enjoy the wildlife.

From our very first meeting we became great friends and enjoyed each other's company wholeheartedly due to our interests in the same things. At the end of the first six months, Candy had grown into a very nice-looking dog, and Miss E thought she was something special. Then one day another dog walker stopped me on one of my many trips down by the river. He asked if he could look at Candy and asked a few questions before saying that I should consider showing her because he thought she was beautiful. My curiosity was aroused and I asked our old friend what she thought about it. She said there was a dog club in Farnham a few miles down the road and suggested I joined and learned the art of showing. So I did, and for one night each week, Candy had the opportunity to mix with many other dogs, young and old, which was to be a good grounding for when she eventually entered a show ring. Present each night were many top-class breeders and very experienced show people.

Every year the club held a show for all the members. It took the form of a knockout match for any breed as long as the dog was six months or over. Members could enter as many dogs as they wanted and all the names were put in the barrel and drawn out in pairs. A fully qualified judge was booked for the day and he or she decided which dog out of the two was the better and that dog's name was put back in the barrel to be drawn out again as each round was completed. That carried on until the last one standing was declared the winner. On that very first show, Candy was judged the winner. It was no mean achievement because there were almost sixty dogs on show that day and many were established show dogs. There were also quite a lot of up-and-coming youngsters bred by some top breeders. From that day, I had the bug, as Miss E said I would. I started to learn everything I could about dog showing.

The very first real dog show I entered Candy, was the Kingston Open and I put her in the puppy class. On that particular Saturday morning none of the family could go with me due to other plans, so off I went to my show, very excited and unbelievably nervous, just hoping that all my daily training on the local football field with Candy would be a success. The judge for the day was a gentleman named Terry Thorne, who went on to become one of the top judges in the world, and who actually judged the best in show at Crufts.

The time of my event duly arrived and once inside the ring with all the other entrants I went through the routine of standing Candy on a loose lead with the other pups before walking her around the ring. By that time, I was feeling pretty relaxed and gaining in confidence. Then came the part where I had to stand the dog square on the floor for Mr Thorne to give her a final inspection. That meant I had to bend over her with one hand under her chin and the other under her tail to offer the dog to the judge, showing a good bodyline. By that time I was feeling confident, or cocky to be more precise, and I forgotten the golden rule for bending over, especially when the dog being shown is so small. I did not bend my knees.

When I was at full stretch, it happened. I felt the tension about my nether region being released revealing everything in slow motion to the spectators around the ring. My trousers split down the rear centre seam from waistband to crotch. Thank goodness I was wearing underpants and many thanks for my little Irish mum's number one rule which I always followed – "Ensure your underwear is clean at all times. You never know when you may be in an accident." I doubt if she ever envisaged so many spectators the first time her rule was tested. The crowd certainly seemed to enjoy it, but I will never know if the 3rd prize awarded to our pup on the day by the judge was for the dog, or just compensation for my embarrassment.

By the end of her first year, I thought it was time I took her to a championship show so off we went to Bath. It was truly a show to remember, not only because Candy received a fourth place but more for a comical situation.

The judge that day was a very well known gundog expert from

Yorkshire. When he entered the ring there were bouts of stifled laughter and people talking very rudely behind their hands. He was wearing the most ridiculous wig ever. It was made of thick red hair and was very obvious – hence the laughter. He was about halfway through judging a puppy class when suddenly his wig fell off. The young dog he was handling at the time was standing there as it had been taught, saw the large ball of hair fall and being a gundog could not contain itself and sprang to life. It grabbed the hair and shook it vigorously like some form of prey. That stirred the whole line of young dogs into action and within seconds half a dozen of them had broken away from their unsuspecting owners and joined in the game, grabbing and shaking until each had a piece of the judge's wig. The audience around the arena had erupted in laughter, but the gentleman judge was a true professional and carried on quite unperturbed. On completion of the class, he received a terrific round of applause from the audience.

During my teaching period at the school, I was kept very busy with one course after another and I enjoyed every single moment. But, every once in a while one of us teachers was allocated a different programme. One Monday morning I was asked to go and see the senior civilian instructor who asked me to do a one-to-one two-week course with an Arab prince from one of the oil states. It was to be a short time, briefing him about the Rolls engines, which were installed in some of his country's vehicles. The following day I was introduced to a very smart young man who seemed very keen to learn but the more we talked, the more I became suspicious of how much English he actually understood. I tried many times to confirm if he understood all I was saying to him and always received a very positive "yes" in very good English. My job was to cover as much as possible in the two weeks so the following day we made a start and he wrote constantly about everything I told him. Come the lunchtime I asked him where he was having lunch and after a few attempts I managed to find out he was going to the Officers' Mess. So as it was on my way home I offered him a lift and dropped him off outside the Officers' Mess telling him I would pick him up at the same place on my way back after lunch.

A few days had passed and a young subaltern came to see me. He said he was just curious about why I dropped the young Arab off outside the mess each day and then picked him up on my way back. "Nothing unusual, it is just an agreement between us. I drop him off for his lunch and then take him back to school with me."

At that, the young officer started to laugh. "Now I can see and tell all the other mess members who have been curious and I can tell you that the young lad has been sitting on the kerb for one hour each day after you have dropped him off until you return." My thoughts about his lack of understanding of our language were confirmed, and he had not eaten any lunch for almost a week. I dread to think what he told his parents on returning home about the strange English custom where they leave you sitting on the kerb for one hour each day. More puzzling was what did the young Arab constantly write in his little book?

Another time, I had three young soldiers from Uganda, a corporal, a lance corporal and a private, for a month's training. All three were very nice lads who spoke very good English and were very keen to learn as much as possible. I reached a part on the course, which dealt with the fuel system of the vehicle, in particular how the petrol pump operated. I was showing them how the pump diaphragm was pulled down mechanically creating a depression in the pump chamber, which was then filled by fuel being pushed from the petrol tank by atmospheric pressure. Suddenly, one of the young lads stood up and with a very serious look on his face told me there was no atmospheric pressure in Uganda. No matter how much I tried to convince them otherwise, it simply fell on deaf ears. So, it was time for a little experiment and off we all went to the welding bay, where I found a small can with a screw top. I partially filled the can with water and put a lit blowtorch underneath to bring the water to boiling point. After a few minutes, the steam started to come from the open can. At that point, I told my small class to watch and see the effect of atmospheric pressure. I turned off the torch and immediately screwed the cap into place and waited. Suddenly the can started to buckle and I was explaining to them what was taking place but when I turned I was all alone – not a student in sight. I found all three of them back in the classroom staring into space in what seemed a kind of fear. I never did convince them about atmospheric pressure. When the short course came to a conclusion, we had to set them a test paper so that a result could be taken back to Uganda.

The morning after the test I read out the results to them and what was usually a very cheerful atmosphere became very cold indeed, so I asked them what was wrong. The results had come out with the private having gained the highest mark followed by the lance corporal and finally the corporal. The private asked me to change the marks about so that the corporal had the highest otherwise it would not be good for him when he went back home. After a short discussion with the senior civilian instructor, we agreed and the three of them were back to their normal happy selves again.

During 1974, the inevitable happened; my tour at the school was complete and my new unit was to be a workshop in Cyprus as a WO2. The move would be great for my career and, if successful in such a prestigious position, a promotion to WO1 was there for the taking.

The island of sunshine would be great for the family but – what about the dogs? A year before, we had purchased another pup which the girls christened Tina. It was something we had always dreaded. If I asked Miss E, I felt sure she would have given them both a home at her beautiful cottage because by that time she had lost two of her old Springers and Winkle, the griffon, to old age. Stupidly I went down another path and made a terrible mistake, one, which I regretted and have had to live with every day since. I somehow managed to talk myself into believing that it would be wrong to lumber our new-found friend with two young dogs.

Later she told me that she had been very upset at not being asked. Instead, I managed to find what I believed to be a nice lady who was very keen to provide Candy with a loving home. We had a couple of visits along with the dogs to her home and were very pleased at what we saw. So we agreed to leave our lovely dog on an unwritten agreement that, if she so wished, on our return we would take Candy back. Once more, I was not thinking because we had no idea where our next posting would be. In Tina's case, we planned to take her with us.

Unfortunately, things did not go according to plan. Cyprus was suddenly in a political turmoil and on the 15th of July, the Greek

National Guard carried out a coup against the Makarios Government. On the 20th of July, the Turkish forces invaded the island. My posting was brought forward and on the 14th of July, I was out there earlier than expected, without the family.

Moira and Miss E outside the cottage

Candy (red) and Tina at Miss E's 1973

Moira outside the cottage

*Miss E with our dog Tina
and guest*

CHAPTER THIRTEEN

Off to Cyprus 1974

Everywhere was chaos, and fighting of the very worst kind took place. The Greek Cypriots initially outnumbered the Turkish Cypriots and a large number were either killed or driven out of their homes.

My new job was I/C of the workshop inspection team, which consisted of a number of highly qualified technicians on every kind of military equipment the army were using at that time. Our job was to ensure that all that equipment was being looked after and correctly maintained by the users, to a top-class standard. To achieve that, we as a team had to present ourselves, with very little warning, at every military base and outpost over a period of time and inspect everything on site. The results were sent to HQ Cyprus so that the top brass knew exactly what equipment they had at their disposal at all times.

All the British personnel on the island were put on a war footing and the Sergeants' Mess became host to dozens of reporters who were sent out from the UK supposedly to keep the British people fully informed of what was taking place. Scroungers, I called them. From the very first day they started to arrive they thought that they were very special and demanded that everyone in the mess should be at their beck and call. We senior ranks soon nipped that in the bud. We did however allow the bar to stay open all hours seeing as how they never went very far from it, and certainly not from the security of the military base.

The majority of stories about the conflict printed in the British newspapers at that time were the result of questioning soldiers returning from active areas. Reporters would ply the lads with drink to tell them what they had seen. It very soon became a game to many of the soldiers; the better the story they told the more attention and free beer they received.

One sergeant in particular was well known for his outrageous imagination long before any troubles had started, and he fed some of the most far-fetched stories ever to the press. The following day, there in the papers, would be Bill's fairy stories, as witnessed first-hand by one of the reporters, who had faced bullets and hardship in order to let the people of Britain know what was happening. What a load of old rubbish that was, and no doubt for that they were highly paid.

The invasion by the Turkish army took place, led by paratroopers who took a large area in the north of the island and within a very short-time almost half the island had been captured, including the one and only airport at Nicosia. Many of the Government buildings were destroyed, so any hope of getting Tina out there had gone. Moira and the children would be flown into the RAF base at a later date, when things had settled down. Upon hearing that news, Miss E stepped in and said Tina was staying with her at the cottage. It was a very sad time. I should never have left Candy with the other lady and things became worse because we hadn't been in Cyprus long when we were informed she had given our dog to a milkman. Not many days pass without me thinking of our lovely dog and even today, 40 years later I have a picture of her very close by.

We were aware that the Turkish army's plans were to invade Famagusta in the east of the island so all British civilians, except those living within the base, were told to be ready to evacuate their properties within one hour, with one suitcase only per person. There were doctors, teachers, actors and even footballers, all either working out there or living in holiday homes. The plan was, that the rest of their belongings would be packed by a group of designated soldiers and sent to the addresses in the UK, which they had been asked to leave behind in their properties. It was all very sad because many of them had lived out there for many years and had various pets, which were simply left behind to fend for themselves, never again to see their owners. Later, Cyprus had a large population of feral cats all of which Moira seemed to take care of, and it was quite common to open the patio doors and have a budgie fly into the house. Many of those ex-pats suffered big time financially. There was no way they could possibly get their cars or boats away from the island and the chances of selling them for any sort of decent price at the last minute was highly unlikely. For many months after the invasion, soldiers were trying to locate vehicles and place them into secure compounds until the owners could be found. It was chaos, a part of active service the general public are unaware, is just another part of a military task in such situations.

The Turks moved their tanks across the northern plain toward Famagusta and hundreds if not thousands of Greek Cypriots left their homes and possessions behind and entered the military base for safe refuge. As they entered, each one was searched for weapons before being placed in a refugee camp, which had been prepared by the Royal Engineers in a place called Athena Forest, which had the lowest number of trees I have ever seen in a forest.

Every refugee family was supplied with water, food, tents and blankets plus utensils and sufficient tools for them to set up a camp. It soon became very obvious that they were content to sit around smoking, eating and talking. Most of them were able-bodied men and women with young families who needed warmth and shelter, yet they did nothing to help themselves. Instead they insisted that the soldiers did it all for them. I really thought anyone in such a situation would move heaven and earth to look after their families. How wrong I was.

Moira and the family arrived in the September of 1974 and their journey was not without problems, mainly because the Greek Cypriots had formed into groups to take revenge on the British because we as a country had not stopped the Turkish invasion. Lone vehicles or personnel were the targets. Once the family arrived at Akrotiri RAF Base they were loaded, along with others, into military coaches and driven under escort across the island to a hotel where it had been arranged for the husbands to meet them. During our waiting time at the hotel, some crackpot decided to open fire with a heavy machine gun. Luckily, for us he was a lousy shot and only managed to knock hell out of the brickwork above our heads.

We soon settled into very nice quarters overlooking the Med and the kids started at their new school. Meanwhile, outside the base, sporadic military action took place on a daily basis but life for the families was uninterrupted. We even had ENSA send out various shows; Frankie Howerd, Ken Dodd, and Harry Worth came over at different times, the shows were very much appreciated. After the Harry Worth show, Moira and I sat down to dinner in the mess with the star and his manager. He was a very funny man on the TV and on the stage, but a dour little man when not performing. In fact, he was the most difficult person to have a conversation with that I have ever met. On the other hand, Ken Dodd declined a meal but came into the mess. There, he spent four hours at the bar chatting and telling jokes almost non-stop. That was after doing two one-and-a-half-hour shows. That night nobody left the mess early; he had them all in stitches. What a great comedian and what fantastic company!

Moira and I spent every weekend in the Sergeants' Mess in the company of many wonderful people. There we would enjoy far too much drink, but the majority of it we danced off outside on the patio until the early hours of the morning to the eerie haunting sounds of Demis Roussos singing "Mourir Aupres De Mon Amour", Charlie Rich or Suzi Quatro, John Denver and many more, blasting out across the Mediterranean Sea. When finally we succumbed to muscle fatigue the gentlemen would give the ladies a lift home on their backs or dance all the way home finally finishing in one house for coffee – the last thing we needed at four in the morning.

During that tour, I had the great privilege to be involved in the annual island run from Akrotiri RAF base in the south to the top of the Troodos Mountains in the north. Military Teams came from all over the world to take part in the very physical orientated type of race during the heat of the summer. It takes great fitness and stamina to complete the run. The race is held over two days and teams of three leave the airbase at about three minute intervals starting at 6am. Their aim is to reach the ski lodge at the top of the mountains before dark at about 7pm.

The course itself is within a seven-mile corridor and at least six checkpoints have to be visited during the trip. The positions of those checkpoints determine more or less the distance covered. What could be a thirty-mile run by the straightest line may turn out to be thirty-five after negotiating all the checkpoints. Once a team has arrived at the lodge, showers, food and drink plus medical attention is available for all before a good night's sleep. The following day the journey is repeated with the checkpoints situated in different places.

A sorry state, having just completed a 35 mile run/walk up the Troodos Mountains Cyprus 1974

Competition was very fierce with teams from almost every regiment one can think of, including Special Forces.

We trained for the week prior to the race day and I lost ten pounds in weight. It was the most fantastic team-building exercise and one I would not have missed.

Early in 1976, I was promoted to WO1 and informed I was to be posted to Bulford in Wiltshire where I was to close down an LAD prior to an RAC squadron being disbanded. We said our farewells and left a most beautiful island where we had enjoyed ourselves as a family for almost two years.

CHAPTER FOURTEEN

Back to Bulford 1976

Arriving back in the UK during a very cold January was a great shock to the family who had never before experienced such a rapid change of climate. In addition, the house we took over was nothing less than a tip. One night in that place was enough and the following day I presented myself before the RQMS who apologised profusely and moved us immediately to other quarters. The cold weather lasted for two weeks, during which time Moira and the kids remained very close to the fire and did not venture outside, if, at all possible. Meanwhile, I completed my take-over duties and collected our car. I had been very fortunate to be able to put it on a landing craft returning from Cyprus to the UK a few weeks before leaving. It had been collected on my behalf by a garage, serviced and cleaned, before being delivered to me at the camp.

Although our stay in Bulford was to be a short one, we were determined to have a good time in another of England's beautiful counties, Wiltshire. The family could not wait to visit Miss E, take Tina off her hands, and thank her for being so kind. Once again, I lived to regret what I did at that time. The dog and our dear friend had been constant companions all the time we were away, I was absolutely thoughtless and had never given any consideration to where our next move could be. Afterwards, I realised how much I must have hurt both Miss E and Tina but neither showed it at the time. We visited the cottage on a very regular basis always taking Tina with us and more or less carrying on where we left off before going to Cyprus. Once again, we enjoyed the garden and the lovely walks and we actually took the opportunity at Christmas 1976 to drag a reluctant Miss E away from her lovely cottage to be with us for a family Christmas Day, something I don't think she had experienced for a good many years. I like to think she really enjoyed herself.

On arriving home from the workshop one evening, Moira said she had received a telephone call from a very well spoken lady, who asked if we would bathe and groom her Cavalier King Charles spaniel that night. It was a hobby, both of us had become very interested in, during our short period of dog showing not for any real financial gain but more for the experience because we had both talked about having kennels once I retired. The address she gave Moira was Bulford Manor, which meant nothing at all to either of us, as we were so new to the area. So, I went to one of our new neighbours and asked the directions.

At six that evening, the time agreed between the two ladies, I drove through an archway into the very fine courtyard of Bulford Manor. Standing there, ready to meet me, was a very dapper grey-haired gentleman waiting with the dog on a lead. He introduced himself as Wynn, or that's what I thought, we shook hands and he explained what they wanted me to do to their little pet and off I went.

A couple of hours later I returned with a much smarter sweeter-smelling dog. Wynn answered the door and invited me inside his splendid home where he introduced me to his wife and daughter who seemed quite pleased with our efforts on their canine friend. I was asked to sit down and the lady asked if I would like a beer. We had a nice cosy chat about dogs in general and after an hour and a couple of beers, I thanked them for their hospitality and stood up to take my leave. Wynn took me to the door where we shook hands again before he casually asked what I did for a living.

"I am in the Army," I replied.

"So am I" – then he said his goodnight and I was on my way back home my head in a spin. "Who in the forces lives in a house like that?" I thought.

The following morning as ASM of the workshop, I was on parade awaiting a visit from the Commander in Chief of the UKLF as part of the unit's closing-down procedure. Such visits normally took the form of the main visiting officer, my CO and an entourage following very closely behind. That morning was no different. I had forgotten all about the night before and as I'd been back in the UK for such a short time had no idea of who the CinC was.

It came as one hell of a shock when I saw him and it was none other than Wynn, the very gentleman I told Moira about the night before, saying "I think he must be Welsh with a name like Wynn."

Once his eyes met mine he left his following behind and entered my workshop. All he really said was that his wife was delighted with the dog. But, while that was taking place the colonel and the gaggle of followers were standing where he had left them, watching with mouths agape and straining very hard to hear what he was talking to me about. The look on their faces was quite unbelievable, especially when Wynn patted me on the shoulder and said goodbye in a very friendly manner.

Needless to say, that when the CinC UK LF, had left the camp – I found out later who he was; it was Dwin he had introduced himself as and he wasn't a Welshman – my telephone rang and I was asked to report to the CO immediately.

He was sat behind his desk when I was shown in to his office. "ASM, what was that all about this morning with the CinC?" he asked.

"Nothing really, sir. We were just talking about last night when we had a couple of beers together."

A blank look spread across his face followed by a nervous laugh before I was dismissed. I don't think he ever believed me – and the subject was never mentioned again.

During January 1977, I and twelve of my staff decided we would like to do something for charity before we finally closed down the workshop and left the area. So after many discussions it was decided that we would run a sponsored relay run from John O'Groats to Land's End and all the money collected would be donated to Salisbury Hospital. A hollow baton would be passed from man to man and inside would be a scroll signed by our colonel at the start and again at the end. We planned the run in three-mile stages. Following on behind was to be a very visible vehicle which would also be used as our quarters for eating, washing and resting at certain times during the course of the long journey. It would contain medical kit and spare clothes as well as a couple of volunteer medics. Everything was planned, down to the very last detail.

Unfortunately, at the last hour one of the police forces on the route refused to let us run through their patch, on the grounds that it would be too dangerous during the night. We had to change our plans very quickly but our great friends, the RAF came to the rescue. Together we selected an area on Salisbury Plain and they marked out a three-mile circuit with ground lights. We settled on a figure of one thousand miles in the week, 48 circuits per day, and set up a tent including a shower unit to do what the support vehicle was originally set to do.

As stated, it was January and the temperatures on Salisbury Plain dropped to minus 10 degrees. Each man ran dressed in combat trousers, shirt, jumper and military boots. We started with twelve men and the target time for each circuit was 30 minutes, about twelve miles each man every day. The nights were horrible; apart from the lights, the whole area was pitch black. The ground was rock hard, each step boomed through our heads like the beat of a drum and the crackling of the grass plus the usual night noises were eerie. From the very first day, the surface of our skin and clothes was crystallising due to our body moisture and the very cold air. During the week, we lost four team members with stress-related joint injuries, which increased the daily mileage to 18 miles for the remaining lads. However, we finished on time and were met by the colonel and other dignitaries plus the press. But most important, we made £500 (a lot of money in the seventies) for the hospital who used the money to buy an instrument for internal checks of the bladder for cancer. I was very proud of my young lads and felt very privileged to have served with such fine young men.

My tour at Bulford was coming to an end, and my workshop and the squadron were in the last days. But before we finally bowed out, we had one last visit from the Colonel in Chief of the RCT, Princess Alice, Duchess of Gloucester, the Queen's aunt. All the mess senior ranks had the great honour of entertaining the Princess to a buffet lunch and we were able to chat with her for quite a time about our thousand-mile run. It was a very proud time in my career.

CHAPTER FIFTEEN

Borneo 1977

March 1977 and once again, we were off on our travels, this time to the island of Borneo in the South China Sea. The excitement was unbelievable. The mere thought of all that wildlife to me was like a chocoholic being given the freedom of Cadbury's. The sun and the sea were enough for the rest of the family.

Shortly before we left, the euphoria gradually turned to apprehension. Were there any shops? Where were the schools? Those were just two of the questions we discussed but no matter how hard I tried to find answers I could not find anyone who had been on the posting or indeed knew of anybody who had. So, completely unaware of what lay ahead, we found ourselves at RAF Brize Norton on a very cold, wet morning in March. From there we were flown by RAF Comet via Bahrain and Hong Kong, with very short stops at each just to stretch our legs while the aircraft was refuelling, finally arriving over the island twenty five hours later.

The memory of my first view of the island out of the aircraft window, as the pilot made his approach, is still very clear in my mind. What a fantastic sight. So many beautiful shades of green as far as the eye could see. I doubt if it is like that now or ever will be again because of the rain forest logging and the development projects to attract the tourist trade, which had started before we left.

My new job was that of Garrison Sergeant Major to the Sultan of Brunei's Garrison, which consisted of a battalion of Gurkha Rifles, a REME workshop and a jungle warfare school. To successfully run the garrison there were 600 military personnel from all kinds of regiments. Our concerns about schools and shops were very quickly answered. Within the compound in Seria was a Commissariat to cater for all our needs.

Vegetable and fish market

The small towns of Seria and Kuala Belite had a very good range of shops plus a very smelly meat and fish market, which was educational just to walk around and see what other people actually eat.

Our girls went off to a world-class boarding school in Singapore, along with all the other British children and the Sultan's family, all part of my posting. They were flown there either by the Royal Brunei Airlines or the Sultan's private jet. There, they received a wonderful education for two years, which only the very richest people could have possibly been able to afford.

We had a beautiful house secure within its own private garden. Moira had an amah who did the cleaning, ironing and washing, and, if required, would sit with our son Clive at night if we had to go out, which because of the job was almost every night. Within the house was a bar-room, which could accommodate thirty people and was used on a very regular basis for parties when we were not at one of our many friends' houses. The social life was unbelievable. Although we were in a Muslim country we were never bothered within the areas we had been

Borneo House

allocated. Not only were there military people in Brunei but about five hundred oil workers from the USA, Australia, UK and other countries. Also within the state, was a trade school and a very fine hospital both run mainly by professionals from Britain.

The very beginning of my tour was a bit awkward, as I needed to deal with problems in the management of the mess and the poor morale, which resulted from this.

The Sergeants' Mess

I had to take a firm line to develop the mess into more than a shed with a bar in the corner. It took me a good six months, with the help of some good guys, to win over the majority into believing that we could have a good community a long way from home in the jungle of South East Asia.

Eventually the management and morale problems in the mess were sorted and a place to be proud of was made, by refurbishing the whole building and making a nice bar and social area. That is what we did with the help of some of the Chinese labourers we had on site. It was amazing what talent came to the fore once they were asked and in a very short time, they transformed our shed into a palace. On completion, we decided on a programme of monthly mess meetings whereby only military members ran the mess and correct procedures were adhered too. One of the outcomes of such meetings was a two-monthly Regimental Dinner so that all newcomers could be welcomed to the garrison properly and those leaving could receive all our best wishes for their new postings. At each of such dinners, we would have a special guest decided on by all members. This could be a visiting dignitary, a senior officer or civilian.

At one such dinner, the agreed guest was one of the elders of the local Iban, jungle dwellers. He was very well known to most of the lads, especially the jungle warfare trainers and anyone who cared to travel a few miles into the undergrowth. When the day of the dinner arrived one of our chopper pilots and I, flew out to pick him up.

Such trips were a delight to me as an animal lover and I was very fortunate to have many during my tour. Once above the canopy of the jungle I had a very special view of a diminishing world of great beauty. The noise and the downdraft of the helicopter blades was enough to bring the huge green carpet to life. Then Ray, the pilot, and I saw the most exotic display of colourful birds quickly followed by hundreds of fruit bats taking flight and every so often the sight of an orangutan making its way through the thick emerald foliage like an enormous ginger caterpillar.

We landed in a clearing immediately adjacent to a longhouse, the home of our dinner guest for the night, the chief of his people. We were instantly surrounded by a large group of Ibans including women and

Longhouse home of our mess guest, Chief Iban.1978. Taken while sitting on 'chopper' skid.

children. They were just a few of the jungle dwellers, once notorious headhunters, who had been recruited by the British during the Second World War to help fight the Japanese. Evidence of those sad times could be seen at various places along the Tutong River, in the form of cages filled with Japanese skulls like some macabre trophies.

Although very friendly people they had animistic beliefs and, hard as it may be to believe, a genuine fear of the very jungle in which they lived. They had a very hierarchical culture; from the time they were very young they were taught to do everything for the good of the family and the rest of the village. Respect of elders without question was always paramount.

Moira's amah always insisted on being home before dark. On the times when she stayed to look after our son, I had to take a very terrified lady home afterwards. The whole journey for her was one of searching the darkness for whatever. She constantly told my wife that evil spirits came out of the jungle at night to take people away. I think those Iban people who stood before us that day really feared us but did not let it show. Their bodies were covered in tattoos, and most of them had bones or rings through their noses and split earlobes hanging down to their shoulders, which when in full dress, would hold wooden discs.

Parked nearby under the trees stood a very modern Mercedes car, covered in dust, leaves and bird droppings. Through the doorway of the longhouse, which had a nice bunch of leaves hung at either side to ward off the spirits, I could see the flashes and hear the sounds of a television. At least I had two questions to ask our guest on the flight back to base.

Suddenly there was a gasp from the people and standing in the doorway to the longhouse was the Chief himself. Regimental dinners for military personnel are very fine occasions where we dress in our mess uniforms, consisting of white shirt, black bow tie, red waistcoat, black trousers with a broad red stripe down each leg, and finally a black dinner jacket, adorned with medals and badges of rank.

We had not mentioned any of that to our guest, thinking that he would come in his traditional dress whatever that was. Before us barefooted, stood four-foot-six-inches of tribal chief dressed in a skirt, a beautiful white shirt, black bow tie and a black dinner jacket, also adorned with medals, and carrying a huge parang – a single-edged machete. He was nicely shaved and in his ear loops were large decorated wooden discs. His small community seemed quite speechless. During the flight back I asked him about the car and the TV. He told me both were bought with a Government interest-free loan, which really meant 'never paid back.' The car had run out of petrol so he had lost interest in it – but the TV was great for the children to learn English. His medals were from the British and the Sultan for his headhunting during the Second World War against the Japanese and against the communist insurgents in Brunei during the sixties. He then showed me a series of dot tattoos around the base of his thumbs, each dot represented a head removed.

Once back at the mess, I took him on a guided tour of the area, during which he told me that the semi-wild dog situation we had round the camp area was not good; dogs which have been kept previously by humans and returned to the wild neglect themselves and suffer from lots of horrible problems, which we had already noticed. He offered to send one of his warriors to cull them with his blowpipe.

A few days later, true to his word, a hunter arrived carrying a six-foot blowpipe and escorted by one of Brunei's finest policemen. Before the Iban got to work, the policeman counted every dart the hunter had and then made sure that he took the same number away with him. Within a very short time, every dog had been blowpiped and killed with the exception of one. That particular one had been hit but the dart fell out leaving the animal bleeding profusely. he hunter picked up his equipment and left very quickly mumbling to himself. The next time I went into the jungle the elder told me the dog had not died because it was carrying an evil spirit and his hunters would never dart that dog again for fear of upsetting the spirit. More than likely, the answer was quite simple – the dart had opened a major vessel and the outward gush of blood had pushed the dart and the poison back out. Not as good as the Iban version.

I digress – back to our dinner night at the mess. As a gift my guest had brought me a second-hand VAT 69 bottle full of Tuak, a very sickly-sweet extremely potent rice wine. I accepted his present knowing full well that I would never drink it, having tried some previously. That night when I returned home the bottle was placed in a corner of one of the bar shelves and quite quickly forgotten. My gift to him was whisky all night, which he really enjoyed and of which he consumed a vast amount without showing any change from the moment he arrived until he left. That night he slept in the mess and the following day, after he had been fed a Full English, my pilot flew him back to his people deep in the Borneo jungle.

Although we had the most fantastic social life with lots of eating and drinking the majority of the soldiers and their wives were very fit. Almost everyone played tennis or badminton. The swimming pool was constantly full and we could take swimming qualifications because we had an Army PTI, fully trained to instruct and pass people on examinations. The result was that the majority of soldiers and their wives had gold or silver certificates. Many of us ran every day and most of the soldiers were involved in football or rugby, played in extreme temperatures at least twice a week. The ladies had a Hash Team, which followed a five-mile paper trail through the jungle three times a week. I, or one of the other senior ranks, would lay the trail with the toilet paper as markers. Unfortunately, we had one or two problems, which resulted in the Hash team getting lost and search parties having to go out and search for them. Unbeknown to us on those occasions, the Ibans had watched the trail being laid and when the person laying it had gone the paper was gathered up for a much better use.

Brunei Rugby Team 1978 – Me, second right, back row.

After playing rugby against the New Zealand Army (facing up to the Haka is something else I will never forget) both teams, plus many spectators, made their way back to our house for a good party. That particular night, among the civilian oil workers, who had been spectators or simply arrived for the beer, was one I had never seen before – but that was no problem because everybody was most welcome. One of my young workshop lads took over bar duties, which was something they liked to do.

Everything was going very well for a couple of hours until the stranger, who it turned out was an American, changed from being a bit garrulous and enjoying himself, into a jabbering idiot before becoming paralysed from the neck down – except for his bladder and his bowels which everyone who was there that night can verify worked very well. We had among us the garrison doctor who like me had played that afternoon. So I asked him to do the honours and give a diagnosis. After looking at the chap, his answer was, "I have not got a clue."

By that time, the guy was a complete gabbling jelly.

"Never seen anything like it," said the Doc. "What the hell has he been drinking?"

So I asked the barman.

"Well! he insisted on drinking VAT 69 out of that funny shaped bottle," was his reply. "At first I told him we did not have any 69 but he recognised the bottle and that was it" reiterated the lad and with that he passed the bottle over to me, the present from my jungle dweller. For a few seconds I was speechless and thanked God I had not been tempted to try the stuff one more time. Needless to say, our new-found Yank friend was carted off to the hospital where he had his stomach pumped before being kept in for a day for observation. We never did have the pleasure of his company at a party again.

My love for the wildlife grew with every passing day. Everything that lived in the rainforest was huge, colourful, vociferous or deadly, and everything was targeted by the locals for their menu. Any living creature that dared to try to cross the highway was deliberately run down. Then the car would stop and someone would leap out and collect the prize, before the car behind beat them to it.

One morning on my way to the unit, I came across a small group of locals gathered round a reticulated python, which they had battered, on the head with a shovel. It was so beautiful I could not accept them turning it into a dinner so I gave them a few dollars and they were well pleased. I opened the car boot and lifted the poor creature inside and there it was, left in the dark and quiet until I returned home that night. At the time, I had no idea if it was alive or dead, not having had the time to carry out any checks. What I did know was, it had an enormous lump on its head. Although I would have been sad if it was dead, I still wanted Moira and Clive to have the opportunity to see such a beautiful animal close up.

That night on arriving home, I opened the boot and was delighted to see it was moving, but very disoriented due to meeting one of man's tools head on. I called out to my wife and son to come see what I had rescued from our tiny jungle friends. After more than twenty years of listening to me eulogise about all kinds of animals, Moira was not surprised any more at what I might have brought home. I pointed inside the boot and curled up in the spare wheel was my good deed for the day. I tried to lift it out, but at my touch, the snake went straight and rigid like a pole. For a few moments, I must have looked like Charlton Heston as he came down from the mountain in the film Moses carrying the tablets in one hand and the staff in the other. No matter how I tried, I could not get the python to relax so I had to give it the best inspection I could with my very limited knowledge. On completion, I was reasonably happy that apart from the lump on its head there was no reason why it could not be released to return to its home in the jungle.

The jungle trees started fifty yards from the house but I still had to carry one rigid ten-foot python, the thickness of my arm, over that distance, thank goodness no one was watching. Once inside the tree line I laid it down and stepped away. After a short time it came to life and slithered off into the thick undergrowth, I felt a great sense of pleasure. Later that night all the houses in our area had a power cut. The following morning everything was back to normal but on the local radio it was announced that a power cut had taken place in our area; the cause of which had been a python climbing up one of the pylons and shorting out the power, in the very place I had let my dizzy reptile go on its merry way. Moira and I had a laugh although the snake must have died; at least he had paid back in inconvenience, those who had battered him.

I took the golden opportunity of living among such a variety of animals to study for an A Level in Zoology. After studying very hard for more than a year, I applied to sit my examination. It was agreed that I could take it out there in the jungle and the powers-that-be back in England decided that the garrison doctor could adjudicate. One of my choice questions on the paper was to sex fruit flies, Drosophila Melanogaster and answer certain points about genetics. Those flies were critical for the test and were sent in a bottle from the UK along with the test paper. When the time came for me to determine the sex of my flies, I duly placed them on a slide in order to view them under the microscope, completely forgetting that almost every building in Brunei had overhead fans, which were continually in operation, and the Doc's surgery where I was taking my test was no exception. It just never occurred to me because we lived with the situation all the time. So! when I placed my slide under the scope and looked in the eye piece – nothing! It took me a good few seconds searching for the absent flies before I realised the culprit was spinning above my head.

That particular part of my paper had to be delayed, until I was given an alternative question. Finally, the question came and I had to beg my Chinese gardener to persuade his Iban friend to drop everything and with great urgency catch me a rat, to dissect. That was completed within the hour and what he brought back to me strengthened my belief about the jungle animals being bigger than those found in other places. That rat did not disappoint – it must have been eighteen inches long without the tail. Unfortunately, that part of my test did not go very well. I had not studied much about rats, and I do not think the examination board back in the UK really believed the story about the fan, so I only received an 'O' level pass in Zoology. Not to worry – at least I achieved something worthwhile during my stay.

The seventy-mile long road between the capital of Brunei, Bandar Seri Begawan, and Seria was policed by the Sultan's police force. They were on average five feet tall, dressed immaculately in black leather suits, jackboots and white crash helmets, plus the obligatory shades. Their mode of transport was the Harley Davidson on which their main duty was to catch speeding vehicles and fine them on the spot. At least twice a month they would put up a roadblock and stop all cars. Then they would carry out a driving licence check and make all drivers remove any form of window stickers before allowing them to continue their journey. It was really their show of authority, usually a long process in the heat of the day. So knowing that they had the greatest respect for the garrison personnel, I always left my spare cap on the rear window ledge of Moira's car. As a result, when she was caught up in one of their regular games one of the 'Mini Chips' would see the cap and immediately apologise to her before moving all the traffic aside, so that she could proceed without delay. We were made to feel that we were very important people.

Whenever one of my garrison soldiers was caught speeding, the policeman instead of fining them, brought to me every Monday morning the speeding chits. I had to give him an assurance that I would deal with the culprits most severely. Then he would ask me for a nice cold drink before tearing the chits up and throwing them in the bin. The following week, when he had more chits, he would always ask what punishment the previous week's speedsters had received.

One particular Saturday morning, Moira and I were taking a beautiful wooden carved German clock to the town of Seria in the hope of finding a clock repairer who could fix some damage, received in transit. As we were about to alight from the car in the town car park, I noticed in my driving mirror the very familiar white crash helmet and the black shades pull up right behind me. I opened the door fully expecting to be told that I had committed some crime when he spoke;

"Where are you going?" he asked. I explained and showed him the clock on the back seat. He immediately parked his bike before reaching into the car and picking up the clock." Follow me, "he said, then strode away in front of us both, clock held firmly to his chest as if he was carrying a bomb.

As he walked, he ordered people to step aside or prodded them with his white baton out of our way. By the time we got to his destination, we had quite a following; it was like something out of a film. Once inside, he took it upon himself to tell the shopkeeper what he wanted for his friends (us) in a very commanding voice.

"It must be mended quickly and failure to do so is unacceptable." He then went on to say that, "I would collect the repaired clock in two days time". When I returned two days later the clock was ready, but the poor shopkeeper was quite terrified and refused to accept any payment. I do not know who he thought I was, but it took me quite a time to calm him down and get him to accept the due amount and only after a promise, that I would not tell my friend in the large crash helmet.

As already said, at the start of my tour there had been many problems, a lot of ill feeling and a lot of very childish things done. By the Christmas of 1977, I thought we had a very happy garrison, but then the doubts returned. I received a card with the inscription. "Sorry for your illness." I simply thought it was someone just being silly and let it pass.

A few days later one of my WOs told me his wife had been quite upset at Christmas because they had received a card, which said, "Sorry for your bereavement." He mentioned there were at least two others he knew of, who had got similar type cards. Altogether, we managed to find nine such cases and decided we had a very silly person among us and could not help but think someone was trying to dole out some kind of retribution, for what had taken place during my early days. So I drafted a letter to be placed upon the notice board, telling whomever what I thought of such infantile behaviour.

Nothing more was said, or heard about the subject. Then during May 1978, one of the Chinese gardeners who had a very good command of the English language stopped me as I was approaching the mess. He introduced himself as Peter Wong and told me he was the husband of Clementine, one of the cooks in the mess. He then went on to say that one of his friends, who was cutting grass nearby, liked his English boss (me) and had asked him to ask me if I liked the 'Clissimas' card he had sent me and my family.

"I didn't receive a card," I told him.

"Well, he said he sent one," said Peter as he returned to his friend.

I had started to walk on to the mess when he called out again.

"He says he also sent all your friends one."

I immediately turned back and asked both gardeners to accompany me to the Commissariat, the only place I knew of where he could have got Christmas cards. Once inside, I asked them to show me where he had bought the cards. There was a really good selection of cards for every occasion due to us being in a Muslim country. He started to point to cards in the section that covered bereavement, get well and various other things – but not Christmas cards. I then thanked the two men and assured them that the cards had been received and now appreciated.

We had mixing in our group, a number of very wealthy Chinese businessmen. One in particular was a local food trader, and I say that with tongue in cheek. He sold anything that could possibly be eaten and anyone who has lived in South East Asia, knows that covers a vast range – much of which most Europeans would not go near, let alone eat.

One particular friend of ours who had not been out there very long, told me his family fancied a goose for Christmas and he would like to find one and surprise them, but he had no idea where to find such a bird. So,

I took him along to the food trader whose knowledge of the English language was on a par with our Mandarin. We tried every way to explain to him what we wanted, but to no avail.

By that time, the trader had gained quite an audience around his stall. Unfortunately, they were of little help but they seemed to be enjoying themselves at our conversation, and kept trying to repeat our words. Then my friend came up with the idea of using his party technique of charades. He positioned his arm like Rod Hull's Emu and by opening his hand emulated the mouth, then, by moving his arm up and down, the movement of the neck. The spectators were in fits of laughter and along with the trader, were copying every movement. At that stage, my friend decided to go the whole way.

Every time he moved the neck he said, "Goose" – followed by the crowd shouting "Gus Gus" in between fits of hysterical laughter. Then, as he extended the neck, he made a hissing sound.

After more laughter the actions seemed to be successful and by that time all the Chinese present that day, were holding up their hands and hissing and finally seemed to understand my friend's needs. I wrote down the address and delivery date he required the 'gus' – I mean goose. Then we all shook hands with the businessman on the deal, and many of the audience who had played such a wonderful part in our game of charades.

I wasn't there when the delivery arrived at my friend's house but true to his word, my friend told me that on Christmas Eve there was a knock on his door and on the step was a large basket with a lid. He took it inside the bungalow, placed it in the middle of the floor, and called his family to come see what he hoped, would be a great surprise of an oven-ready goose. As he unfastened the lid and slowly lifted it, to give the very best effect for the family surprise, he noticed a pair of eyes shining through the darkness from within. Once fully open there was indeed a surprise for his family; before them, and now risen up to its full height of almost six feet and swaying back and forth, was a beautiful king cobra. Needless to say by then, the family had disappeared and did not return until an Iban had been brought to catch the snake and return it back to its jungle home.

On another day, the same senior rank left his place of work and went into the mess just to have the odd beer. The problem out there was, that one beer in the mess usually led to quite a few more, due to the heat and the company. That night after dark, he finally staggered out of the bar and climbed into his car to drive the ten miles home along a very dark road with dense jungle at one side and the South China Sea at the other. About halfway through the journey he felt hot breath on the back of his neck and something started to lick his ear.

When he told me the story, he said he almost needed a change of underwear. He immediately stopped the car and leapt out, taking with him a torch from the passenger seat. When he finally picked up enough courage to return to his vehicle and very carefully shine his torch into the constantly open window, facing him was one of the many semi-wild dogs that lived around and under the mess.

Our social life in Brunei was one big party, which gave Moira and me the opportunity to meet a great many very important people. We were guests at the British Embassy on more than one occasion.

To celebrate the Birthday of

Her Majesty Queen Elizabeth II

in Her Silver Jubilee Year

The British High Commissioner
requests the pleasure of the company of

WOI & Mrs Horn

at a Reception at the Residence on 11th June at 11.30 am

Dress: Lounge Suit

Regrets Only Tel: 22231

A great honour

I attended the Sultan's birthday party at the royal palace in Bandar Seri Begawan two years in succession.

To this day, I have hanging on the wall in pride of place, one of our invitation cards. If you are ever fortunate enough to see it, you will note that it is a bit the worse for wear – nothing to do with its hard life in Brunei or its numerous journeys, until I finally retired. It is the result of me taking it to a photographers to have it reduced in size to fit in this book. Unfortunately, I put it on the roof of the car so that I could open the door and simply forgot it was there. After a couple of miles, it dawned on me and I retraced my journey to find it lying in the road where a tractor had run over it.

During lunchtime sessions in the mess, we often had very important people there, usually on a visit to the Sultan in the first instance but later joining us for lunch. As senior member of the mess, I was very privileged to meet a great many dignitaries such as General Sir Roland Gibbs, Chief of the General Staff, Sir Martin Farndale from the MOD, and Sir Roy Redgrave, Major General C. in C. forces Hong Kong.

General Sir Roland Gibbs at mess lunch 1978

How could I ever forget Sir Roy Redgrave who came to visit the unit from Hong Kong. On that particular day, I asked the Gurkha cooks to do the catering for the guests' luncheon. It was of course a curry, made with wild boar meat. Before the lunch, when Sir Roy and I were chatting I thought it might be a good idea to make him aware how hot these guys could make a curry, even more so when there was a visitor. It was like a challenge for them to create a red-hot surprise.

When I mentioned that to my guest he simply laughed and said, "Don't worry, I have eaten their food before." When the food arrived and we had all been served, I was watching very discreetly for the General's reaction and I certainly got one. As he withdrew the spoon after his very first mouthful, I saw his face start to change colour from a nice healthy-looking suntan to a bright scarlet, that looked about to burst. I also noticed the smiles on the faces of the Gurkha-Cooks. To be fair to my guest, he had a good laugh about it afterwards. But, for those few minutes I had been a bit worried at what his reaction might be; he came out of it with flying colours, a true officer.

In July 1979, we left Borneo behind, having spent more than two years among some of the nicest people one could wish to meet. We had become great friends with the Chinese gardener, Peter Wong, and his wife, Clementine, who I promoted to chief cook in the mess. They both loved to cook and every party we had from our very first meeting was fully catered for, by them.

After we returned to the UK, we kept in touch with the couple and quite a few years later, we were able to meet up again. Clementine's sister lived in Leicester and her daughter got married. Moira and I were invited as very important guests for them; it was indeed a great honour for us to be invited. The two of us, plus another of my colleagues from Borneo, were the only English guests among one hundred or more. The reception was magnificent and a credit to our Chinese friend who had been responsible for all the catering.

A couple of years later our two friends came to the UK again to stay with us for a short time, prior to moving to Canada, where she made a name for herself not only as a fine cook but also as a senior officer in the trade union. There she died of a brain hemorrhage during September of 2012.

Our friends, Clementine & Peter Wong

Moira with Gurkha WO – 1977

Brownie – wild dog tamed by Moira

Our bar

Meeting Sir Roland Gibbs – General C-in-C.

Some of the rescued orangutans

CHAPTER SIXTEEN

Northern Ireland 1979

From Borneo to Northern Ireland – now that was a culture shock. Although the Military Camp and the married quarters were well situated, in a quiet area just outside Belfast, we felt very restricted. It was not a good family posting because fear and suspicion abounded. Whenever my wife went out shopping with the children and they were heard talking, eyes immediately turned toward them and whispering usually followed, creating a feeling of discomfort. The girls had all finished school and were eager to start working but employment was difficult to find, for obvious reasons. Clive went to school but was bullied on a daily basis, by both sides of the religious divide, and not made at all welcome by the teachers.

I remember very clearly, quite early in my tour, being asked to go to the school to see one of his teachers. On arriving, I was taken to a classroom by a secretary who knocked on the door, then opened it and announced me, at the same time as a voice from within asked me to enter. Before me, at the front of the classroom, I could see a pair of Doc Martin boots or to be exact the soles, because whoever it was in the boots was lying flat in a chair with their feet up on a desk. As I got closer a young girl, whom I took to be the teacher I had come to see, raised herself up. Starting from the boots and going up to her head were; yellow tights, a mini skirt, a bright red jumper and a really weirdly made up face, topped with a head of blue hair. My first impression was one of shock. Then I thought, perhaps this was some kind of wind up. But no, she was indeed Clive's teacher. The reason she had asked me to the school was she believed that our son was a liar, a rather startling statement after him being in her class for such a short time.

Her story was that, during the English lesson the class had been asked to write a composition on places they had visited. With the exception of

Clive, the rest had run out of words after a page. As the lesson had come to a close, he was still writing and he was on his tenth page.

"So I have come to the conclusion that your boy is prone to exaggeration," and she handed me the papers. I quickly read through and was very proud at what my son had written.

"I see nothing wrong with that," I said to her.

For a while she was deep in thought – or at least I think that is what was happening. I could not be sure, having been met by what looked more like a clown, than a teacher, who started a conversation with such an outrageous statement, and had now entered a trance of some kind. Suddenly, she landed back on the planet again.

"No sorry. I can't accept that he has been to Cyprus, Germany, Hong Kong, Singapore and Borneo. The furthest anyone else in the class has been is Portrush." I was completely dumbfounded and tried to explain, but it was to no avail.

I had only one year to do in the posting before returning to the UK for my last six months and that little fiasco triggered me into action. That very night, Moira and I decided we would return home for a few days and try to buy a house where she and the family could live and I would complete my time living in the mess. So, that is what happened. We purchased a house in Wilsden near Bradford, the city where Moira and I, and the two eldest girls had been born. The countryside was very beautiful with woods, hills, rivers and a few waterfalls.

It was hard to believe that just a few miles in either direction there were stagnating wool cities such as Bradford, Huddersfield, Halifax and Wakefield.

Once back in the UK, Moira settled the family very quickly. The three girls found work and Clive got his wish to attend a school where he would be able to play football. Because we had left our dog Tina with our dear friend in Hampshire, the family insisted on a dog for the new home. This time, it was nothing expensive or high-class so they decided on a Jack Russell dog, duly christened Spike.

I settled down in the mess and, because there was no regular weekly sport due to the troubles, I decided to join a golf club, Carnleigh, with the intention of learning the game and keeping myself reasonably fit.

Neither was a great success. One weekend per month, I flew back home to be with the family; the other three and some part of everyday I played golf, or tried to. I had the great pleasure of playing on some very fine courses such as Portrush, Helen's Bay, Bangor and Holywood which was to become famous many years later for producing one of the greatest golfers ever seen – Rory McIroy. It was not for the lack of trying that I never progressed at the game I really loved, and still do. I was not flexible enough and my fitness went backwards due to my age, the constant use of the nineteenth hole and living in the mess.

Once the family had settled down, we were able to make regular telephone calls to Miss E at Caines Cottage and visit her as often as military duties would allow. That year and every year after during the summer, Moira and I spent at least one week with her and Tina in the beautiful county of Hampshire. There we lived the simple life that our host did every day of her life. Each morning of our holiday, we would awaken in the tiniest of bedrooms in the five-hundred-year-old cottage to a cacophony of bird song. For me, just to look out of the window meant I had to get down into the kneeling position because it was positioned at floor level. The ceiling was so low I had to walk about stooped and once outside the sleeping quarters, we had to negotiate the narrowest staircase I had ever seen. My shoulders touched the walls at either side.

Downstairs Miss E, who always rose at dawn, would be waiting patiently to start her daily routine. Breakfast was simply toast and tea then out into her beloved garden. We would sit and talk or the two ladies would wander off to go gardening or discussing plants. I would often sit and relax listening to the beautiful sounds of the birds, or spend time painting. Occasionally, but not too often because of the age of our host, we would all set off for a walk across the gorse-covered heath returning along the banks of the river Wey, where if we were lucky we would see the kingfishers on their daily hunt for sticklebacks.

On returning to the cottage, we would enjoy a nice glass of wine before having a simple sandwich for lunch. Our main meal would be in the evening, when the two ladies would cook something like lamb chops or fish with nice new potatoes accompanied by a side salad.

They were the most idyllic holidays one could wish for – so relaxing and peaceful but most of all so informative.

It was a very hot summer evening in August 1983, when we arrived at Miss E's for one such holiday. She was quite aware of our timetable and time of arrival so it came as a shock when we pulled up outside the cottage and there was no one on the premises, not even Tina. But, there was a large estate car, which I did not recognise, parked on the drive. We really started to worry after searching the garden and down by the river, the only places our friend ever really went, and having no success. Then we decided she must have taken the dog for a walk across the heath and because it was now starting to get dark, we worried that perhaps she had been hurt in some way. So off we set on a rescue mission. We had walked no more than half a mile, when we saw two very tiny tired-looking figures staggering toward us out of the gloom. Then Tina was alongside us wagging her tail followed very closely by a long tailed Springer spaniel.

Then our friend and an even older looking lady, duly arrived. Both were loaded up with tripods and camera as if they were on a safari. Miss E introduced her friend, and if I didn't know otherwise I would swear that day I met Margaret Rutherford, the film star – my favourite Miss Marple – right down to the voice and the flexible lower jaw. Our old friend assured me it wasn't. She was simply a fanatical lepidopterist who Miss E had known for many years but had not seen for a long time. She had turned up that very afternoon, completely unannounced, and dragged our host on a marathon to try to find and photograph some rare species she had heard was in the area. She stayed one night only – but what a wonderful character. The two of them together, along with a bottle of sherry, made that night one to remember. They both had a rare knowledge of wildlife.

During late October 1981, I had returned to the UK to serve my last six months at REME Records in the Midlands. From there, I could catch a train home every weekend. The idea of that period of time, is to allow myself and other Senior Ranks the opportunity to find a job and settle back to civilian life before actually signing off.

When I arrived at the Records Office I was very surprised to find that my direct boss was a captain who had served with me previously as a

PH and CO – Northern Ireland 1979

WO, before he took his short service commission. Little did I know at the time, he was to be a key figure in my transition from the military back to civilian life.

It was a Thursday morning and I had just arrived from the mess to start another boring day of shifting documents. My mind was on the following day when I would catch a train home for the weekend with the family. After all, time was passing and I would soon be retired and hopefully have found a good position in civilian life.

The telephone rang and brought me out of my dreams. I was asked to report to the CO's office, "Good morning, ASM. Yesterday evening after you had gone for the night to your mess I received a telephone call from the head of the transport department of a county council. He said he had been given your name by a REME officer, and he asked if you would give him a call on this number," and with that he handed me a card.

I thanked the Colonel and returned to my office where I rang the telephone number. The gentleman asked me if I would meet him at 1300 hrs the following day at the council workshop where he wanted to put a proposition to me. That was all he would say. I told him that I would because by that time my curiosity was killing me. That night I went home to Wilsden, curious at what the morrow would bring.

The weather that Friday morning in December was really bad. Blizzards were blowing in Wilsden but that was a very wild area of Yorkshire so perhaps it might be different further south, or so I hoped. I had worked it out that it would take me about two hours to drive there but because of the weather, I decided to allow myself four and left home at 9 a.m. Unfortunately, the weather along the way turned out to be far worse than I ever expected and I did not arrive at my destination until 3 p.m. I had my doubts that the workshop would still be open and, if it was, my contact Colin would have given up on me. I was wrong on both counts, which showed the measure of the man. He had noted the weather conditions and where I was coming from and furthermore his assessment of my promise to him on the telephone. There he was, waiting patiently with sandwiches and hot drinks ready.

The story he told me that evening was quite daunting. In the council workshop, there should have been fifty staff, plus supervisors responsible for the commissioning, resale service, and the maintenance of over a thousand vehicles and plant of various kinds, used to carry out the needs of the county council. The whole department had collapsed and the morale of those who remained was at rock bottom.

The transport system for the county was simply grinding to a halt. School buses, fire and police vehicles, along with highways and tip site equipment were becoming no longer fit for use. The question put to me that evening was, "If I let you have a free hand to recruit, reorganise and develop the workshop can you do it?"

"Why are you asking me?" I replied.

"Because, I was told by a very good friend of mine who was an officer in the Army that if I was looking for quick results, Senior Warrant Officers in the REME such as you, were where I should be looking. All my requirements in one package." were his words. Especially, there was the need to move things along very quickly and that was the way the forces had to work.

"That is exactly what I need," I told him; so he phoned REME records and they told him there was such a guy ready to leave the service – you. And they gave him a number for me to ring and here you are."

At least this chap has done his homework and knows what he wants, I thought.

"Can you do it?" he asked. At that stage of my life I was not going to say no because to approach any position with lack of confidence is just wasting time.

My answer was affirmative and his face lit up. At that moment I felt as if I had won the pools, I had the chance to start a good job with a challenge and end my military career.

"Good. We will give it until April as an open contract then we will meet and if either of us is not satisfied at the way things are going, we can call it a day as friends. Until then you are the boss of this department. I will visit weekly for a coffee and a chat – no interference whatsoever. Agreed?"

With that, we said our goodbyes, shook hands and went our separate ways.

TO: WARRANT OFFICER CLASS 1 PETER HORN

Now that you have reached the end of your service after 26 years, I am writing on behalf of the Army Board to thank you for all you have done for the Army during your long and loyal service. You have had to take your share of the arduous duties which so often fall to the lot of the British Army and you may justly claim to have played your part in upholding its age-long traditions and in fostering loyalty and pride in your unit, your Corps, and in the Army as a whole.

In sending you my thanks, I am taking this opportunity to express the hope that all good fortune will be with you in the future.

George Cooper.

ADJUTANT GENERAL

CHAPTER SEVENTEEN

A Different Life

That weekend both Moira and I were on a different planet. Everything had happened so quickly. One day I was a soldier thinking about applying for jobs and hoping there was a good one out there for me – the next I was a civilian with a top-class job. Colin was true to his word; he never once bothered me. Every member of the workshop staff I recruited or promoted his administration staff dealt with, without question.

The forces' management teaching at senior level is all about leadership so the job I had undertaken required very little technical knowledge because that could be recruited or brought out of the personnel already there. I simply had to lead them and encourage team spirit in order to develop a desire for achievement.

During April, Colin and I had our dinner together as promised and the very first frank discussion since that first day. The result was that we were both very pleased at the way things were progressing.

Eighteen months later, with a completely reorganised workshop, lots of new staff and training programmes in place, we had a workshop of top quality. The efficiency was better than it had ever been which was really no surprise, when we took into account how much time and equipment had been wasted previously. We had developed a system whereby ten per cent of all work across the board was sent out to private contractors, so that we could constantly prove to the council that the workshop was giving value for money to the ratepayers. As a result, there was no justification to turn to privatisation, which seemed to be the way most councils, the length and breadth of England, wanted to go at the time.

As Colin would often say, on that wintry day in December we both pulled the handle and three cherries dropped. All the time I had been at Market Rasen I had commuted between there and Bradford on a daily basis, eighty-five miles each way. My start from home was five thirty each morning and I arrived back at seven thirty each night. Moira and I had discussed moving nearer to my work but the children were all settled and, at the time, mortgages were almost impossible for most people to get. I was all right because there was a rule at the time that ex-servicemen should have some priority on building society lists, but we could not find any buyers for our property who could find a mortgage.

Almost two years passed and Colin had provided a caravan on the workshop site so that I could stay down during the week and go home at weekends that way saving on fuel, wear and tear on the car and me being constantly knackered. But it was becoming too much and not fair on the family, so with Colin's blessing I started to seek employment nearer home.

I applied for a position with another council near to home. The job was a step higher than my position at the time; in fact, it was equivalent to Colin's and my jobs being combined. I was duly informed I had been shortlisted without ever seeing anyone, and was awaiting an interview. Then one Sunday morning, when I was out with our son at football, Moira received a telephone call from the personnel officer of that council. He told her the shortlist had been reduced, to me and one other person. Then he asked her if I was in receipt of a military pension, which was rather strange for two reasons. First, I had told them in my application that I had served twenty-six years in the forces, which would tell anyone with half a brain that I must receive a pension. Second, I had also told them in my application that I had one and exactly how much it was. My wife once again told him those details to which he replied that unfortunately the council could not employ me because I was already receiving a wage, which was ridiculous because the amount was nowhere near enough to live on. He apologised and rang off.

When she told me, I found it very strange that the list had been reduced to two, without seeing anyone. In addition, telephoning my home on a Sunday morning was not the usual practice one would expect from a senior council officer.

About a month later, and once again on a Sunday morning when I was away with my boy at football, Moira received another telephone call from the very same personnel officer. That time he told her that the post I had been unsuccessful at had now been deputised, and they would like me to apply for that position. Needless to say, I did not reply to them.

Two weeks later, I received a call at work from the clerk to the personnel officer who liked to telephone my wife on a Sunday morning. She thanked me for attending the interview for the initial post, the one I had been turned down for, on grounds of having an Army pension. She went on to say the council were very sorry that I had not been successful and wished me all the very best for the future.

Later that day, I was talking to Colin on the phone. He asked me how my job search was going so I brought him up to date about the council not interviewing me due to the pension, and the later offer to apply for deputy to the same post, and finally the thanks for never attending an interview.

"It seems to me they employed the wrong man and the offer of deputy was for you to carry him – and what happened to the pension rule? As far as attending the interview is concerned, I would ring them back and ask for a claim form for expenses for attending," Colin replied.

I immediately telephoned that particular council and asked for the form. The lady who answered was the same one who had rung me earlier. She seemed quite shocked and speechless at my request and said she would call me back.

Within a short time, the telephone rang and that time she was obviously very well briefed and said she had spoken to the boss. He had said, "Please accept our apologies. We now see you never attended the interview." I think that would have been very obvious from the start if there were only two of us on the shortlist.

Afterwards, when Colin and I talked about it we were both of the same opinion; that the council who made the statement on its paper headings that they were an equal opportunity council really wanted from me confirmation that I had been treated fairly.

In January 1983, I attended another interview with a local council near to my home. The post was that of transport manager and my CV and application had been good enough to get me into the last half dozen of sixty plus applicants. The job was to manage fifty staff, looking after three hundred vehicles and specialist equipment. If successful, I would be responsible for the transport budget, including purchasing authority, and selling of old equipment.

My interview took place and I thought it went very well, and once again, I had made it very clear on my application that I received a military pension, which was by no means a living wage. I even told them exactly how much, and at no time was there any comment about it. Furthermore, my application was supported by a fantastic reference from Colin and the leader of county council. At the end, I was told that I would be informed one way or the other within one week.

Time passed and I had applied and been shortlisted for two more positions but had been unsuccessful. Then on 1st March, I received a letter from the council, where I had been for the job interview in January. The letter was to tell me that I had been successful and asked me to telephone a certain officer as soon as possible.

I did that at the earliest opportunity and was transferred to the senior officer who was to be my head of department. We had quite a long chat during which I asked why it had taken such a long time before calling me. He informed me that I had been chosen for the post a few minutes after the final interview on that day in January, but once again, the narrow-minded Labour Councillors on the board would not accept the holder of a pension. So, during the three months since my selection the council board had been advertising the post and interviewing but the officer I was speaking to had simply refused to accept anyone, other than the choice he had made in the January. The result was, the councillors finally gave in and I was appointed as transport manager. Once again, it was a case of a council broadcasting to all about being an equal opportunity employer and then doing what they wanted.

I started the job in April 1983. Before I left Market Rasen, an unusual but most rewarding event took place. I had put my notice in, but Colin and the council agreed that as a token of thanks for what my team had achieved they would allow me to go to my new post as soon as they had found a replacement for me, providing I partnered Colin on the interviews. A few weeks later on a Monday morning, I left home to carry out the swiftest of handovers and returned home on the Tuesday ready to

start my new job on the Wednesday morning. During the Monday, one of
my young charge hands came into my office and asked me if I would go
to the football club that evening for a farewell drink with him, so I
agreed. After all, I had recruited him and he had been a great success for
me and the council.

That evening, he picked me up from the caravan, and drove me the
short distance to the club. As he drove into the car park I thought he must
have made a mistake because the place was closed; no lights, no sign of
any other cars. He led the way to the door and, to my surprise, opened it
and as we entered all the lights came on and the place was packed. Not
only were all my staff there, but all the administration staff were also
present. Even more surprising, when my eyes became accustomed to the
light, was who was sitting with Colin? None other than Moira! I found
out later there had been a party plot for a week and she had not let the
secret out. The Monday morning I left, one of the young lads had
travelled to my home to pick her up and she had been at Market Rasen
all day with my secretary who had conveniently arranged a day's holiday.
That night was one hell of a shock. To be appreciated by one's direct
bosses for doing a decent job is one thing, but to have a full turnout of all
the transport staff was something I will never forget. It was a very proud
moment in my life.

For almost two years, I had worked for a fantastic council and had the
good fortune to work for a boss like Colin who had allowed me to
manage the way I had been trained. I also had the best team of workers
one could ask for, who were fully dedicated to doing everything possible
to ensure the county ratepayers received value for money.

In 1985, we were informed by a friend of Miss E that she had been
taken into hospital with a heart problem. We made the journey to
Hampshire without hesitation, only to find that she had returned home
to her cottage a few hours before our arrival, complete with a stock of
tablets. The very thought of taking tablets or any kind of medicine was
quite abhorrent to her. She had detested being laid up, albeit for a couple
of days only, and she did not want to be fussed over and she certainly did
not want to be among a lot of whining geriatrics (her words) even though
by that time, she was in her eighties. Unfortunately, there was worse

news. Tina, our beloved cocker spaniel, had suffered a heart attack just prior to Miss E's problem and was not very well. So, when our old friend thought she was going to be away for a period of hospitalisation she asked her vet to put Tina to sleep. That day another chapter of our lives came to an end and our beautiful cocker spaniel was laid to rest in the cottage garden, near the river and the woods she loved so much.

Miss E continued to tend her garden, but alone until 1994, and we continued to visit her for a holiday at least once a year. Then, I suspect very much against her wishes, she was taken into a nursing home. We had noticed her deterioration but she would not accept any kind of care. During her time in the home, we made the trip to visit a couple of times but it wasn't our old friend, so full of energy and love for her garden and the wildlife; she had gone. What remained was a bird in a cage. I cannot imagine how alone she must have felt after a lifetime with her loving dogs and her garden.

Our beloved little friend left this world in 1996 and, apart from her solicitor and the heir to the trust cottage, Moira and I were the only ones at her cremation, which took place at Aldershot Crematorium. We had been very lucky to have had twenty-four years of friendship with a very interesting person who loved life and the countryside so much. I do hope she joined up with all her canine friends.

My new job was with another council so I had great hopes it would be akin to the forces, thereby continue to help me to settle into civilian life. My very first day I had the misfortune to meet a very self-centred top official, a one-hundred-percent dictator who had surrounded himself with a group of very weak sycophants called managers. It was very obvious to me, during our short meeting that he needed obsequious supporters in order to have no opposition to his demanding ways. The very first thing he told me was that he was in the process of changing the duty cars from petrol to LPG because that was the future, and that I must continue to complete the transition. He had managed to persuade quite enough of his followers with the use of sophistry to convince the board of councillors, who were responsible for ensuring the department spent public money in the best possible way, that his idea was safe and cost effective. But not me; I was determined that such a scheme was not going to be used anywhere I was transport officer. In any case, such decisions I considered to be my job. From that day, I started to put together a good, solid argument for a swift return to petrol or diesel cars. I knew, from what I had already heard that it would be no easy task – especially as a lone voice.

Unfortunately, something happened, which strengthened my case for change considerably. On Saturday, 5th November 1983, there was a shattering explosion at a garage in Morley Street, which I attended in my capacity as transport manager. The story was, that in a storeroom beneath the garage there had been a gas tank similar to the ones fitted on the duty cars, which had been removed from a vehicle and simply stored there. A young lad had been given the job of sweeping the room clean and had inadvertently knocked the valve on the tank open with his brush and gas escaped. He reported the problem and the site was evacuated very quickly and all windows were opened. After a short period of time, the workers returned. Unfortunately, the gas had lingered at low level such as down the vehicle inspection pits and one of the workers used a toilet and then proceeded to wash his hands by turning on an immersion heater. That was all that was needed to completely demolish a very solid two-storey garage, killing two people and injuring twelve more.

We carried out the tests on the cylinder to see how easy it was to create such a leak that could do so much damage. After that, it was fairly easy to convince the powers-that-be that there was a better and safer fuel system for the duty cars. It was becoming apparent to me that, unlike the people at Market Rasen who I had developed into a team, I was now working with a rabble with very little team spirit, who had their own agenda and everything was for their own benefit. I found it quite difficult to come to terms with this, because by then, the lack of belonging to a family like the forces had started to kick in. It could only be likened to a form of PTSD, post traumatic stress disorder. I even got to the stage on many occasions when out shopping with the family, of becoming violent when shown little respect or addressed as 'matey' by some spotty youth of about sixteen. Having served with the very best, I found the attitude of many of the general public and the council I was working with, very hard to accept. However, my military training carried me through.

For a good few years I really struggled to stop the senior managers from spending public money as if it were their own and believing they had every right to do so. Almost all of them insisted that they should have the cars they used for duty replaced, after two years maximum. One manager in particular, put forward a case that he was expected to carry out his duties using a high mileage car. His car speedo had 29,000 miles recorded. Then the models did not suit them, or the engine size was wrong. Fortunately, none of them had the brains to bring their boss round to their way of thinking; the main reason was that he had a better class of car and couldn't really care less about them.

When I first started in the job, the admin staff who supported the council departments were looked after by a senior clerk who had a secretary. He and the CEO had full control of all the budgets and it was all overseen by a board of two or three county councillors.

There was something else I found quite alien. During my time at Market Rasen, when I travelled anywhere on duty for the council I recorded my mileage, and if I stopped for lunch, I got a receipt. At the end of the month, those records and receipts were sent to the finance manager and I was reimbursed. At my new place I started to do the same but was quickly told to simply tell them how many miles I wanted paying for and that if I had a snack or a meal there was a fixed figure for a lunch, dinner etc. The first time I tried to claim for fish and chips when I went on a visit, I was told I must claim a ridiculous figure, about four times what I had actually spent. From that day on, I would allow my sandwich or fish and chip bill to reach the amount quoted to me, before making a claim. Perhaps my thinking was wrong but I, like to think not. However, as time went by, I became aware of swimming in a pool alone, as I had been all those years before in Borneo.

For seven years, I struggled to come to terms with their strange ways of so-called management, which was the only way the hierarchy seemed to understand. From day one, with very few exceptions, everything they did was not about achieving, but more about what they could get for themselves. Throughout those years, I felt as if I was walking in treacle, and more than once seriously thought about leaving. But I knew the CEO and his deputy were due to retire and I hoped their successors would want to make a cost-effective service for the people of Yorkshire. Both positions were duly filled by people from outside the county and, as I hoped, they were indeed good forward-looking managers who could handle staff and budgets for the good of the people. More important from my point of view, was that once again I was given the freedom and the responsibility to manage my department.

From the very day the two new senior managers moved in, things started to improve in every way. However, always lurking in the background were a number of department managers yearning to go back to the lazy, outdated ways they had enjoyed for years, or worse, eager to find new ways to waste public money. Fortunately, they were kept at bay until 1990; then a major change took place. A new Labour council took over and what had been minimum interference by councillors to the council departments, changed dramatically in a very short time. A left-wing element took control and money was wasted like pouring water down the drain. That was what a vast number of department managers had been waiting for.

A number of 'yes-men' were recruited and empires sprang up, almost overnight, like mushrooms. The 'management' to use the word very loosely, more than trebled. Car schemes were developed to give them perks. Many of the very efficient workers were forced out of their positions by corporate bullying.

For my part, I resisted them, until they finally found a heinous way to remove me by compulsory redundancy – even though the council policy was no redundancy under any circumstances. Then when I had left in 1996, they published in the council news that I had taken voluntary redundancy. The final act before leaving was that I had to sign a confidentiality agreement. Having served Queen and country for twenty-six years, I found it hard to believe that so much low-life operated within local government under the guise of working for the people. I never received a word of thanks or any other kind of recognition.

For fourteen years I had the privilege to be part of a great team, like the one at Market Rasen, which had turned a non cost-effective workshop into one that not once overspent its budget in all those years and annually received top-class reports from the the Audit Commission. So readers must draw their own conclusions as to why, with six years to go to my retirement age, I was made redundant.

CHAPTER EIGHTEEN

Retirement 1996

For a few weeks, I felt very lost and useless but I was happy in knowing that for the last fourteen years I had done my best for the people of Yorkshire. Moira and I sat down and listed all the good things we would do now that I no longer had to work. We both had a love for gardening, bowling and walking. But, the main question was where we would go, because where we lived in Bradford did not appeal to either of us as a place to spend our retirement years.

We wanted a bungalow with a small plot of land to allow the dogs playing space. By then, we had a miniature Schnauzer and a Springer spaniel; poor Spike had died a few years before, after contracting hepatitis. Scotland was our initial choice but after talking to Moira's two sisters, who lived there, we decided against it. The alternative was Lincolnshire where we had wanted to go many years before. The following day, during an over-the-fence conversation, Moira told our neighbour about our plans to move. To our surprise, that evening the neighbour's daughter came to visit us and made an offer on the house that we could not refuse. Then she told us she wanted to move in three weeks' time because they had sold their house. The following day it was all telephone calls to estate agents in the Market Rasen area, to acquire as many brochures as possible as quickly as we could, but when they arrived we could not see anything we wanted and almost every property was on an estate.

'Plan B' now went into operation. We had to go down to Lincolnshire and search more estate agents and also have a good look around the area. After two days and ten properties viewed, we had to spread the net further away from Market Rasen our first choice area. Once again, we spent a whole day looking at numerous bungalows without success. Then as night began to fall, we arrived at the very last one on our list, in a village by the name of Old Leake, ten miles out of Boston on the

Skegness Road. It was a three-bedroom bungalow on a third of an acre of land, split almost equally either end of the property. To the south, there was a garden and to the north, a yard containing a small concrete shed and a building, which in days gone by had obviously been a cottage, now converted into what was supposed to be an office and a double garage. What we actually saw was a mixture of pleasure and pain. 'Toad Hall', such a beautiful name and very appropriate with Moira's love of frogs, unfortunately, the property did not live up to the name. At first sight, the bungalow appeared to be well built but the surrounding area of garden and yard was a complete disaster. At some period of time the garden had been surrounded by panel fencing; very few panels were in place, they were scattered either inside the garden or on the side of the road, all in a very poor condition. There was a wide gateway but no gates. The yard itself was nothing more than a tip site with various old farm implements and an old car simply dumped among huge piles of soil, overgrown with chest-high weeds and wildflowers, and with just a narrow pathway to the bungalow door. The rear garden was covered in nettles as high as Moira (not very high) but exceptionally so for weeds. A huge pile of wooden boxes, obviously for burning, littered the area and rats were playing hide-and-seek, quite oblivious to the fact that perhaps their future landlords were watching them.

I turned and started back to the car. "Make them an offer, the bungalow looks good, doors and windows sound, it will give us a challenge to start our retirement and forget the past". If the property owners had been looking out at that time I don't know what they would have thought as I grabbed Moira and gave her a huge kiss. My darling never ceased to amaze me. No hesitation, no discussion, a decision made and when she did that, which wasn't very often, she was usually right. I do not think many wives, who had the money as we did to buy a ready-to-move-in property with all mod cons and in great condition, would have done what she did that day, and we had not even seen inside the bungalow. I knocked on the door and an elderly couple invited us in.

I think buying a new house is like buying a car – one is drawn to the good points but is oblivious to other things, especially when tired and a little bit fed up.

After viewing the interior, we were quite pleased; walls and floors were very good, there was central heating, which we were unable to test due to a lack of oil, and Moira had plans about decor as well as a new kitchen and bathroom. So, apart from the garden and the so-called yard, we were reasonably pleased and there and then, in accordance with Moira's wishes, I made the couple an offer, which they readily accepted. We gave them a date for us to move in, based on our buyers' wishes and, to our surprise, they readily agreed.

On the 30th of August 1996, almost six decades since the start of my wonderful journey, apart from the two-year blip, I was unaware of being about to finally join the 'unimportant people'.

In a small way, I had, unbeknown to me, already moved into that area the day I joined the workshop staff at Market Rasen. Fortunately, Colin had eased the transition from my having responsibility for a large number of highly trained soldiers to a position of being told almost everything I had to do by council hierarchy with little or no training in leadership, management or engineering. He had done this by allowing me to manage the workshop in the manner, which I had been trained. All that came to an end, once I made the move to Yorkshire. Not that I was aware, it would happen at the time of accepting the position. In fact, I understood quite the opposite. Every time I think back to my days in that council I think of fourteen wasted years of doing everything within my power to save public money for it all to be taken and misused after my departure.

I had the consolation of knowing that I had stalled them all that time and they had only managed to move me out with my help. They did not realise it at the time, but I was so fed up with their constant manipulating and whining to get their own way, I thought OK I will go, but on my terms.

Moira and I made our move and settled down to a life of retirement at our new bungalow in Old Leake, where for the next twelve months we were very happy working every hour possible, carrying out lots of alterations, repairs and, in some instances, major overhauls of our property and gardens. It was a blessing that left us little time to worry about the heinous way (although manipulated by me) our lives had been changed, and really proved to me how bad civilian management was.

Each day when the weather allowed, we would be in the garden. If the weather was not so good, we would work indoors or go shopping for the many things Moira wanted to buy to make our home nice. At the end of each day, we had a nice meal and a glass of wine as we watched quiz programmes on the television, finally collapsing into bed and sleeping like babies.

Everyday the number of garden birds increased. We even had a couple of pheasants visit the garden and Moira, as usual, managed to win the confidence of one so much it came to the back door to be fed. Almost every evening we were treated to a wonderful aerial display by the vast number of swallows and house martins in the area. That alone went a long way to convincing us we had made a good decision in buying the property.

Outside the lounge, rear window was a field and each morning we had the pleasure of watching up to twenty rabbits feed. We even watched a stoat do a ritual dance in front of them in order to put one into a trance so it could make a kill. Unfortunately, Moira allowed it to get very close then knocked on the window and spoiled the stoat's day.

In 1998, we joined the local indoor short mat bowling club to give us some form of relaxation and to meet some of the locals. (Alas, the start of that was a bit daunting; for the first six weeks before play began there was a minute's silence for one or more of the members who had died, I was dreading my name coming up). However, like many of our ideas, things escalated. What started out as one afternoon a week became two nights playing in the league plus weekend competitions. We became quite good, winning a couple of mixed pairs trophies, and when the summer arrived we were easily led into joining the local outdoor flat green bowls club at Wrangle. We spent a year there before moving on to the next village club at Friskney. Every day we became more and more involved with bowling and all our other pastimes, such as my house maintenance and Moira's never ending list of hobbies – flower-pressing, jigsaws, gardening, music and her PlayStation – and our dual love of all quiz programmes, we were fully occupied; yet that did not stop us joining the indoor bowls club at Skegness. We never went on holidays because when I left the forces

Moira made a vow never to travel again; she had seen enough airports, hotels and motorways. For the first time since we married she really had a settled home. However, she did make three concessions; twice to visit our daughter Tracey when she lived in Sardinia, and once to visit our daughter Linda when she lived in Australia.

CHAPTER NINETEEN

Moira

Readers Note: Throughout this chapter I have indicated a pause; || at various poignant moments which is my way of asking you the reader, to stop and think about what you have just read, then reflect on the experience and impact for my Darling and her carers.

Please understand that as my 'Rock' and I travelled this painful journey, it was one we did in our own humorous way.

We were having a great retirement until one day in 2003 when I arrived home from a bowls match Moira told me she had hurt herself. She had been using an extension on our upright vacuum cleaner and was kneeling to reach behind a cupboard when the cleaner fell over and the very heavy solid rubber handle hit her on the mastoid bone behind the ear, we both thought it was just bruised. A few days later, the left side of her face had literally collapsed; her eye was almost closed and seemed to be lower down her cheek, her mouth had dropped and she could hardly talk. The GP diagnosed Bell's palsy and referred her to a specialist, which took about a week. He confirmed the same and said it should clear up in about six to eight weeks. Later, she had to go for a scan to ascertain if it had been a stroke but they found no evidence. All that took many weeks meanwhile she was given no treatment at all. In hindsight, I don't think she received the best kind of medical 'care', a word that was going to play a major part in our lives from that day. The facial disfigurement remained.

Moira was devastated. She had gone from being a very beautiful woman in every sense of the word, so full of life, to being a depressed person who simply hated going out or having to face people. She didn't like the grandchildren looking at her and she withdrew into herself more as each day passed. She did however, force herself to play a limited amount of bowls.

One afternoon, whilst we were both working on the garden, she returned to the house for a break. After ten minutes or so, she rejoined me in the garden. I popped back into the house and noticed the smell of burning coming from the living room. I found she had left a cigarette perched on the edge of the ashtray sitting on the arm of the settee, having forgotten about it. It had burnt down and slipped onto the arm, and started to smoulder. By the time I had found it, there was a large burn-hole the size of a fist. This was out of character, she'd normally smoked her cigarettes to the finish.

Around 2005 she began to show signs of character change and became very abusive to our son-in-law over 'where' he had walked our Jack Russell terrier, it wasn't really the 'where' but the fact he had taken her the wrong way round a circuit, such a trivial thing, but to Moira it was terrible. Then later she fell out with a couple of ladies at the Short Mat Bowls Club, about a small matter appertaining to the rules, and she walked out, never to go back. Her speech began to deteriorate; not the pronunciation of the words but the putting together of sentences. By 2007, it was becoming quite bad and she finally agreed to see the GP.

That was followed by a visit months later to the neurologists. After more examinations and a brain scan, she was diagnosed as having Broca's aphasia and progressive frontotemporal dementia, neither of which could be cured. Life for us went on as usual, apart from Moira becoming reclusive, spending more and more time sitting alone doing jigsaws, working in her garden or walking her beloved Tina, our Jack

Russell. At that time, she was still reading six books every two weeks and playing games on her Nintendo. Then suddenly she did not want family members to visit, or even to talk to them on the telephone. She was becoming quite oblivious to the fact we had grandchildren and great-grandchildren. I knew in my heart that I was rapidly losing my beloved friend, the love of my life and the rock I had depended on for so many years and the very centre of all my goals, to achieve any kind of success since 1960. She was fully aware of what lay ahead and asked me constantly not to put her in a home or leave her at the mercy of a hospital. There was no chance of either happening as long as I was alive, and I told her so many times.

One morning, without giving it much thought, I took her into Boston to buy her some new trousers. In the department store, I helped her select one or two nice pairs, then it struck me she had to try them on, there was no chance I could go in the dressing room with her and she was unsteady on her feet, and could be quite confused. I asked one of the young female assistants if she would be kind enough to help her in the changing room. I suddenly realised my wife was so shy and reserved there was very little chance she would agree to being helped, our daughters would find it difficult with her. The young assistant came across, took Moira's hand and like mum and child they walked off together, the girl being the mum. It was then when it really hit me how serious her illness was becoming. I could have choked on the lump in my throat.

After the diagnosis from the neurologist during 2008, I had made it my duty to read about Moira's illness at every opportunity, in the hope that I could help her in every way possible. Much has been beautifully written about dementia, by many established authors, journalists and even celebrities. However, I think my darling's story, because of her cocktail of diseases, is worth writing about.

Readers Note: This part of the tale, I have predominantly taken from diaries, albeit I have not baffled or bored you with unnecessary dates.

By late 2009, I was finding it very difficult to communicate with my darling. The dementia alone is a horrible imposition for any human being. But the aphasia was so difficult, just to see her so frustrated at trying to explain even the simplest thing was heart-breaking. She was also becoming more unsteady on her feet and had one or two minor falls, but still insistent on doing as much as possible for herself. Then, right out-of-the-blue, during September 2010 I left her early in the morning to go to a bowls tournament at Skegness. I kissed her goodbye and told her I would keep her up to date with my progress, and what time I would be home, something I had done so many times before. At 12.15pm that day, I was knocked out of the tournament and tried to call her on my mobile phone to let her know I was heading home. When there was no answer after five attempts, I knew something was wrong she had never missed one of my calls before. Every one of those fifteen miles I raced back home, seemed like a hundred.

Upon my arrival, Moira was coming out of the garage, that alone was unusual. She had never been able to open the up and over garage door before; if she wanted to garden when I was away I always took her equipment out for her before leaving. She had in her hand, a piece of the garden hose about ten feet in length, which I found out later she had cut from the main hose. I asked her what was wrong and why she had not answered the telephone, she was very evasive and not like my Moira at all. After a bit more prompting the story came out, she had tried to take her life by use of the hose and her little car, which had been sitting in the garage for almost six months. Fortunately, for me (I think selfishly the wrong word because I knew her wishes) the car had run out of petrol within minutes of her attempt to gas herself with exhaust fumes. She told me she had been planning to do it for quite a while and was just waiting for me to be away from home.

I contacted the doctor and he referred her to the psychiatric consultant and, as a result of my promising not to leave her unattended for any length of time, she could stay at home. A nurse was organised to visit her monthly and Moira was prescribed medication. The reason for the attempt was that she felt not only was she ugly, but she knew in her heart that she was going to get to a stage where she would have to be looked after. She didn't want the indignity of being like a child, having to be washed, dressed and taken to the toilet. Although she promised me and the children there would be no repeat attempts, I gave up the indoor bowling and anything else that took me away from her for more than a very short period of time.

2011 – By this time I was doing all the cleaning, cooking and shopping. Moira was still doing a small amount of gardening but by then she was also suffering from OCD (worsened by her dementia) which is of no use to anyone, but to a gardener it was absolute torture. Every leaf that fell down with the wind had to be cleared, immediately, and she could not pass a weed, it had to be pulled out. Then her falling, albeit minor, became too much so the gardening she loved became minimal.

During the summer of 2012 the lady next-door looked after her a few evenings to allow me some respite so that I could play a few games of bowls. Unfortunately, she was in her eighties and her mother had suffered a very violent type of dementia before being taken into a home, where she had died. I think just the thought of looking after Moira was simply too much for her, or perhaps it brought back too many memories. Whatever it was, she went very cold on us and once I told her it was all right not to sit we saw very little of her again.

Many nights I lay awake and railed against Moira's illness but it was a waste of time and energy. Moira had quite a few falls during this time, due to her OCD drawing her from her chair in an attempt to straighten something quite insignificant to me, but crucial to her. I was very lucky really, in as much as I could always make her laugh by pretending to have a conversation with myself or telling her I was thinking of buying a parrot. We had found a means of communication by the language of humour.

2013

Our youngest daughter Linda died of cancer shortly after her fiftieth birthday in 2013. It was a very sad time of my life and today, I still think of her at least once a day. I miss my weekly chats about all the wonders of nature that we both loved so much. When I broke the news to Moira, she showed no emotion whatsoever. That night she told me with great difficulty that she could not cry. I did however know what turmoil was taking place within her mind. People say dementia sufferers are in a world of their own and do not understand. I do not believe that is so, I have seen deep within my darling's eyes, the windows of her soul.

Each day there was some change taking place within my girl. She was becoming more agitated about what the future would be like for her. She would continually grab my hand and make me promise that I would not put her in hospital or a nursing home. By then, I had taken to carrying out all her daily ablutions for her including her dressing and undressing.

As the next few months passed, it was becoming obvious that her balance was quickly deteriorating. I had stopped many activities and we survived on my quick trips to the village shop. The number of times I left her in her beloved garden doing a simple job, such as weeding or dead heading, minor tasks which I felt sure she was safe doing, only to return home to find her upside down in a bush with her legs up in the air. The laughs we had.

From then until early 2014 I noticed slow progression. We were still going to bowls together, albeit not as often and one of the club members would be kind enough to sit with her, while I played. Moira was still doing her jigsaws, very slowly and at times with great difficulty, which she never had before. She constantly had her beloved music on but how much she listened to; there was no way of knowing. In fact, any visitor who saw her at first glance would think apart from her face, there was nothing wrong with her, and that, is the way she wanted it to be. Then she started having more falls, luckily nothing drastic but enough to tie me even closer to her.

Every day seemed to bring something new. She would have a few days feeding herself, which she insisted on doing, although I knew it was becoming very difficult for her. Numerous times, she had difficulty swallowing or she would spill her drink or tip her food dish all over herself, or on the floor. Then she would become very agitated and I would have to calm her down. Just to hold her beautiful hands and talk to her was tearing me apart, I could feel everything she was going through. Quite often she would put her hand on my cheek and manage in her own way to say sorry. So many times, I had to leave the room, my heart breaking. What on earth was she sorry for?

I always returned to my darling with a smile and a cuddle plus ten minutes of funny rubbish simply to take her mind off everything.

‖

2014

March 2014 – It was by pure chance that I found help, nobody tells you any of these things. The doctors knew our situation, the Dementia Society knew, but not a word of advice was provided. I had a mobile mechanic visit to fix a small fault on the car, during the time he was there I had to leave him to pay regular visits back into the house to ensure my wife was safe. Now Moira was going through what I called, the 'walkabout stage'. Either she would be watching TV or asleep in her chair when I left her to do small tasks, but there seemed to be a switch, which would turn on the moment she was left alone. Quite often resulting in her getting up to follow me or set-off on another venture. Usually ending with either a fall or knocking something over (we had a beautiful seven-piece frog orchestra that one day became thirteen pieces). After a very short time of me going back and forth, the mechanic asked what was wrong and I explained; "I know a lady who does caring, she may be able to help, I will ask her to call you."

That was the start of a wonderful leap forward for Moira and me. That evening a lady visited and agreed to sit and care some evenings for me. She told me that Moira should be entitled to some help from the county council so that I could have some respite breaks.

The first council number I telephoned could not help, but passed me to another department. That morning, I was on the phone for almost an hour, which in itself is very stressful when you are trying to listen for and look after someone with my darling's illness. Little did I know that this would become a regular annoyance in the years to come. When I did finally get through to someone who could help, I was told an assessor would contact me. A week later, I received a call during which a date for the assessment was set for two weeks later.

‖

The big day arrived and after two hours of questions and form-filling the assessor agreed that Moira could have 12 hours per week of respite care paid for.

One month passed and I still had not received the confirmation or final documentation, although the assessor had said to go ahead and pay for care, ensuring I would be paid from the day of the agreement. That is quite daunting, to see that amount of money being paid out of our bank, at the end of that month I had paid out £560. The first payment from the council was paid into the bank 13 weeks after, by which time I had had to find £1,751. How many people in our situation have that money to pay out? I suspect, they most simply had to wait until the payment was made before having the use of a carer, and would have struggled on. That was repeated with every reassessment as my wife's illness progressed.

||

Once I had the OK, and the money to pay for at least one carer, the council must have passed my name to private agencies and they were on the telephone within a short time, wanting to run the fund on my behalf and organise carers for me. I had already tried a private care company when I was told I could be able to pay for extra care. So, I politely refused. Now I had two very experienced carers looking after my 'Rock' and I could have some respite knowing that she was in safe caring hands.

||

The more time I sit and think about my darling's young life and the more information her brothers and sisters passed on to me, it seemed that it was violent and very upsetting, all of which she kept to herself. I did however, notice that the girls of the family were all gentle like their mother, and the boys simply frightened of the father. Over the fifty-four years we have been together, I have noticed bits of a true personality being born. Now her illness seems to have created a wonderful blossoming of what should have been.

Tadpoles have hatched in the pond Moira had me build for her seventeen years ago, to encourage her beloved frogs to live in our garden. Quite a surprise because that is only the second time it has happened in all those years.

We had a good laugh today. I like to show her photographs at regular intervals to help keep her stimulated. Today we were in Borneo once again, one photograph was of Moira playing badminton with a very dear friend of ours called John, whose parents were from Africa (one-time non-stop walking world champion). This is you and John playing badminton, she pointed to John and clearly said; "me?"

We were supposed to have a visit from two of our children, but unfortunately, had to cancel. It is always nice to have visitors, someone to talk to. It is so difficult, having someone you love sitting alongside, never speaking or being able to answer, and if she does, it usually ends up in a screaming session because she becomes so frustrated. Then, I have to dig deep into my memory for some of the oldest jokes on the planet to change it into laughter.

||

This morning I sat Moira down on the bed after her morning ablutions, but too near the edge for safety, so I asked her to jump up and back a little, in order to help me dress her and to seat her safely, not really expecting any response. To my surprise and complete disbelief, she made a super human effort and her legs shot up in the air, resulting in her completing a full backwards somersault and disappeared over the other side of the bed. What a sight in full flight, we were both in stitches. Who knew she could have been a gymnast!

We had laughed our way through the earlier years of two or three visits to see the consultant neurologist. Twenty-nine miles in each direction for ten minutes of his time during which he would ask;"Are you all right Mrs Horn? "I could even see the laughter in my darling's eyes. If she could have answered yes or no, there was no way he could check if it was the correct answer. Then he would have her very reluctantly raise her arms up high (she was never keen on PT before her illness) and I could sense she was being stubborn, one of her many lovable traits. I would often tell her, long before her illness that her ears were growing like a donkey's. Then came the grand finale – the walking test. I had told him she tripped up very easily when she was outside; off she toddled like a four-year-old. His face was a picture of success, and my darling's about to burst into laughter. At the end of the walk, she did a turn, which would have been a delight on 'Strictly Come Dancing'. So, I politely pointed out to him that his beautiful linoleum-covered floor was nowhere like the roads or pavements outside, full of notorious potholes and the pavements full of cracks, just waiting for someone to trip and file a claim.

||

Twenty-nine miles back home and we laughed all the way. That was the best treatment my wife ever got from the NHS. After the next few tests at the two hospitals, I stopped taking her, it was not fair on genuine cases awaiting treatment to waste valuable time that way. I believe there are very few in the medical profession who know anything worth knowing about dementia. The real knowledgeable ones are the genuine carers and in most cases, I exclude the ones who work in care homes.

At that time, I decided that our eldest daughter and our son had to sort out Power of Attorney for Moira and myself. Just the thought of something happening to me and my wife being left at the mercy of a council was hard to imagine.

Her illness had by then reached a stage where I was about to embark on a journey of complete ignorance of what lay ahead. I took everything on board so that I could be with her all the time. Much to my shame, I think I manipulated certain people at every opportunity to help.

Dear Frances, a retired school teacher who lived a few hundred yards away, volunteered to bring me a Saturday morning newspaper, so I used that offer to include milk or other small items. That developed into asking, "If you are in town this week would you mind picking up?" She was so willing and genuine about it. I have always been so independent so I felt very guilty.

||

I booked an appointment to see the doctor about total hip replacement (THR). What little sleep I had last night, I was very disturbed by my constant listening for Moira. I swear my ears are getting bigger as each day passes. Usual day not much change. At night, I played bowls first game of the new season.

During the summer months, I managed to play a few more games of bowls, dependent on who I could cajole into sitting with Moira. With me, being from the old school, I married Moira for life, and it was my duty to look after her, I made the vow. But, most important she was the love of my life. As I cuddled my darling in her chair, my eyes were drawn to the window and the field behind her. There, I could see a dozen or more swallows skimming across the grass. The music playing in the background was one of her favourites, Demis Roussos singing 'Mourir aupres de mon amour'. I hope heaven is like that if there is one, and I am allowed in. At times like these, the mind can fully relax and think of all the beautiful things our world has to offer. I feel for my darling, I know from being with her almost all the time, her thoughts are blocked inside her mind and available to her alone, simply because she cannot communicate in any real way.

||

Today she has played constantly with Linda's bracelet on her wrist. At night, I was awakened with the most painful cramp in my exterior ligament – a result of Peripheral Neuropathy (which the consultant had diagnosed but told me he did not know much about the reason for – a bit like a Tommy Cooper sketch). It took quite a time to clear, walking around the bedroom and then the bone-to-bone grinding inside the hip joint was horrific. I must have this hip replacement, if the surgeon will even see me.

We moved some of the furniture out of Moira's room to allow easier movement of the walker. Moira has been helped with her breakfast and has settled down in her chair to watch the TV, and I go into the kitchen to clear up. On my return she has her hearing aid in pieces, and part of it is missing. After an extensive search, I finally find it. What she hides things there for, I will never know.

Today, one of our granddaughters visited with her two children. They grow lovelier each time they come. I can see you my darling in all the grandchildren and great grandchildren. The beautiful blonde hair on most is inherited, from you.

I wonder what it must be like, for all of them being frozen out of your life? They have never, and will never know the beautiful Gran or Nan whichever they choose to call you. If they had, they would have been overwhelmed with your kindness, the willingness to partake in transporting them back and forth to any activity they chose to do, in their young lives. 'Super Gran', someone who would have played computer games on a par with their generation, someone who would have never tired of listening to the many imaginary problems life will throw at them. Unfortunately, my darling these joys have all been denied you.

So sad my darling cannot enjoy them, she shows no interest at all. That night after being settled down in bed after the visitors had gone home, she not only managed to climb out of bed but out of the bedroom. I looked up and behold she was standing in the doorway using the bookcase, by the living room door for support, with a big smile on her face, like a naughty child. Although there was no reaction during the family visit, something had stirred inside her mind. I managed to get her back into bed after much pushing and pulling and the use of a slider sheet, but she had a very restless night. If only I knew what goes on inside my darling's mind.

‖

This morning, having taken the opportunity to slip away down the yard while Moira sleeps on, as I was filling the bird feeder in the shed I had the strange feeling of being watched. I raised my head and looked out of the window of the shed into the field behind, and less than two yards away, stood looking at me with its head on one side and an expression of great curiosity, was a Rhea (a South American bird like a white ostrich with the most beautiful blue eyes) the last remaining one owned by a neighbour. She had always kept them in a pen a long way from our property, but had now decided to let this one roam around the field. Not everyone has a joy like that to start the day.

‖

Tonight at 10pm, I gave Moira a new tablet prescribed by the doctor to stop her screaming and banging on the bedroom wall. At 1010pm I helped her up onto her walker to take her to the bathroom for her final ablutions for the night forward but her legs never moved. I could not pull the trolley back because her arms were locked, and her whole body was horizontal. How I managed to get her to the toilet and then to bed, is a complete mystery but that night something was on my side.

‖

Bright and early this morning I heard a Spitfire flying nearby, unfortunately I could not see it. Strange how I can still remember the sound of that engine seventy years after watching them high in the sky as we made our way to school. The memories came flooding back. So long ago, so much and all good.

During the day as I sat holding Moira's hand I thought never once did she tell me in any depth anything about her parents. Her mum's history was very vague. All I knew was her family were tin miners who lived in Cornwall and when the mines closed, they moved to Newcastle to work in the coalmines. Mum-in-law herself came across to me as a very beautiful lady, who had been bullied into complete submission, doing and saying only what her master (her husband) allowed of her. Her dad, I knew a little bit more about, as a result of a trip my darling and I took to the north, to where her remaining relatives lived. He was one of a family of six boys, all professional boxers, and one girl. The boys were known as the fighting O'Keefes. During that visit, we managed to acquire a small book titled 'Liniment and Leather', which includes their names and many of their fights. Two brothers only were still alive, Tommy and Eddie, and we had the pleasure of meeting Eddie and his wife from whom we heard a couple of nice anecdotes. She told us how her husband, a ten-stone fighter at the time, had knocked out three huge miners with four punches one night outside a public house for saying something rude to her. "Oh! that's right" replied Eddie who was in his eighties and very frail, "I missed with the first punch".

Later that day, when we sat down to dinner she told us that Eddie fought twice one Sunday down on the beach, first in the morning, then home for refreshments. While he was having them, she stitched up his facial cuts before he fought again in the afternoon. What a remarkable man! I was very proud to be married to his niece.

Tonight I sat watching Moira, as she was being made ready for bed by one of the carers, while she played with the buttons on her cardigan completely oblivious to everything around her. Just to see her helplessness tears me apart. She is fully reliant on care for the rest of her life now, how hard for her. If I had a dog in a similar situation, the vet would release it with dignity. Why are humans so cruel?

Everybody should have the right to make a 'life will' while they are still capable and have it witnessed in a lawful manner. I was always taught as a child; I am responsible for whatever I do, I am responsible for myself, and my actions. Not some unknown, who in most cases hasn't a clue about life, saying no to my actions, you must suffer. Why not, it's my body, why can't I decide when to go?

||

Tonight I put my darling to bed before I gave her the tablet; we had enough fun last night. 0200 am – crash, bang, Moira is up and out of bed, once again it was a real struggle to get her back between the sheets.

A carer sat with Moira this morning so that I could visit the consultant about my hip. I agreed to let him operate. Then on the way home, I had second, third and even fourth thoughts, about going ahead with an operation, a few reasons were playing on my mind. I had looked at some of the nurses on my visit, their turn out and their attitude rang the 'infection bell'. The consultant also said, that apart from the pain and the bones being in the wrong place, he had never known a hip even as bad as mine fail, which had been my greatest concern. Final thought; every moment with my darling is so precious to both of us. Meantime, I will continue to push the pain barrier by using my weights to exercise my hip and keep the muscles good.

My thoughts from last night broke my heart, because we all have a selfish streak, and I dread the very thought of losing my darling. I want her to stay, even though she wants to go. But, everyone should witness what happens to dementia patients. Inside their minds' they must have to absorb their worst nightmares of having to be treated like something completely useless. With the help of the carers, I do everything possible to make every one of her days good. But, I know when I settle her down at night she is tortured inside, going from being an independent strong person to this shell.

This morning I telephoned the surgeon's secretary and cancelled the appointment for my hip surgery. We are now on first name terms, I bet he really loves me, and I doubt if the time ever comes, he will operate on me.

Worried about my darling today, she looks very tired and is extremely vague. Very little response to anything, even with two of us; myself and a carer constantly prompting her. I was supposed to play bowls tonight but I have cancelled to stay with her. When alone after settling her down in bed, I cried for her as I often do. This illness is so cruel.

||

Moira tried very hard to help herself in every way today; I could see it in her eyes. Unfortunately, her mind was not responding. Tonight I held her in my arms for such a long time until she dropped off to sleep, then I laid her head gently on her pillow, gave her a good night kiss and she never moved again until the morning.

||

Such a beautiful morning, I have had a nice walk around the garden while Moira still sleeps. It is such a busy time of the year for nature. We have a nest of fledgling blackbirds hiding amongst the plants, waiting for their parents to arrive with their regular food visits. Tina, our Jack Russell is confined to the house or brought out on a lead; she has the constant urge to kill anything that moves. At times like this, I reflect back to memories of our dear late friend, Miss E, whose house in Hampshire sat alongside the River Wey. We had so many beautiful summer holidays there.

Flowers have been arriving much of the day; it is my darling's 74th birthday. Thank you friends and family. Perhaps somewhere deep within her tortured mind she will understand and realise they are for her.

Once again, I have problems with elderly help. A district nurse arrived to administer my three-monthly B12 injection but she did not have the serum with her, she said it was my job to collect it because she is not allowed to carry it with her, but a 'man with a van' can deliver drugs every week, and not just mine!

I telephoned the surgery staff to ask if, during one of my respite periods, I could call in and have the injection carried out? No!, I was told that I must make an appointment. The injection takes all of ten seconds, less time than it does to type the appointment on the PC. When we arrived here twenty years ago the surgery had six very experienced doctors, now it has two main partners and the rest are junior doctors or locums. They tell me that is more cost effective, I do not believe those comments at all. However, I would have thought the main concern would have been for the patients who see a different doctor almost every visit.

||

What better time and place to start this phase of our journey than awaking at five thirty on a beautiful morning, near my lovely wife of fifty-four years.

She had started her night at 11pm by constant banging on the bedroom walls, one of the many stages of her progressive dementia. At 1.30am, she finally succumbed and is still sleeping heavily, and I am exhausted.

||

The dawn chorus I love so much has not long started and my favourite bird the Mavis, or if you are not from the countryside the Song Thrush, has been making himself heard above all the others. I was completely mesmerised by the range of his singing. Over the years, I have had the pleasure of hearing many but never one with the repertoire of this beauty, completely mind blowing. One of nature's many beautiful gifts to start the day on a happy note.

During the night, the smoke alarm starts bleeping, initial panic, but after a good look around everything is OK. Now I have a dilemma, the battery is going flat and it is bleeping continuously. To remove the battery I have to climb on steps and I feel pretty useless having to restrain myself from doing something so simple. If I fall and hurt myself, where will my darling be? Meanwhile, every few seconds 'bleep, bleep'. I do hope it doesn't wake Moira. After a short time the bleep starts to fade, good – no such luck, it starts again.

Come the morning, one of our granddaughters arrives with her partner. At last, the cavalry has arrived! He tries to remove the battery, but with no success so he removes the whole unit from the ceiling and puts it in a drawer. Lovely – silence, unfortunately Moira has now awakened and starts screaming so the family depart. This seems to be the only solution we have found, to calm her down in these situations.

I shower her and then make her comfortable in her chair, 'beep beep' from the drawer again – it has come back to life. I leave Moira to make a cup of tea, I can hear a string of unrecognisable words and see her pointing toward the toilet, surely not, she's been already, but to calm her down I stood her up on her walking frame and made the trip again. Once inside the bathroom she started pointing frantically and erratically. The bathroom window is not open wide enough, and the picture on the wall is not straight, OCD is no joke. She must have spotted those things on her first visit and remembered them.

Moira is trying to eat breakfast by herself, I must allow her to be independent as much as possible. I sat next to her sorting her medication for the day when suddenly her spoon flew up in the air and she screamed out "pee pee pee" about ten times. She had startled me so much I had dropped all her tablets and I was trying to pick them up before Leah, our rescued Staffordshire bull terrier, managed to find them. Meanwhile, my heart rate and blood pressure had rocketed to a record level. Once again I thought, off we go to the bathroom again, but she calmed down as quickly as she screamed out and carried on eating her breakfast with her hands, as if nothing had happened. Luckily, for me, my heart seems to be capable of taking such shocks, we had a laugh together. I told her as a result of that shock, the next time I went shopping I was going to buy a Lord Nelson suit, red jacket and brown trousers, as he had requested before going to battle. The red jacket did not show the blood if he was wounded and would be good for the men's morale, and the brown trousers? – work it out – an old joke but it made her laugh.

||

A very quiet Sunday. Moira very agitated and pointing to herself, so I started asking lots of questions. Is it a pain, are you hungry, do you want a drink and many more, before I finally understood she wanted some sweets, the only ones I dare let her have were soft chocolates. Luckily, I had some in the fridge, because she had not been interested in any sweets for many weeks, it was so nice to see she actually wanted to eat something she loved in the past.

At night, Moira dismantled her hearing aid once again. When I put it back together she started screaming, I keep trying to tell her one of the switches on it is preset, and no matter how much fiddling, she cannot adjust it. Then she tried to get out of bed, half an hour later I had managed to quieten her and cuddle her off to sleep.

||

Very wet today. The carer sat with Moira for a couple hours doing a 500 piece jigsaw, a come down for my darling who used to do a 2,000 piece every week not so long ago. Nice to see her trying once again. The carers are very good and make every effort to keep her stimulated. Moira looks so tired and the carers are concerned.

Carer took Moira to Skegness for a fish and chip lunch, eaten in the car looking out to sea, a view my darling loves so much.

||

What a beautiful sunny morning. Unfortunately, I had a painful night, as a result of my arthritic hip, which I should have had replaced many years ago. However, at the time I chose not to, on the grounds of as long as I can manage, leave well alone. Then when Moira was diagnosed, there was just no way I was going to leave her. Now it has reached a stage where the two bones do not like each other when they meet and have to take my weight. A few twisting and wiggling exercises of the hip and leg usually solves the problem. I just have to hope it doesn't happen in the supermarket or crossing the road.

Moira awake very early and had breakfast in her usual way, a bit here, a bit there, then the odd coughing and choking. Not too bad, she seemed pleased with herself. Shower time – something she always enjoys. As I was drying her I asked her, "How about you and me doing a nude run through the village, and see if we can get any response from the locals?" Well that started her day off very well. She laughed in her own very restrained way, which we have all come to recognise.

We gave that idea a miss and I settled her into her chair to watch the TV then I gave her a cup of tea and a piece of cake. I had fully prepared her with a bib and I turned to sit next to her, then crash, the tea went one way, the cake another. Once again, I disappointed the dogs by retrieving the cake before they could get to it. My fault, I should have helped her more. Unfortunately, I am still not accepting what is happening to her and how far I can let her do things for herself, all I know is my heart cries out for her with every day that passes.

At 8pm she is in bed calling out unintelligible words. That lasts for more than half an hour during which time I keep looking in on her, to see if she is trying to escape. I know that sounds awful but it is a joke between us, which I think sometimes is not a good idea because it encourages her to try. Then again, it always makes her laugh and it must help in some small way to keep her mind active.

||

Moira has had a good night and is still sleeping at 9am, I take advantage of the respite to attempt to cut Leah's toenails. I managed to cut one last week, it would be easier to fight twenty pythons, I have to be very deceitful with the clippers, by hiding them behind my hand. I manage to cut just one more and then she went into a series of backward somersaults, followed immediately by forward rolls and a grand finale; a circuit of every room in the bungalow, all in a space of ten seconds, or so it seems. A sight to behold.

Last night I had a long one-way talk with my darling before she went to sleep. It is said, that sufferers such as my girl do not know what is happening because they are in a world of their own. Sometimes, when she asks me the football score when she is watching a drama on TV, she is in another place usually at the Emirates Stadium watching Arsenal. But, I often look into her eyes and see hurt and mental pain and then I know that something deep in her mind has come to life and I feel so useless.

||

Moira awake at 0815am calling out for me quite clearly, quite unbelievable. When I sit her up in bed, she is very agitated and looking at me with a strange vague expression. Once again, she called out "Peter" then she gripped my hands – this is a very rare occasion.

We have a nice sunny morning to start the day, but very misty for about two metres above ground level. Reminiscent of a scene from the film Great Expectations, when the convict Magwitch came up the river in a boat; (creepy). It frightened me as a child and I still find it very disturbing.

Moira had a couple of screaming sessions during the night. From the little I was able to glean, I understood she was concerned that I was leaving her. So, this morning we had a reassurance cuddle.

The carer took Moira out to a garden centre for a look around, followed by some lunch. Good respite for me and a change for my darling not having me to look at, for a couple of hours.

Today was one of constant demanding from Moira, much of which I could not help her. In the evening when she was watching TV, I took the opportunity to slip away and have a quick shower. On my return, I noticed she had a cushion on her chair that had been on the settee when I left her. To retrieve it meant she had to stand up and move it across. Initially I was really upset with her, what if she had fallen? It also leaves me with no option but to cancel another small task, in order to stay even closer to her. I felt very guilty at being so sharp with her, but at night after a few good hugs and a sorry from me, she went to sleep with a smile on her face. I think she does these tricks on purpose to wind me up.

||

Very quiet morning, granddaughter and her two daughters came to visit in the early afternoon. Moira seemed to enjoy them being here and actually gave them a hug, which was so nice to see.

At 3.30pm we had a most wonderful hailstorm, the stones were dancing all over the lawn for a good five minutes, such a joy to watch.

That night, my darling went to sleep without screaming or wall banging. Once again, the visit of the children must have been a good tonic for her. Although upsetting, and knowing that the majority of the time she did not seem to know who they were, it was lovely to know that there was still something within her mind, which just needed a certain time to bring it forward.

||

What a beautiful start to the day. Then, as a result of all the damage to my hip and back, one turn too fast and my knee locked up. To release it requires a lot of painful twisting and bending. Moira seemed to understand and I think inwardly was having a little laugh as she did each time I was injured playing rugby.

Today I purchased a small blender and a selection of fresh fruit to make my darling smoothies, in the hope I can improve her fluid intake to keep the dreaded urine infections at bay.

We laughed and hand jived to some of her favourite music, or I did, while my darling looked at me in a very strange way, I think she thinks I am daft. That night, I was very tired and aching all over, even that small amount of exercise can have an effect when one is almost eighty.

||

I awoke very early with Moira foremost on my mind, not unusual because today is our fifty-fifth wedding anniversary. We laughed a lot during our nonsense half hour and just waited for the flowers to arrive, which in due course they did. I do not think she understands what they are for. Every time she strokes my face or squeezes my hand, I think of a wild bird in a cage. It is as if, suddenly she realises the door is open and she can be free and then as she reacts and makes a move towards freedom the light seems to go out and the door closes.

||

Moira woke up with a very heavy cold. I sat her up at 6am but it was quite impossible to get her to cough and clear her throat to help her airway. So, I put an inhaler mask on her face to try and help. We will have to see how the day goes.

A few weeks ago, I applied to the council for help to convert our bathroom into a wet room. Unfortunately, I was refused on the grounds that I had more than one pension. The wet room is essential for the safety and cleanliness of Moira, she can no longer step in and out of the shower safely. Strange how my pension is ignored when assessing my darling for care. I was told, that was based on her income because she was the one who is sick. However, if I had been on handouts and in rented accommodation, that would have been OK, making the landlord better off by one nice new wet room. I can actually have it converted by a local builder at a quarter of the price three other builders were offering, when I thought the council might help out, and they knew who would pay the bill. The mind boggles.

Moira seems to be a bit better this morning, she dirtied herself during the night, I cannot imagine how she feels. Never mind, I still make her laugh, but today that was not a good thing. It made her cough and as a result, she wet herself. Every time I enter the kitchen with my arms filled with washing, I imagine the washing machine screaming and trying to make a run for it.

Tonight I put her to bed very early because she was really tired. As we did every night, I sat talking to her and then gave her a kiss and a cuddle. I will probably have the cold in the morning – who cares.

||

Today, with help, I moved all the furniture, except the bed, out of my darling's room to manoeuvre her walker, and eventually any other equipment she may need. She had spent much of the night coughing and I was with her numerous times to help her. Then to finish off the night, I was awakened with the most painful cramp in my exterior ligament, which the consultant told me to expect when he diagnosed peripheral neuropathy. To get rid of it I had to walk about the room, then the hip went bone on bone. The joys of getting old – one thing about old age, it doesn't last long, not to worry there are lots worse than us. I must get this hip sorted.

Today I really did see the lack of team spirit in civilian life. For a few weeks, I have had an extra part-time carer as requested by the other carers, to help them out. Unfortunately, she lacked in knowledge but she made up for it in kindness and willingness to learn. However, the two main carers were not willing to help her or bring her into the team, they have constantly niggled about her inadequacies, finally making it so uncomfortable, she walked off the job. Now they are not satisfied. "What are we going to do? We have no 'bank' now, we can't manage, we must have time off to rest". That means another carer is required, a new face for Moira creates panic in Moira's mind. I have told them, continuity of care is essential, unfortunately they always know better.

From the start I discussed with both carers as professional as they are, that to make any group of people work together successfully requires team spirit. The result of that was, they knew all that and didn't need me to tell them how to run the system. I could not see any point in being firm about the subject, as it would only lead to me losing one, if not both of them. They simply did not know the meaning of the word 'team'.

Great day, I managed to find another carer. Unfortunately, she has not been trained on handling and hoist work. It seemed to me to be a very simple task for anyone who has had more than a week of use. Nevertheless, as before, neither carer was willing to train her in readiness, if a hoist is finally required – more lack of 'teamwork'. It was by now quite obvious to me that neither wanted anyone else taking hours, except if they needed to be off for some reason. I called in a private company to train the new lady, I now wait and see if they can work together. None of this has been good for my wife and has highlighted a basic flaw in their good carer status.

||

I spent a long time reading and talking to my darling. We went down memory lane, all the way to the beautiful island of Cyprus again. I told her how I remember with such fondness the day she was towed out to sea behind a speedboat on a small board, no bigger than a tea tray. She, as per usual, was the first to volunteer, "Nutcase" as one of my young soldiers said very quietly to his friend, unaware that I could hear him. I must admit I agreed with him, you had no fear of anything.

Come bedtime, my darling was not walking very well on her frame. I finally managed to move her into the bedroom, only for her to try sitting down, where there was no seat. It was a terrible strain trying to hold her; thirteen and a half stone. She thought it was very funny, unfortunately, I was in no mood for laughing as much as I love her, and I was very sharp with her. When I finally settled her in bed I was very ashamed and I cuddled her for a good long time.

||

This morning my love has not recognised me at all, maybe she is getting her own back for last night. We had a very quiet day together watching tv; Moira keeps drifting off into sleep. At night I have to ask one of the carers to help me put my love to bed, because she is finding it very difficult to stand and walk with her trolley, even with my support. I must now find another way to manage her, the carer suggests I speak to the occupational therapist and arrange for delivery of a hoist. My heart sinks because I know it is another path of no return, but there is no other way.

Telephone call to OT nurse, the only department that has been helpful, since my darling first became ill. Hoist arranged.

That night I had planned to go bowling while one of the carers sat with Moira. During the day, she was very agitated and kept screaming, and making hand gestures but I could not understand what she wanted.

I went to the bathroom to get ready to go out and she was still calling out. When I came back out she was flat on the floor, I could not raise her, so I called one of the carers who came very quickly. They have been unbelievable for me, no agency could ever care like these girls, such a shame they lack in team spirit. Together, we managed to get her back into her chair only to find she had dirtied herself, hence all her gesturing.

What a conclusion to life. Needless to say, I cancelled my bowling that night and a carer helped me to put her to bed.

During the last few minutes before I settled her down to sleep, I reminded her of how she took on the SAS boys and others from the jungle warfare school in Borneo in the welly-throwing competition on Jubilee Day in 1977, and she won. That's my girl.

||

My day started at 5 am I heard Moira moving about. When I opened her door, she was struggling to stand up at the side of the bed. It was a very tricky operation to support her before she could turn and bring me down with her. No use, she fell onto me and I was lucky to remain upright. Once again, I had to call a carer and between us, we washed and changed my darling before putting her in her chair. Later that morning, I telephoned the council with the intention of getting extra carer hours to help me with her ablutions and every day movement. True to form, I had the usual run around from department to department before I finally found someone willing to take some responsibility – that was another hour wasted. That time, one of the ladies I managed to contact, actually moved quite quickly and gave permission to have 24 hours per week care. But as always, the money wasn't paid into the bank until 6 Aug 2015 by which time I had to find 9 weeks @ 24hrs x £11.32=£2445. So incompetent, I wish I did not have to rely on them. Unfortunately, it is the only way I can have my girl looked after safe and with dignity.

I have now received a hoist and a special bed for Moira, all thanks to the OT team. Unfortunately, the bed was delivered without side rails and the engineer did not notice until he had dismantled Moira's original bed and erected the new one. He made a telephone call, but they cannot deliver until tomorrow. I will have to be extra vigilant tonight.

The carers are showing change, once again they have suggested that we need another carer, what they call a 'bank', who can allow them to have days off, or take a holiday. That makes good sense to me, so I advertise with very little results, except one or two who are on a par with agency carers, who I had dealt with previously. I struggle to make Moira's present carers understand that if they want a 'bank' the 24hrs care I had been granted, must be shared three ways in order to attract someone. They were insistent that the 'bank' did not have any hours, just simply to be on call, for whenever needed. I asked them who in their right mind would sit waiting for hours with no pay, to work at short notice? Once again, they knew better. As I said earlier, the way civilian life operates puzzles me, not only was I learning about Moira's illness and another way of life, but also selfishness, a trait I did not particularly like.

||

Moira seems quite happy with the hoist and shower chair, thanks to the OT team. Now the two carers are complaining that the hoist is difficult to move on the carpets and they may damage their backs. So, I call in two men to rip up a very good carpet, and lay a wooden floor. Meanwhile, I have seen another type of mover for Moira called a 'Sara Stedy'™ and put the idea to the two carers, the fact that I would prefer this for my darling because it will ensure she has to stand up to be moved, at least four times a day. That will ensure exercise for her, plus the opportunity for the air to circulate around her back and bottom, which can reduce the chance of pressure sores and lesions. (I cheated really, because I had read up on it). This was met with resistance – "No way, it is not the way it should be done, it's impractical and dangerous to try and lift her, plus it is our job". They more or less told me keep out of it!

Later that day, I telephone the OT department, and asked if they would come on a visit to show my carers how to move Moira safely on the steady.

0940 am. My love is still sleeping after a good night. As I look out of the window, a young blackbird is sitting on the edge of a flowerpot underneath the overhang of a rose bush sheltering from a morning shower. Just such a sight is quite comforting, the world really is beautiful, especially our garden.

True to form, two OT operatives arrive to instruct my carers on how to stand and move my darling. It was with great reluctance that the carers listened. They were determined the hoist was the best way and not the 'Stedy', I had to step in and say that I wanted her moving with the 'Stedy', for as long as possible.

I read an article yesterday about a scientific research into animal communication. They could have saved money, simply by watching any household pet, especially if there is more than one. The love between each other is special, and they do not have to be the same species. We could learn so much from them if only we could accept that we are not superior.

This morning my love and I played a game, and I had her laughing. We tried to use tapping as a form of communication, one tap for yes, two taps for no. I don't think she got the hang of it. She has now started doing something different. She taps on the table constantly at the side of her chair, I can see it becoming annoying, but currently it is good, I know she is trying to make contact or simply just to annoy me, and whatever – she is thinking. Unfortunately, she cannot make use of the tapping to answer any questions.

A day which has become quite regular, feeding, cleaning, choking, refusing to drink, pouching and bringing food back up. Forgive me my darling if that sounds awful, not meant to be; just my day and I do it with every bit of my love.

At night, a carer and I put my love to bed. All is very quiet for a couple of hours, then the 'church bells' start to ring – she has activated my latest purchase, an escape alarm situated under the bedside mat, she had stood on it. Fifteen minutes later, I had her settled back in bed with the use of the lift and a slider sheet.

||

I opened the kitchen door this morning to a layer of dog vomit and urine. Looks like Tina our little Jack Russell has had a stroke, I took her out in the garden but she was back into her bed almost immediately and back to sleep. She is very old now, so I hope that she passes peacefully in her bed at home, I will not take her to the vets.

Moira slipped in the shower this morning and made a very nasty groove in the soft tissue on her shin, there must be two of us for this task in the future. During the afternoon, my darling has gone very vague and is showing a complete lack of interest in anyone or anything. Each day, my darling seems to go a bit further into her own little world. If there is some other power, please look after her.

Tonight when I put her to bed she grabbed hold of my hand and squeezed so hard, then she started to adjust my shirt collar and stroke my hair and face, she is trying so hard to tell me something. It's just too much, I had to leave the room for a few minutes.

‖

Tomorrow I am having the bathroom converted to a wet room, anything to make life easier for my little 'Rock'.

This morning I witnessed the most wonderful flying display by more than twenty swallows all around the property. I have not seen that since the first week we moved here during 1996.

‖

The wet room is up and running, much better for all, including the council, who have saved a lot of money. Not that they would ever think of that, it is not their money.

Moira quite alert today taking notice of most things, and engaging with carers, which is so nice to see. Unfortunately, at night, another Moira has arrived and managed to have five sessions of wall banging.

8 August 2015 – fifty-two years ago, today we were blessed with our youngest daughter, Linda, she died from breast cancer. I still do not know if Moira understands.

All our children and grandchildren telephoned today, the anniversary of Linda's death, to ask if we were all right – nice thoughts cost nothing.

‖

Lovely start to the day, Moira is going to Skegness on a day out with two carers. For a few days after these trips, she always seems to be more stimulated.

The swallows are gathering on the telephone wires. I do not know why, because it is far too early to be thinking of their trip to South Africa, plus, they do not travel together. Perhaps it is some kind of a planning meeting, if so, I hope they have more success than our leaders; otherwise they could finish up in Siberia.

Tonight, I listen and watch as the carer gets my darling ready for bed, always a heart-breaking period of time. I had to take a firm hold to stop from crying. My little partner of fifty-five years (not so little now due to her immobility and diet) has been so proud, shy and self-reliant, now she has to have everything done for her.

10 pm – The house is filled with snoring, Moira plus two dogs. Those are the sounds of contentment.

||

Today I employed a lady physiotherapist to massage Moira's legs and feet each week, hoping it may help with ILS (irritable leg syndrome) and circulation. I will do anything possible to give my love some quality of life and comfort.

Moira had a good night and after breakfast I settled her down in her chair to watch one of her many murder programmes, she had seen numerous times before. I took the opportunity to get the steps out and dust the tops of the wardrobes, a much needed job, (forgetting about the rule I had made previously of not taking risks). No more than a couple of minutes after starting, "wee wee wee" blasted my eardrums. I literally jumped in the air and turned around forgetting I was over a metre from the floor on a pair of steps, gravity took over and I landed on the floor, thankfully on my good hip. When I limped into the living room, Moira was quietly watching the tv. Never a dull moment however, it was a wake up call for me, another job I had to refrain from doing myself.

Some days there is little or no pleasure in opening the mail, but not today. I had a quick read then sat beside my darling to read the bundle of joy right on my sense of humour wavelength, that our postman had brought to my attention.

1. From the Cooperative Society; *How to plan my funeral?* Do they know something I don't?
2. Sun Life – *How to start a policy, no medical required for up to 79-year-olds.* Dash – just missed that.
3. This one filled me with joy – *Where to buy tablets for my prostate problem*
4. *Where to buy Haemorrhoid Cream.*
5. Sales pitch for a lifetime watch – *Buy one get one free* – The mind boggles.
6. Finally – a luminous alarm clock, *saves switching the light on to see the time.* This one I bought, only to find out the numbers are luminous, the hands are not! We both started the day with a good laugh.

Moira very quiet now, at a stage where I have to feed her all her meals and drinks, and toilet trips are becoming more difficult. When she is sat in her chair, she insists that I sit beside her all the time. If I get up for the slightest thing she becomes agitated before screaming, the carers get the same treatment.

I must not read or use the laptop. If not careful, I will lose the use of my legs.

||

After breakfast this morning, I took a little time teaching Moira about confidence. Myself and the carers have noticed that her weak foot has started to turn outwards and seems to have a mind of its own, making it difficult for her to step onto the 'Stedy'. I told her to be very assertive with it and each time she stands to say, "turn around Prat". I went through this with her a few times with no response, with the hope that somewhere inside she may give it orders. Ten minutes later the carer popped her head around the door and said; "Good morning Moira" she received a nice clear answer "Prat".

This week I purchased a small pedal machine with the hope that we can encourage Moira to use her legs while sitting in her chair.

Yesterday the council finally paid the money into the bank, which I have been chasing for months. Just to prove how incompetent they are, it was paid again today. Unbelievable, they have paid twice. I contacted them and got their bank details to return the second payment immediately. Afterwards, I thought I should have just left that in the bank to see how long it would be, if ever, before they realised what they had done, or else used it as payments, the next time Moira is reassessed. That way I would not have to spend hours on the telephone chasing the increase.

Tonight my darling dirtied herself and soaked her chair; once again, it had escaped the protection covers. Just another job to do before I can go to bed tonight, it did not matter, I would not have slept, she was banging on the bedroom wall for almost an hour.

||

Moira very rarely tries to speak but this morning she actually said "Sorry" which alone tells a story, we hugged and had a good laugh.

Overnight snow has fallen over our little piece of the world. It is so white and beautiful, as far as the eye can see.

As a result of an advertisement I put out for carers, one is coming to see me tomorrow.

A wren woke me up this morning at 0530am singing his little heart out. My mind thinks of those people who constantly complain about how difficult life is. That little bird is no bigger than a 50p piece and has to face a world so full of danger and yet he has the temerity to tell the world he owns this little patch of our garden. Great!

This morning a lady arrived for the carer's job, not very experienced but willing and lives very near, so I set her on, much against my present carers' wishes. They are now trying to tell me, that should be their job. Now I wait with bated breath, to see if they will put the team spirit into action.

This morning, I telephoned the receptionist at the doctor's surgery to re-order Moira's prescription. After waiting what seemed like a lifetime, a young lady eventually answers; "Sorry Mr Horn you are on the wrong line", and tells me to telephone 'extension two'. Another lifetime waiting for an answer, then a young lady with a familiar voice answers and I ask "Can I please re-order my wife's prescription?" "Certainly" she answers. Then I asked, "Did I just speak to you on the other line?" "Yes" was her reply. Unbelievable! Why didn't she just stay on the first line?

Moira is coughing and choking lots when taking her meals and drinks (even though we use thickener). I must stay with her throughout meals now to ensure her safety.

I spent almost the whole day reading to her, which usually ends up sending both of us off to sleep. At times like this I know what effect I have on people.

Before bed tonight, my love had a pointing session, which I could not understand, so it ended in five minutes of screaming along with her becoming very agitated. My poor darling, I do not know what she wants. But it is so difficult to know what is troubling her because she constantly changes her point of focus.

||

A big day today. After months of council telephone assault courses, I have finally managed to get together for an assessment meeting the people responsible, to allow my darling continuous health care and respite hours. It was quite a shock when all the parties involved arrived at our home, they actually do exist. I really believed they were just names on paper, something to blame. Two ladies from the county council and one from the NHS, a senior district nurse, the leader of the team, and a psychiatric nurse plus my eldest daughter, who came along to record everything from the meeting which was to be held in the kitchen. Having been employed by a council for the last fourteen years of my working life, I am very aware of their lack of integrity. They have a wonderful way of promising, but they never follow up.

The meeting went quite well and all indications were that the NHS and the county would share the cost of Moira's care from that day on. I am very happy I now know that my darling will get all the professional care she needs for the rest of her life.

The only disappointing thing about the whole meeting was with the district nurse, the lead on the panel. All the others had met my wife at some stage, but she had never seen my wife before, and whilst filling in the final questionnaire and completing her notes prior to leaving, she asked my daughter; "Is your mother Caucasian?" to which my daughter's response was; "Why don't you go in the living room and have a look?" She was leading a team and didn't even know if my wife existed. For all she knew I could have been doing a Norman Bates. She still left the house without seeing my darling.

I wish I could tell the council to get lost and pay for everything myself. Every step feels like begging, and every step is delayed in every way possible. My son tells me off for trying to get financial help he thinks I can manage without them. But I am old school and have paid into the system since I was fifteen years old, I feel I am entitled to what I paid for. But now, it seems that anyone who has not paid anything into the system is given help more easily than my generation. It would appear that the highly paid bosses who make such decisions (I will not insult the good managers by calling them such) surround themselves with obsequious sycophants.

||

When I entered Moira's room later that morning she was awake, staring at the window. No movement, or recognition that I was there. When I spoke to her, there was no answer, not even a movement. Wherever she was at that time, it was not with me.

Human beings? I do not know how we can call ourselves such. Brief definition; humane, considerate and understanding. Inside that shell, my darling of a 'Rock' is hurting for both of us but we must keep laughing.

Today, I actually saw a squirrel on the bird table, that is certainly a first. Not many about here due to the lack of trees. My back is bad and I find it quite difficult to walk, but I must soldier on.

Later, one of the carers sat with Moira and together they wrapped small presents for the great grandchildren. Just trinkets they had collected over the year during Moira's trips out. Throughout, there was no change in my darling, her eyes were just fixed on the presents. Afterwards the carer tried to involve her in doing a small jigsaw, but to no avail.

Later that day, Tracey arrived and together we put on a nice buffet lunch for Moira and her carers in appreciation of what the carers do, beyond their normal duty. The first signs that day, that Moira was with us.

||

I telephoned the hospital reference my total hip replacement. They tell me nothing yet has been received from my doctor, later in the day he tells me a letter was sent a month previously! My fault really, all the times I've cancelled, they've every right to ignore me.

This morning I stood over Herman, our little Schnauzer's grave in the garden. Strange how long forgotten thoughts come back, I remember being asked by a man doing gardening for us, "Was he a big dog?" to which I replied; "His exterior body was very small, but internally he was huge". I remember very fondly what a little character he was.

Our previous house was situated at the top of a very steep hill and on his daily walks I would take him into a field nearby which had a really vicious decline, stretching down to a sty which led out into a country road. Before I let him off the lead, I always checked the road for cars and people walking, an easy task, because I was literally looking down onto the road below. (He was mad on people, especially children.) Once set free, off he would go, right down to the sty some two hundred yards away, turn and race back up the hill. That particular day for some reason, my mind was elsewhere. As he made his rapid descent, I heard laughter, and walking along the roadside in the distance were a number of children and behold, a car was travelling towards them. Herman heard them and no amount of my whistling had any effect, through the sty, he went, at the same time as the car was passing. BANG! My heart missed a few beats, he had been run over. I covered that ground in seconds. On arrival a car was there, driver's door open and a distraught lady stood apologising to me, "I am so sorry, I never saw it coming, I am so sorry"; "Where is he?" I asked, and in chorus the children called out "He is in that field." Back through the sty I went, expecting to find he had died somewhere, which is common for animals hit by vehicles. No sign. Then there was a movement among the long grass, out came Herman. Oh my god what a horrible sight his face was, completely knocked over to one side and his lower jaw well out of line, badly broken or even worse. Before I had chance to think what now, he stood up tall (as tall as miniature Schnauzers can) and vigorously shook his head and everything fell back into place. Much to the delight of the children, who by that time, were alongside me. They cheered and made a fuss of him as I went back to console the lady. Then I saw her car door had the most horrendous bulge in it, Herman had run head first into it. She declined my offer of payment, saying she was only too pleased our dog was all right. That was only one of his many incidents throughout his life.

Moira is having great trouble walking with the trolley, even with the two carers to support.

Still knocking on the bedroom walls a bit at night, but less than in the past and she is sleeping better and longer.

||

Today I tried to put a spreadsheet on my laptop, must seem strange to my children and grandchildren, but having been brought up during the times of horse and carts, coal ovens and an old zinc bath hanging on the outside wall, I find it difficult to understand why, when I put something on to my laptop, it often vanishes, never to be seen again and it has cost me two hours of my life, with no result. My grandchildren simply say; "just press a button, you won't break anything". That seems to me to be a very strange way of doing things.

||

Another birthday, mine. I still enjoy every day, even though I never imagined that our life together would come to this. Physio arrived to work on my left knee; my left leg is now considerably shorter than my right and is causing many problems. It's my own fault, it pains so much sometimes when taking my full weight.

How my dad, who lost a leg in WWI, managed to hop up and downstairs all his life is unbelievable. The only help he ever received, other than the most horrible prosthetic leg, was to have a handrail fitted to help him down the series of four steep concrete steps leading to the front door of the house.

At one stage today, Moira suddenly screamed out quite clearly; "Want to miss it". The words themselves were quite unusual but the fact she could say them so clearly after such a long time of no word clarity, was unbelievable. I tried everything to understand what she meant and after about ten minutes of pointing to almost every ornament and item in the house, I finally pointed to the alarm clock. Then she suddenly became very excited and I realised what she had tried to say was; "What time is it?"

Moira banging on the wall for only a few minutes tonight, then off to sleep. She also had long periods of sleeping in her chair throughout the day, during which time her limbs kept going rigid or her face and jaw became distorted, as if in pain or in spasm. When I told the carers that this had happened two or three times during the day, they said it was possibly TIA's (Transient Ischaemic Attacks). I mentioned it to the doctor who says it possibly was, and offered for her to go into hospital for tests, which I declined. I don't want her sitting around, nothing they can do, it's part of the disease.

When my love started becoming ill, I started missing her for short periods, but now it is different, she is drifting away. I had a game of bowls tonight; one of the carers looked after Moira until my return. When she was in bed and the carer had gone, I stood in the kitchen and remembered times when we bowled together. Sorry to say I lost it, I hope it eases the tension.

Had a long chat with the dogs tonight. They sat looking at me as if I am daft, they are probably right, but loneliness is no joke. It is true what is said about dogs helping to reduce stress, I watch and listen to them as they snore the night away as they lay beside me, each one has a single ear standing upright and every few seconds it changes direction slightly, always listening.

Call from the lady from the council once again, payment for Moira's care delayed, yet again. The council creates stress beyond belief, eleven weeks now since the agreement.

||

Each day it becomes more difficult to get Moira to drink, and I have to liquidise everything and all drinks have to be thickened to stop her choking. During the day, I constantly give her teaspoons of juice, tea, ice cream or lollies to help the fluid intake. In two days time, my darling is 75 years old, and 55 of those we've been together. I've been so lucky.

Tonight, when I put my darling to bed with the help of the carer, she managed to tell me in her own way that she did not feel very well. The carers agree it best to keep an eye on her throughout the night, which I did at regular intervals.

||

This morning she told me by way of our many hand signals, thumb up or down, or short bouts of excitement when we struck the same cord, that she did not want the doctor, she did not want to be messed about with anymore. I know this may sound awful to some, but my little 'Rock' wants to pass with dignity.

||

Today Moira seems better. I heard a cuckoo in the field behind the house. For the first ten years after our arrival one had a territory behind the house and one in front, and that continued every year until 2006.

At last, the National Health Service have begun their payments for Moira's care.

||

I awakened this morning to the smell of smoke in the house, a big worry until one of the carers said that the cause was the stamens on the lilies Moira had been sent for her birthday. She cut these off and within minutes, the air smelt fresher. You learn something new every day.

I telephoned a care company today, in desperation for another carer to help, let the other girls have a break. I had vowed many times I would never use a private company again, but my adverts in the papers are having no success.

||

The area manageress from a large care company came to see me. Having spent more than a quarter of a century in the forces and 16 years as a senior manager in civilian life, I wasn't very impressed with her turnout or presentation, seeing as she was seeking work for such a large company. Never mind, I may be a bit harsh, I needed a carer. She told me the cost would be £16.50 per hour, which meant I would have to pay £4.00 per hour myself. Not to worry, my wife is my number one concern. Then we got to the part of, how soon could she send a carer, today being Friday. "I will be interviewing three girls on Monday, then they have to do extensive training, so you could have one next Wednesday". I was absolutely speechless.

"Will that be all the training they have?" I asked? "Don't worry they are extensively trained by me personally" she replied. "Oh by the way" she followed up, "do you have any carers now"? "Yes", I replied. "Well, they will not be able to work with my girl, as company policy states they will not be up to our standards". At that stage, I had to speak out. "The carers I have at present are very experienced ladies with over 40 years of experience of working with every kind of patient, your girl of three days cannot work with them. I am pleased that you have made that statement, as you would have to pay me, for my carers training your girl." That was the end of the meeting, much to her disgust. I knew I was right about care agencies.

||

Nature is very strange, for a good few years Moira and myself have been trying to replace a beautiful flowering plant called a hypericum, which was in the garden when we arrived. But it died, our efforts to replace it have been unsuccessful, each time we bought one, it died off. This week, there are two successfully growing in the garden, obviously planted by the birds who know more about planting than we do.

Today, I paid for a special wheelchair-adapted taxi to take Moira and the carers out for the afternoon.

The evening was very sad, Tina had to be put to sleep at 1810 hrs, no more pain. She is now at rest and will be missed more than words can say; Bye `Shorthouse`, until we meet again. As I sit here tonight and Moira has gone off to sleep, there is a lump in my throat and I feel the whole world has collapsed. My little friend of 14 years lies outside in a grave under the cherry tree with the rain pouring down on her. I felt so guilty, could the vet have saved her? But I did not want her to have any more pain. It will take a long time, if ever, before I accept her absence. Many times during the following weeks, I call for her or hear her feet clicking across the kitchen floor.

||

There has been very little communication or recognition from my darling all this week. I cuddle her every morning and every night, but she does not seem to know who I am.

Another carer started today, very good, with all the relevant qualifications. Moira seems to like her and that's the most important thing to me. My darling has now found a new toy with which to annoy me, she has an alarm around her neck in case anything happens to me, one press and help will arrive, she does not need to talk. Now she has realised she can get my attention simply by pressing it. A speaker comes to life in the hallway to accept her call and tell her help is on the way. I have to quickly intervene and stop it, with the excuse that I am just testing the system. After three times during the course of the day, I finally take the press button away from her.

Cheryl, daughter number two, arrived today to clean the pond out for me and as usual, she brought me a present, a bottle of Auchentoshan whisky. Later that night, after the pond job was complete and Moira was asleep Cheryl said; "I will taste a drop of that whisky, I have never had any of that brand before". Her tasting stopped three hours later when she was flat on her back in the conservatory. When she was back on her feet, off to bed she went. During the night, there was a loud bang and then silence. Come the morning she told me she had fallen out of bed and slept on the floor. Never mind, what a night, fantastic – Cheryl, good on you girl. The best respite I have had for a few years.

Moira slept almost the whole day, my heart cries out for my girl. I had a telephone call from a bowling friend of mine, he lost his wife today. She had a very violent dementia, it was very sad and a wake-up call, knowing it's only a matter of time before I lose my darling. Tonight, Moira is not very responsive, the carers are concerned, but we know it's no use calling the doctor, we understand it's the progression. It is heart-breaking to be so useless, just sitting holding her hand. I feel like crying for my little 'Rock'.

||

This morning, as I looked out of the window into the garden I remembered our little Jack Russell doing her morning walks anti-clockwise around the perimeter of the lawn, something she had done for 14 years and always made me smile, creature of habit, the way she stopped every few yards to listen and bark at goodness knows what. She would toilet then return back indoors and beg for my breakfast, how I miss her. Strange thing, since she died Leah goes through the same routine, only she goes clock-wise.

Moira not responsive at all today, she really frightens me. She has now started falling asleep whilst being fed, very awkward with food in her mouth, it's horrible. I feel for her every minute of the day and night, when I am awake.

||

I am very quickly turning into Victor Meldrew. I have purchased a jar of top quality baby beetroots only to find more than 50% of them were rock hard. So, I telephoned the company to speak to a young lady in customer service who said that it's the end of the season and the quality is very poor, I told her that on the jar it states "only the best quality" and the price has not been reduced. "I am very sorry" she says, "I will send you a voucher to purchase a couple more jars". I shall really look forward to some more hard beetroots!

At last an offer to sort out my hip at a private hospital. I have been trying to teach my regular visitor, the Rhea, to come to my whistle. This morning, I decided to give it some windfall apples from our trees, thinking that she would peck at them and eat them in pieces. Not so, she immediately picked a whole one up, threw it in the air, caught it and swallowed it and repeated this with about 10 others, with each one she swallowed, she gained lumps along her throat and I was quiet perplexed that her owner might be chasing me for compensation having choked her Rhea, nevertheless it is quite funny to see.

NHS gave the okay today for me to pay for taxis to take Moira, wheelchair and carers out for a day once a week. Fantastic, Moira really loves the seaside.

My darling much more responsive this morning, she held my hand for quite a long time and occasionally gave it a squeeze. Such a small thing, but it gives me a wonderful feeling.

||

Today I drove my car for the first time since my hip operation. What a difference, no effort and no pain. If I tell my son he will say; "Silly old sod, I told you to have it done years ago". If I had my time again, I would do no different. Every moment with my little 'Rock' has been precious to me, who could say that everything would have gone as well, years ago.

Today, I read about the gentleman whose wife was in a dementia home and told him she had no wish to live any longer, as a result he shot her. My heart went out to both of them; it must have been an awful dilemma to find oneself in.

During our journey together, I have found that councils and government bodies really do not care about the elderly, no matter how many costly pamphlets they distribute, and units they set up. If they did, there would be no private nursing homes, except by choice. They would provide council-run care homes with good, effective management and properly paid carers. (We spend £12 billion on foreign aid.)

Privatisation very rarely works. A large portion of all funding is lost immediately to pay shareholders if there are any, or taken for profit plus high salaries for very incompetent management. But, and most important, whoever has the responsibility on the council for elderly care has a large part of his/her annual salary to do a successful job. Instead, they simply farm it out to whoever, in most cases with contracts that are useless. Hence, the majority of care homes are a disaster and the money is wasted.

Another year is coming to an end, I should not grumble but I know I do, it is my pressure release. Me and mine are far better off than most. Until we meet again next year ...

> *May the road rise to meet you*
> *May the wind be ever at your back*
> *May the sun shine warm upon your' face*
> *and the rain fall soft upon your fields.*
> *Until we meet again may God hold you*
> *in the palm of his hand.*

A great start to a new year. Sophie our great granddaughter is off to hospital, as a result of pushing 'Blu Tack' up her nose. God only knows what the doctor will find, her finger is always up there, but then again most little children are preoccupied with their nose, and various other parts.

There has been little evidence of Moira understanding anything for many days. I spend as much time as possible to engage her in a range of things to stimulate her. She used to attempt to play her favourite game of Scrabble with the carers, unfortunately, that became too dangerous (who would think). She had started hiding the tiles in her mouth, once in there they are difficult to retrieve because my darling is into another phase of this awful disease. She has started clamping on anything that gets near her mouth, glasses and cups are no longer used, anything she can break or chew off with her bite which is unbelievably powerful, is banned (we have to be very careful with our fingers).

OT department brought Moira some safety toys, made for her by a lady and her friends. How nice of the ladies and the OT girls for thinking about my darling. Most days, one of the toys gets locked in her mouth. Sometimes, she is taken to the shower with a lovely stuffed penguin clamped between her teeth.

Then the game starts, myself, or the carers have to remove whichever animal it is, in order to shower her and put her to bed. We have to trick or bribe her with a chocolate, but she soon understands and our tricks have to change on quite a regular basis.

Tonight the two carers hoisted her to take her to the bathroom, contrary to me asking them to use the 'Stedy' as much as possible (they are determined to do what they want). Unfortunately, they made a mistake positioning the sling and as a result, Moira left a trail of excrement all across the lounge floor. (There is a saying; what goes around comes around). If my darling knows what has happened, she will be crying inside.

||

Today my darling started pouching a lot, she takes a spoonful of food, goes through the actions of swallowing, then she accepts another, at which time I can see her mouth is empty, that is also swallowed. The carers are elated at the fact she is taking food. Some thirty seconds after the last spoonful, everything she has taken comes trickling back out of her mouth. The brain is not going through the normal procedure, I may be wrong, but none of the carers or the doctor seem to know much about it, or why it happens.

I watched my darling attempting to do certain things with a carer. She was trying to hammer wooden pegs into a pegboard with a mallet, just like our four-year-old granddaughter had done a few weeks previous. The difference being, my love could not do it. My 'Super Gran' as the grand-children call her, is now reduced to being a young child, with little or no control at all.

||

When Moira has been settled for the night, I watch the most beautiful sunset. Our neighbour has a host of baby trees inside plastic tubes in his field, and the sun is making them glow like fire sticks – how beautiful.

Up at 01.30am to change my darling's pad, very wet, I must protect her skin. It is a vicious circle, push fluid down her to stop urine infections, result – more pad changing to stop pressure sores or moisture lesions.

Today not a good start, the latest and the better of the carers who spends a lot of time stimulating Moira, is leaving. She has been offered another job with more hours, she will be a big loss. I know Moira really likes her and that is very important.

||

During the day, I change Moira's top three times due to pouching and the out-pouring always manages to get past the bib.

The final move of the day, she has wet so much and it has escaped her pads. That means the chair, the cushions and the cover have to be washed and dried tonight, ready for the morning.

Another bright start to a day. After ablutions and breakfast I spent a lot of time talking to my darling about her garden, how I did the maintenance and she spent the whole day chasing weeds. Sometimes, she seems to be listening, other times she goes off to sleep. Then I quite often hold her hand and marvel at her beautiful skin, which since day one has fascinated every one of the carers. They make comments almost every time they shower my love, about her skin and hair. She is in her mid-seventies and does not have a blemish or a varicose vein at all, and her hair is still as blonde as the day we met, with no artificial aid at all.

||

I tell them perhaps it is the way she looked after herself, she showered only every other day and used the very minimum of basic soap, anything else damages the skin and hair, was her comment to me, and she was very sparing with all forms of make up or creams.

Carers took Moira out to Parrot World, I think she enjoys her days out. The main thing is, she has time out in the fresh air and a change of scenery.

||

Today I feel a little bit down and I think, depressed. I never thought I could ever feel this way, I have always preached positive thinking to all my family and it was a key word for all my life-coaching clients. But unlike anything else in life, I know there is no positive outcome for my darling and I know she is in real mental pain. I will however pick myself up, each day becomes lonelier and then the mind starts to play tricks.

My love has just managed to remove a paper towel I left under her chin, and she has very quickly stuffed it in her mouth. I must retrieve that very quickly or she could choke, I hope I have all my fingers left at the end of this process.

No sooner had I succeeded with the towel task and started to feed her some drink to overcome a dry mouth, than the spoon was clamped very firmly between her teeth. Now it is a matter of waiting, the more I try to remove it, the tighter she clamps.

April 2016

I saw my first swallow today, after its long journey to South Africa for the winter. Once again I had a deep feeling inside that life starts again, if only it could for my darling.

Each day my body seems to be changing since the hip replacement. The feeling is returning to my feet and legs, which I believed to be Peripheral Neuropathy. Now I have my doubts, unfortunately nobody seems to know the answers.

This morning Moira appeared to be asleep in her chair, her mouth open wide and her breathing very shallow, I held her hand and started talking to her, she did not open her eyes however, I felt her hand squeezing mine. I gave her a little fluid and tried to coax her into closing her mouth in order to swallow. That normally takes a few seconds or longer for her to react, she tries and I watch her with a heavy heart. I can see the frustration of her knowing what to do but nothing is happening, a simple swallow which just happens without any thought, is now beyond her most of the time.

The doctor visited today and asked if I would like my love to take some swallowing tests, I declined on her behalf, she has had so many and the result is, there is nothing they can do it is a normal progression of the dementia. So, why waste hospital time and resources.

||

A most unusual happening took place today. I have been a very keen birdwatcher and lover of nature all my life, during that time I have only very rarely seen long tailed tits and only from a distance as they flit through the foliage. But today, quite unexpectedly, two arrived at the bird table. After feeding, they both came to the kitchen window and proceeded to peck at the glass. Such shy birds and today I had the great pleasure of seeing such beautiful birds close up. Wow!

Another day and behold the tits are back at the window.

A usual day of trying to encourage my darling, to drink, or eat ice cream or lollies. Then, during the afternoon when she was asleep the horrible twitching and distortion of her body started again. Once more the carers thought it could be TIAs, apart from that she had a decent day and night.

26 April 2016

Elsie-Linda born today, our latest great granddaughter. If only my darling could be part of the family again. Sadly, she shows very few signs of knowing anyone most of the time.

||

Our granddaughter Amy visited today with Elsie-Linda and her two elder sisters Abigail and Sophie. What a change in my darling, she held the baby and hugged the other two, so lovely to see.

Today I had a nice long talk with my sister who has lived in America since 1963. She asked after Moira and when I told her about clamping and bringing food back, she knew all about it. Her son died in a car accident a few years ago, which I was fully aware of. However, I did not know that, as a result of that accident he suffered a Broca's aphasia, the same as Moira. That was only part of what killed him, but it was enlightening to know the doctors in the USA knew all about clamping and the return of food, which they call harvesting.

Our neighbour has bought a small piece of agricultural land between his house and ours, and is in the process of turning it into a small wildlife park. Now in its second year, and after a lot of work, it is looking beautiful. I delight in viewing it all the time to see the many changes taking place. Something else, I think my darling will be missing.

Not many swallows returned this year. Nature is certainly on the decline thanks to man and his greed. No doubt, it will be blamed on global warming, as most illnesses are blamed on smoking and most crime on a poor lifestyle. Bunkum! The majority of old people they are saying live longer today, creating great expense to the NHS and social services, are my generation. We lived through the war, with smoke fires and fogs that had to be seen, to be believed. Almost everybody smoked, and in winter time it was a community 'must' to clear snowdrifts up to ten feet high. Oh yes, we had no antibiotics, or a chemist full of vitamins. I cannot be convinced that those three things are responsible for the sorry state the world is becoming, my belief is the three things to blame are greed, greed and more greed.

Today is dull but very warm. The garden vegetation seems to be growing as I watch. It brings back memories of the Borneo jungle, sitting there at 5 am as the rain falls and rises immediately as steam, not an animal or bird in sight, the sounds my friend sat alongside me is recording, are out of this world. It is very strange how the smallest thing triggers the brain to go searching through the files.

Moira went to bed nice and quietly tonight. After a few minutes of hugging and singing to her, she was asleep (no surprise with my singing).

A nice new day starts with the dawn chorus. After which, I prepare all Moira's needs for the day ahead and I make smoothies each morning to supplement both her fluid and food intake. She seems to enjoy what she manages to retain, I hate to see her dribbling all down her front, we put bibs on but it still manages to wet her clothes. This is a cruel illness.

||

The carers and I, thought it might be a good idea to buy a fish tank and a few small fish as a point of attraction for Moira, another form of stimulation. Once I gave the word, off they went to the garden centre with Moira to select one, returning with a very nice expensive orb shaped bowl plus all the artificial plants and its own air supply and of course, three very colourful fish.

When Moira had her phase of wall banging at night it was disturbing, but now she very rarely does it, I am at a loss and wish she would bang, just to let me know she is there.

||

Today I received a telephone call from Moira's eldest brother to inform me that Moira's twin brother Shaun in Australia was also suffering with dementia, he had recently suffered two strokes and wasn't very well. I thought it best not to tell her, although I had my suspicions she already knew.

Her mum once told me on a rare occasion, when she was allowed to talk, (I think Moira's dad must have been at the pub) that when the twins were young Shaun was the weak one. He was born with weak eyesight, a very poor physique and was not very bright, the perfect target for bullies. Consequently, my darling, although a slip of a girl, battered half the students at Lapage Street School in Bradford on his behalf. Out of all the family, she was the one who had inherited the boxing genes of her uncles – she was frightened of nothing. As time passed, she was always there to help him and he took full advantage of it. When he decided to emigrate to Australia in the early sixties, I thought good, duties over now, look after yourself. How wrong I was. Until 2008, she continued to listen to his drunken tales of woe, usually in the early hours of the morning. By then she was not in a good place, and she told him not to telephone any more unless he had something nice to talk about. The result was, he never called again.

Moira had the 'twin thing', as I called it. The experts call it ESP (extra sensory perception), I never found out if Shaun had the same feelings. When anything happened to him, she could sense something was wrong. Hence, my reason for thinking she knew more than I thought.

Very strange how days can be so different, today Moira ate everything she was given, no clamping on the spoon, no choking, pouching or bringing back. Why?

||

A very sad day, I was informed a very dear friend of ours has died. Thomas Fuller wrote, if you have one true friend you have more than your share, in our case we had four. The one who has died, Barb was a great lady. Whenever we talked on the telephone or met, it was time spent happy and laughing. For forty years, we have been friends. Tonight I had a couple of drinks to a lovely lady who only knew how to be cheerful and enjoy life. Wherever you are Barb keep them laughing, you will really be missed. But I, for one, know you are still very near. See you later.

Another day, but not so good for my darling. She is refusing everything and has spent much of the day sleeping.

Different again today, no refusals but constant clamping. Later when her mouth is finally empty, she is playing with her numerous soft toys which she strokes and cuddles. Much of the time, I now leave her with them because she seems so content. The problem comes when I try to remove them to have her eat or drink, myself or the carers have to trick her into releasing the wet chewed object. No harm really, she seems to get a great deal of stimulation from such games.

My doctor insists I go for a knee x-ray. I will oblige although, I feel sure there is nothing they can do, it is all about repositioning my undercarriage after years of neglect.

One week later and there has been little change in my beloved; each day varies with her moods. Some days she is quite bright for a few hours, at such times she accepts her toys, or partakes a little in games carried out by myself, or the carers. Another time, she just drifts off to sleep. She now has a new toy, which she has taken a liking to, a doll, which the carers have named Toni with Moira's help, named after our dear late friend from Hampshire. She has to have it in her arms to hug and even takes it to bed with her, whatever is safe and brings my love some pleasure is my constant wish.

||

I had my knee x-rayed today, simply to pacify the doctor and please our children, who insist I do as I am told.

13 Sept 2016

Three years ago today our youngest daughter was laid to rest; I am still holding your hand my darling.

I have to constantly tell our children, do not worry about mum and me, we are all right. They have their own lives to live and families to enjoy. Sometimes I need a little help with the computer, that is when the younger generation excel, but unfortunately I cannot understand their teaching method; "Just press a button".

Today Moira's youngest brother was diagnosed with motor neurone disease. Once again, I do not think there is anything to be gained by telling my darling, I do not know what her reaction would be. (Talk about rain and pouring.)

Tomorrow is one of our grandson's military passing out parade, which I promised him I would attend. Unfortunately, the knee is still too painful to take my weight, for more than a few minutes. I cannot take any risks, Moira is my number one priority.

Moira has a very slight increase in the time she is sleeping during the day, and she is clamping and pouching a lot more. I spend most of the time sitting with her and it is playing havoc with my figure. I have to laugh when the doctor says "Rest your knee".

Today I purchased a wheelchair-adapted car so that the carers can take my darling out at every opportunity when the weather is good and is convenient for them. It will be much more flexible than booking a taxi. Why did I never think of it before? I just hope my little 'Rock' enjoys her days out, it is almost impossible to know if anything at all is happening because she very rarely responds. All the carers and I can do is feed her, clean her and CARE for her.

Moira is now deteriorating slowly each day so I can now notice the changes. Today was bad for my love, almost every drink or small amount of food was either, pouched, refused or brought back up. For some reason she was very agitated and continually squeezed my hand. What are you trying to tell me, my darling?

||

At lunchtime the doctor had called and asked to speak to Moira, after all the time she has been unable to speak? Then he asked what kind of eye drops I use in her eyes to stop them becoming sore? He is the doctor and it was he who prescribed them (very sad).

Today the carers took Moira in her wheelchair for a walk in the beautiful sunshine. At night she went off to sleep very quickly, obviously the fresh air had been good for her.

One of the carers left this morning in quite an abusive manner, she refused to stop and give me a reason for such actions. I have always left them to do whatever, with no interference from me as long as it was in an agreeable manner to all concerned. Something has happened which I will have to find out and overcome as quickly as possible.

Early the following morning the original carer has also left with no explanation. Once again, their professional status seems to be questionable. Now I am in trouble, only one carer plus myself and one young lady I can call on if desperate. What on earth has gone wrong?

Today we managed, and in the evening, I tried to contact the carers, in an attempt to find out the problem but to no avail.

Another day, but with a big difference; a shortage of carers. I immediately telephoned the previous carer who left for another job, the one Moira really liked. I asked her if she was still employed, with my fingers crossed. "To tell you the truth, I did not leave for another job and I haven't worked since leaving you," she replied. "I left because I did not like what was going on behind the scenes, and I did not want to cause any upset for Moira". "Will you come back?" I asked. "Not if those two self-imposed seniors are still there," she said.

"Well, they are not" I said. "I will be there in the morning" she replied. At that moment I could have jumped for joy, if it wasn't for the hip and the knee. Now I had two carers and two more names that looked promising, plus a 'bank'.

My words about civilian work ethics were so true. The two initial carers were poisoning the team in order to control all the hours, and I had not seen it by leaving them to organise it among themselves. They were also being very disloyal behind my back. I will, however, never criticise their caring.

After all that, my darling and I had a morning hand jiving session to some of her favourite music without her leaving her chair. Later that day I saw the consultant about my knee, nothing he can really do just carry on as I have been doing.

Moira is spending extra time in bed; she has a small moisture lesion at the bottom of her spine. I feel very guilty because I now know it may be my fault. By turning her on to her side at night, to change her pad I may inadvertently have stretched and torn the skin. (It is very delicate and like thin paper). So now, we leave her on her side without pads for a short time to allow the air to circulate and the lesion to dry and repair.

Today she ate her breakfast of porridge, all was fine until the last spoonful then she clamped tight, for a few minutes, finally releasing and allowing me to feed her a few spoonful's of juice, before opening her mouth to show me it was empty. Then all of a sudden, all the fluid came rushing back out. The look on my darling's face was one of great mental pain and uselessness, and horror at the way she is. I hugged her and consoled her for such a long time.

||

Another Christmas and New Year has come and gone almost unnoticed as far as me and my darling are concerned, Moira is now in a very lonely place and has very little reaction to anything. Even my rubbish humour no longer brings the smile I always long to see. All the days seem to mingle into one.

||

2017

15 Jan 2017
This morning, for the first time in many days, I raise my darling in bed, she leans forward stretches her arm and strokes my hair (what is left of it). Then she proceeds to explore my face before putting her hand behind my head and pulling me into a kiss. By that time my face was wet through with tears, such a long time and now something has awakened.

||

Tonight, when my love was asleep, I did a memory test. I had to set my watch so that I could start and stop after thirty seconds, during which time I had to memorise twenty objects. That I did quite successfully then realised I had forgotten to start the watch. Failed at the first fence, never mind, it helps to keep me sane.

24 Jan 2017
Awakened by a tawny owl calling, letting the world know he is surviving no matter what us humans are doing to his beautiful planet. Each day my darling takes less food and drink, and spends very little time awake. I spend much of my time sitting at her side holding her hand and talking or reading to her.

29 Jan 2017
Informed this morning, that Moira's twin brother had died, the previous day. In my heart I knew more than a week ago, something was happening. After all our years together, I could also tell my darling's feelings. When I told her (I felt duty bound with it being her twin), the reaction was astounding. She immediately perked up, gripped my hand ever so tightly and would not let go for some time.

||

This morning Moira was taking food and drink: a complete change from the past week. Later, when I was talking to one of the carers she said, "That can mean one of two things, Moira may now be a bit better or things could now deteriorate". Unfortunately, from that moment the latter took place.

A week later and my little darling is drifting away. She is eating and drinking very little and is in a deep sleep much of the time. Today I spoke to the district nurse and she said my 'Rock' is in the late stages of her illness, my heart sank. She is on her way to join her twin, and the world will be very dark for me. How selfish even to think that way! I prayed that if there is some form of God; "please do not let her suffer".

8 Feb 2017
Doctor visits today, I told him I was finding it difficult to give her medication – "no worry, I could stop all that now". Those words were like being stuck with a knife, he said he would inform the palliative nurses.

Tonight my darling's wedding ring fell from her finger and rolled across the floor.

13 Feb 2017
Moira is not very good, sleeping with her mouth wide open and she feels very cold, no response at all apart from the choking sounds she makes. Not very good, I say to myself, but there are two ways of looking at it, it is very hard not to feel selfish and I know what my darling wanted. She has suffered far too long, the loss of her looks due to the palsy was bad for her, then losing her speech, followed by her dignity, and finally her mobility and her choking. I do not believe there is a God, at least not as religion teaches.

Our son and daughter arrive followed by three grandchildren. Very bad day – my darling is in a deep sleep, her mouth open and her breathing very shallow. I had sat with her all night and in the early morning I had sent text messages to all concerned.

Another daughter arrived and one of the carers sat with my darling to give me a break. We played all her favourite music very quietly in the background throughout the day and night. The only liquid we can get into her mouth is on a toothbrush, just enough to wet her tongue.

15 Feb 2017

Today the doctor visited and told me she was very weak and it was only a matter of time. He prescribed a medication if needed and informed the nurses. I sat with her through most of the night during which I cried myself dry. Our daughter relieved me in the early hours of the morning, so that I could sleep but it was of little use I was back with my love in no time at all. During the night, I had opened the window and told my darling to go (a belief inherited from my Irish mother in order to release the spirit).

16 Feb 2017

3.15am – and my stubborn little darling is still with me – true to the end; she was going when she was ready.

Her face was very cold and her breathing very shallow and fast. That continued throughout the day, but during the night changes started taking place. Her face and hands turned very mottled with a purplish tinge and her beautiful skin became very tight on her hands and face. Then the mottles faded away.

Finally, she became very agitated as if with possible hallucinations, what was happening? I held my 'Rock', my best friend and the love of my life very close, and asked one of the girls to telephone the Macmillan nurses. On arrival, they gave my darling an injection to calm her down and told us, as we were quite aware by now, my little darling was getting ready to leave.

At 9.45pm my darling finally left through the window and I was selfishly devastated. The disease did not beat her, she left only when her duties as a twin were completed.

So endeth my story of the princess and the frog

tills vi möts igen min alskling

I will never forget the last few weeks together; how I held her in my arms at night; the way she touched my face and stroked my hair, until the time she was no longer conscious; the smell of her hair; the velvet feel of her beautiful skin; even the helplessness of her strained breathing. Yet I could still sense that she was ready to laugh. Many times I had to leave the room for fear of letting her see or sense my feelings for her. I did not know how much she still heard or understood, it was so beautiful yet so cruel.

Where is my darling now, where did she go? The body, which started to fail in the late nineties, had finally conquered her, and much of that time, she had suffered in complete silence. I cannot even imagine what any part of it must have been like.

||

It was very hard to witness the funeral directors arrive with a body bag, place my darling inside and take her away. To them it was just a job, but to me, it was the most painful few minutes of my life.

Life's Log Book

1937–42   The foundation years for a wonderful childhood in Thornton, Bradford, Yorkshire.

1942–44   Junior school James Street, Thornton – Head Teacher Miss Wilkinson.

1944   National School Market Street, Thornton – Head Teacher Charlie Widdus.

1948–52   Secondary School – James Street Thornton. Passed 11+ but football meant more to me at the time than education. Head teacher Mr Twisleton. Other teachers: the magical Miss Rigg, Mr Exley (Art), Mr Schofield, Albert Priestly (sport), Mr Pickles (a genius at woodwork).

1952   Left school aged 15. First job – apprentice overlooker at Mark Dawsons Spinning Mill Thornton.

1953   Went to work at Hazel Crook End Farm between Wilsden and Thornton on Springholes Lane Owner Ernest Leach, wife and son Eddie who had both legs amputated before he was 28 because of thrombosis. Left due to a pig of a story. Joined Bradford Park Avenue FC for one year only. Ran out of whitewash for toilets.

1954   Worked for, or rather slept and sunbathed for, one week for an American Company, United States Metallic Packing Company. Gained invaluable knowledge of how trade unions should not be.

1955 Joined the Army in the REME to be trained as a vehicle engineer. Basic training at Blandford in Dorset – so many wonderful lessons on life. Vehicle trade training – Norton Manor Camp, Taunton, Somerset. Passed-out as Vehicle Mechanic B (qualified to carry out repairs on all wheeled vehicles).

Dec.1955 Posted to Munsterlager, West Germany. Attached to 94 Locating Regiment RA. Passed driving test after one 15-minute lesson. Played football for almost the whole of my three years. Fantastic, but completely wasted.

1958 Demobbed from forces – back to a civilian life and living at home. Worked one year at Thornton Baths as lifeguard – I could not stand being indoors.

1959 Worked for Walter Brook, fantastic man with heart of gold but worst business man ever. Spent most of his days drinking, with me as his companion – more wasted time. Met my Moira, the 'Rock' I was to build my life upon.

1960 Born again on March 26 when we were married at Bradford Register Office. Best man Peter Knott, ex Army pal from Woolwich. Set-up home in Dryden Street, Bradford, almost next door to the abattoir, in an upstairs room of a lady who knew my mother. Had to move away from there very quickly so we saved £40 – the deposit to purchase a back-to-back cottage in Mary Street, Thornton. Brother Danny lived opposite and cousin Jimmie a few doors lower down. At that time, I realised a big change in my life was needed, so I left Walt Brooks and started working for myself. Tracey was born in December.

1962   Cheryl was born in June. The worst winter I can remember with the exception of 1947, and at that time we loved it. 1962 was different as I now had a family to feed, I simply had to find a more successful job because Linda was on the way.

1963   Linda was born in August at the time foul deeds were taking place in Buckinghamshire. Rejoined the Army. Broken promises, heat and cold, lots of travel and so much luck.

1966   Moved to Bordon on Artificer course.
The start of my dream, which almost ended in its early days.

1968   Clive was born in June. Completed course. Posted back to Celle in Germany. Start of a few years among the very best of soldiers and help from our previous enemy.

1972   Back to Bordon to teach at the School of Electrical Mechanical Engineering. A small body made a massive change in our lives.

1974   Posted to Cyprus – a beautiful island in pain, while we danced by the Med.

1976   Posted to Bulford. Had the honour of meeting the boss and dining with royalty – finally giving something to charity.

1977   Posted to Borneo. It was like entering a lost world where everything in nature was huge – but where fruit flies disappeared, along with rations and duty-free.

1979   Posted to Northern Ireland where I met someone from another planet and made a prat of myself trying to play golf.

1980   REME records.

1981   A taste of civilian life; poor management and waste of public money. A wide void between military and civilian life.

1983   Back to Bradford.

1996   Retired to Old Leake in Lincolnshire; the start of being forgotten people.

2003 + Illness strikes my 'Rock' and the walls come tumbling down. Our only protection is laugh.
Heart breaking body and mind changes taking place.

2008   The world stood still my darling diagnosed with Pro Fronta Temporal Dementia and, a Brochas Aphasia – No cure.

2010   My darling tried to leave without saying goodbye.

2010–2017 We travelled the journey together and made every minute of the ups and downs fun.

2017   February 16th at 9.45pm – The log book closed.

There may be embellishments or omissions that are my prerogative as the bearer of this tale, and quite normal according to many eminent psychologists.

Clamping toothbrush

Moira in the Boston Art Shop which was especially opened for her at the request of her carers - such a beautiful gesture.

The beautiful Rhea – my daily visitor!

'WHAT A WONDERFUL WORLD'

I see trees of green, red roses too
I see them bloom for me and you
and I think to myself what a wonderful world.

I see skies of blue and clouds of white
the bright blessed day, the dark sacred night
and I think to myself what a wonderful world.

The colours of the rainbow so pretty in the sky
are also on the faces of people going by
I see friends shaking hands saying how do you do
they're really saying "I love you".

I hear babies crying, I watch them grow
they'll learn much more than I'll ever know
and I think to myself what a wonderful world
yes I think to myself what a wonderful world.

LOUIS ARMSTRONG

Lightning Source UK Ltd.
Milton Keynes UK
UKHW01f1416050918
328323UK00002B/20/P